Arabic Exile Literature in Europe

Edinburgh Studies in Modern Arabic Literature
Series Editor: Rasheed El-Enany

Writing Beirut: Mappings of the City in the Modern Arabic Novel
Samira Aghacy

Women, Writing and the Iraqi State: Resistance and Collaboration under the Ba'th, 1968–2003
Hawraa Al-Hassan

Autobiographical Identities in Contemporary Arab Literature
Valerie Anishchenkova

The Iraqi Novel: Key Writers, Key Texts
Fabio Caiani and Catherine Cobham

Sufism in the Contemporary Arabic Novel
Ziad Elmarsafy

Gender, Nation, and the Arabic Novel: Egypt 1892–2008
Hoda Elsadda

The Arabic Prose Poem: Poetic Theory and Practice
Huda Fakhreddine

The Unmaking of the Arab Intellectual: Prophecy, Exile and the Nation
Zeina G. Halabi

Egypt 1919: The Revolution in Literature and Film
Dina Heshmat

Post-War Anglophone Lebanese Fiction: Home Matters in the Diaspora
Syrine Hout

Prophetic Translation: The Making of Modern Egyptian Literature
Maya I. Kesrouany

Nasser in the Egyptian Imaginary
Omar Khalifah

Conspiracy in Modern Egyptian Literature
Benjamin Koerber

War and Occupation in Iraqi Fiction
Ikram Masmoudi

Literary Autobiography and Arab National Struggles
Tahia Abdel Nasser

The Libyan Novel: Humans, Animals and the Poetics of Vulnerability
Charis Olszok

The Arab Nahdah: *The Making of the Intellectual and Humanist Movement*
Abdulrazzak Patel

Blogging from Egypt: Digital Literature, 2005–2016
Teresa Pepe

Religion in the Egyptian Novel
Christina Phillips

Space in Modern Egyptian Fiction
Yasmine Ramadan

Gendering Civil War: Francophone Women's Writing in Lebanon
Mireille Rebeiz

Occidentalism: Literary Representations of the Maghrebi Experience of the East–West Encounter
Zahia Smail Salhi

Sonallah Ibrahim: Rebel with a Pen
Paul Starkey

Minorities in the Contemporary Egyptian Novel
Mary Youssef

edinburghuniversitypress.com/series/smal

Arabic Exile Literature in Europe
Defamiliarising Forced Migration

Johanna Sellman

EDINBURGH
University Press

Edinburgh University Press is one of the leading university presses in the UK. We publish academic books and journals in our selected subject areas across the humanities and social sciences, combining cutting-edge scholarship with high editorial and production values to produce academic works of lasting importance. For more information visit our website: edinburghuniversitypress.com

© Johanna Sellman, 2022

Edinburgh University Press Ltd
The Tun – Holyrood Road
12 (2f) Jackson's Entry
Edinburgh EH8 8PJ

First published in hardback by Edinburgh University Press 2022

Typeset in Times New Roman by
Cheshire Typesetting Ltd, Cuddington, Cheshire

A CIP record for this book is available from the British Library

ISBN 978 1 3995 0012 8 (hardback)
ISBN 978 1 3995 0013 5 (paperback)
ISBN 978 1 3995 0014 2 (webready PDF)
ISBN 978 1 3995 0015 9 (epub)

The right of Johanna Sellman to be identified as author of this work has been asserted in accordance with the Copyright, Designs and Patents Act 1988 and the Copyright and Related Rights Regulations 2003 (SI No. 2498).

Contents

Series Editor's Foreword	vi
Acknowledgements	ix
Introduction: Speculative Belongings in Contemporary Arabic Migration Literature	1
1 Shifting Frameworks for Studying Contemporary Arabic Literature of Migration to Europe: A Case for Border Studies	22
2 *Harraga*: Mediterranean Crossings in Arabic Migration Literature	46
3 The Subversion of Borders and 'Nightmare Realism' in Iraqi Migration Literature	83
4 Mistranslation and the Subversion of the Citizen–Migrant Binary	109
5 Writing against 'Crisis': Defamiliarising the Refugee Narrative in Arabic Literature and Theatre in Berlin	147
6 Decentring the Metropole: Forced Migration Literature in London and Paris	191
Conclusion: Imagining Mobility	233
References	242
Index	254

Series Editor's Foreword

Edinburgh Studies in Modern Arabic Literature is a unique series that aims to fill a glaring gap in scholarship in the field of modern Arabic literature. Its dedication to Arabic literature in the modern period (that is, from the nineteenth century onwards) is what makes it unique among series undertaken by academic publishers in the English-speaking world. Individual books on modern Arabic literature in general or aspects of it have been and continue to be published sporadically. Series on Islamic studies and Arab/Islamic thought and civilisation are not in short supply either in the academic world, but these are far removed from the study of Arabic literature qua literature, that is, imaginative, creative literature as we understand the term when, for instance, we speak of English literature or French literature. Even series labelled 'Arabic/Middle Eastern Literature' make no period distinction, extending their purview from the sixth century to the present, and often including non-Arabic literatures of the region. This series aims to redress the situation by focusing on the Arabic literature and criticism of today, stretching its interest to the earliest beginnings of Arab modernity in the nineteenth century. The need for such a dedicated series, and generally for the redoubling of scholarly endeavour in researching and introducing modern Arabic literature to the Western reader, has never been stronger. Among activities and events heightening public, let alone academic, interest in all things Arab, and not least Arabic literature, are the significant growth in the last decades of the translation of contemporary Arab authors from all genres, especially fiction, into English; the higher profile of Arabic literature internationally since the award of the Nobel Prize in Literature to Naguib Mahfouz in 1988; the growing number of Arab authors living in the Western diaspora and writing both in English and Arabic; the adoption of such authors and others by mainstream, high-circulation publishers, as opposed to the academic publishers of the past; and the establishment of prestigious prizes, such as the International Prize for Arabic Fiction, popularly referred to in the Arab world as the Arabic Booker, run by the Man Booker Foundation, which brings huge publicity to the shortlist and winner every year, as well as translation contracts into English and other languages. It is therefore part of the ambition of this series that it will increasingly address a wider reading public beyond its natural territory of students and researchers in Arabic and world literature. Nor indeed is the academic readership of the series expected to be confined to specialists in literature in the light of the growing trend for interdisciplinarity, which increasingly sees scholars crossing field boundaries in their research tools and coming up with findings that equally cross discipline borders in their appeal.

Migration; refugees; asylum seekers; refugee detention centres; boats overloaded with refugees sinking in the sea; lorryloads of smuggled refugees suffocating to death in transit – hardly a week passes without some news headlines intimating some disaster or crisis to do with refugees in Europe and the UK. Migration has been exploited by right-wing, white-supremacist groups to advance their xenophobic, racist agendas. Politicians, lawyers, humanitarian and human rights organisations across Europe have had to factor refugee issues into their policies and actions one way or another. Closer to home, migration was exploited to advance the cause for Brexit. Even in the current pandemic crisis, refugees made news occasionally in relation to conditions in their detention centres being conducive to the unbridled spread of the virus. Whichever way we look at it, migration has been a live issue across Europe for a long time and increasingly so since the beginning of the century. Not all migration is from the war-beleaguered, despotically ruled, human-rights denuded Arab world, but a significant part of it is. The many thousands of migrants, exiles, refugees and asylum seekers are not without their talented literary voices; they come from all walks of life including intellectuals and writers. Their traumatic experiences eventually find their way to literary expression, whether in their native tongue or that of their host country. Those expressions are the concern of the volume to hand, a very welcome and timely scholarly attention to the literary reflections of a very current and multi-faceted issue. An added value of this book is the fact that it is focused largely on the last two decades on the one hand, while on the other it focuses again on those parts of Europe whose immigrant literature, so to speak, has not received due attention. This will complement existing research focused on Anglophone and Francophone immigrant literature, while the particular interest shown in speculative and defamiliarising modes of writing brings a breath of fresh air in approaches to the subject.

Rasheed El-Enany,
Series Editor,
Emeritus Professor of Modern Arabic Literature,
University of Exeter

Acknowledgements

It is with a sense of gratitude and appreciation for wide-reaching support and connection that I complete this project on contemporary Arabic migration literature in Europe. I mention names of friends, colleagues and family in this short acknowledgement section and also remind myself that there are many others who have supported me along the way. I thank you all.

I offer special thanks to the writers, artists and creators who so generously engaged me in conversation while writing this book. Mahmoud al-Bayaty, Hassan Blasim, Rasha Abbas, Karim Rashed, Ziad Adwan, Helen al-Janabi, Oskar Rosén and Duna Ghali, thank you for sharing not only your work and ideas, but your time and presence. Author and artist Mahi Binebine kindly allowed me to use one of his paintings for the cover of this book.

This project started out as a dissertation at The University of Texas at Austin. Several mentors guided me in the early iterations of this work: Barbara Harlow advised my MA project and encouraged me as I began exploring Arabic literature in Scandinavia. I recognise Tarek el-Ariss for his transformative presence in UT's Arabic programme and, as my advisor, for sharing enthusiasm, encouragement and his brilliant insights. My committee, Yoav Di-Capua, Samer Ali, Kristen Brustad and Karen Grumburg, provided transformational support and feedback during a time of many transitions. Other members of the UT Austin community made the cultivation of curiosity and inspiration possible. I thank Hina Azam, Yaron Shemer, Ali Issa, Zeina Halabi, Benjamin Koerber, Alyssa Miller and Melanie Magidow for creating a true sense of intellectual community. Somy Kim, Naminata Diabate, Tessa Farmer and Michal Raizen were not only dear friends, but also, in our dissertation writing group, a mutual support system and forces of creative optimism. I am fortunate that Michal Raizen lives close by again and that we can continue to dialogue on literature, work and life. At the Center for Arabic Study Abroad in Cairo, Nadia Harb, Heba Salem, Kamal Alekhnawy and others were the best teachers I could ask for. Tessa Farmer, Amanda Ronne and Anita Husen were constant friends during a demanding year.

At The Ohio State University, I thank Sabra Webber and Katey Borland for inviting me to teach in the Newark department of Comparative Studies as I was writing my dissertation (and for continuing to welcome me). Patrick Visel and Mary-Allen Johnson generously taught me about working in archives and libraries. So many members of The Ohio State University Libraries and MELA, the Middle East Librarians Association, generously mentored me during my three years as Middle East studies librarian.

As Assistant Professor of Arabic Literature in OSU's Department of Near Eastern Languages and Cultures I have had the chance to teach classes and participate in study groups that contributed immensely to this project. I thank Kevin Van Bladel who, as department chair, welcomed me into the department. My Arabic studies students, graduate students in the Migration Studies Working Group, especially Eleanor Paynter and Carolin Mueller, and students and faculty in the Migration, Mobility, and Immobility Project have all been important interlocutors during these past few years. OSU colleagues Lucille Toth, Maggie Flinn, Paul Reitter, Ila Nagar, Danielle Schoon and Magda El-Sherbini have taught me about joy in collaboration. Ashley Pérez and Maurice Stevens enlivened my sense of what is possible in the university and beyond. The SPA-pedagogy group cultivated inquiry into care and mindfulness in both teaching and scholarship. Course releases and research funding provided by OSU's College of Arts and Sciences provided the support necessary to complete this book.

Friends Lisa Bhungalia, Nada Moumtaz, Moriah Flagler, Jeremy Bellay, Noah Tamarkin, Juno Salazar Parreñas and Isis Nusair shared laughter, curiosity and support as I was writing. Collaborative work with friends and colleagues Margaret Litvin and Alexandra Chreiteh has been most rewarding and opened up new vistas. I thank Marcia Lynx Qualey, Jonathan Morén and Amro Ali for rich conversations on the topics of the book. Of course, I thank Rasheed El-Enany, Louise Hutton and her colleagues at Edinburgh University Press, and Douglas Easton who completed the indexing, for so enthusiastically supporting this project and seeing this book through the process leading to its publication. I also appreciate *Journal of Postcolonial Writing* for permission to re-publish my article 'A Global Postcolonial: Contemporary Arabic Literature of Migration to Europe' (54:6) with minor changes.

I wish my father Erik Sellman, who passed away in 2020, could have seen this project come to fruition. It has been a time of grief, change and new beginnings for everyone in his family, and I know he would have appreciated the hard work that all of that those processes entail.

In Columbus, the contact improvisation community and music lessons with Steve Dodge created space for jamming alongside writing and teaching. Ryan Skinner has been a constant and loving partner throughout this project. His intellectual curiosity and love of language and ideas helped create a sense of home that is lively and expansive. I dedicate this book to our children, Elias and Nils.

Note on Translation and Transliteration

In this book, I follow the *International Journal of Middle East Studies* transliteration guidelines and the *Chicago Manual of Style* (17th edition) notes and bibliography system. For Arabic names, I use the most common transliteration in English. When available, and unless otherwise indicated, I cite from published English translations of novels and short stories. All other translations are mine.

Introduction
Speculative Belongings in Contemporary Arabic Migration Literature

In the opening scene of the short story 'Laji' 'ind al-Iskimu' ('The Arctic Refugee'), a weary narrator peers out of an igloo, surveying the Arctic landscape before him. The story, which was written by Sweden-based writer Ibrahim Ahmed,[1] was published in the 1994 short story collection *Ba'd Maji' al-Tayr: Qisas min al-Manfa* (After the Bird's Arrival: Stories from Exile).[2] As such, it is an early iteration of the kinds of novels, short stories and plays of forced and precarious migration that are explored in this book, literary narratives that have been rewriting the meanings and forms of Arabic exile literature from the 1990s to the present. How did the narrator end up in the Arctic? Although he has tried, we find out, the narrator has not been able to apply for political asylum in any of the nations that he has travelled through. Forced to leave Iraq and later, Libya, he is then deported from Germany, Denmark and Sweden. In the dreamlike short story, he now finds himself yet a few more degrees north in an Arctic wilderness, a space that functions as an imagined 'outside' of the kind of community that he had expected to join. The narrator explains,

> When I arrived at the Stockholm airport, the police interrogated me for hours and denied me asylum. I told them that I had come from Libya after the Libyans had terminated my work contract. They told me that Libya was a signatory of the 1951 Geneva Refugee Convention and that I should have applied for asylum there. I was too embarrassed to tell them that I had tried in vain with the Arab brothers to let me stay in their warm and vast country. I even reminded them of our blood ties,

which they used to say were thicker than the ink of conventions. My truthfulness and naiveté had always plagued my life ... I was expelled from Germany because I arrived there from Sweden, also a signatory of the 1951 Geneva Refugee Convention, and then from Denmark because Germany is a signatory of the Convention. Then I was expelled from Norway, a signatory of the Convention like the others. I began to wonder whether this Geneva Convention was written in ink or in mercury, on paper in elegant offices or on my grandmother's gravestone.[3]

In a brutally ironic tone, the text evokes two common models of belonging and citizenship: blood ties and the rights of the refugee enshrined through 'the ink of conventions'. Both the *jus sanguinis* and *jus soli* models of national citizenship, based on the biological family and place of birth respectively, fail the narrator and so does the international rights framework that the Geneva Convention is based on. The space that is left to him is one of imagination and fantasy. His query about the substance of the Geneva Convention also opens up a field of inquiry about the substance of citizenship. If it could be written in substances like mercury, which quickly rolls off surfaces, or on sites of intimate mourning, such as a grandmother's gravestone, what else might our shared belonging and ties to the space of the nation be made of? When the narrator arrives in an imagined (and exotified) Eskimo community, he is interviewed by the chief in a manner that retains the form of the political asylum interview. The chief asks him how animals are treated in his home country, and he responds through metaphors of political oppression, postcolonial conflicts and oil politics. 'How about the fish? How do you treat them?' the chief asks him. 'Very generously, sir. We feed them the flesh of our enemy soldiers and that of our own.'[4] The narrator is welcomed into the community to save him from the indirect cannibalism that eating such fish would entail. In part, the narrator's ultimate welcome into this community highlights how the available models of citizenship and international law created his exclusion in his pre-Arctic life. The community that he joins is, conspicuously, situated both outside the familial model of the nation with its fictionalised 'blood ties' and the social contract model of political community that is aligned with discourses on rights spelled out in 'the ink of conventions'. On another level, the story draws on the resources of the imaginative and the literary to imagine belonging, especially in the outside spaces produced by citizenship.

'The Arctic Refugee' is one of a growing number of Arabic literary narratives that are evoking and reimagining the outside spaces that are often produced for people in contemporary settings of forced migration. While such spatiality evokes the ways that sovereignty and citizenship have often been understood through naturalised links to territory, it is also about ways of being that are situated outside of conventionally understood citizenship. Among the wide range of texts available, I have selected literary narratives that engage with contemporary forms of forced migration through creative defamiliarisation. The different forms of defamiliarisation that we see in this literature can, of course, be situated in a long lineage of writings on the productive role of defamiliarisation in art. Foundational to these is the Russian formalist critic Viktor Shklovsky's notion of *ostranie* (defamiliarisation),[5] which asserts that art intensifies our awareness of the familiar by slowing down and heightening our perception. The playwright and theatre artist Berthold Brecht's concept of *Verfremdungseffekt* (estrangement or distancing effect)[6] refers to techniques that prevent audiences from becoming fully immersed in a play and instead, make audience members critical observers of the concepts presented and the art form itself. On one level, defamiliarisation is a useful way to think of what literature and art does in general. But more than that, it often targets specific concepts and realities. In this book, I have drawn attention to a variety of defamiliarising modes in literature and hold that these techniques – though drawn from different genres – are an invitation to reimagine the often taken-for-granted categories of borders and citizenship that underpin forced, precarious and irregular migration. To see these categories from a distance is also to find space for reflection and, perhaps, movement.

Arabic Exile Literature in Europe draws attention to shifting approaches to writing Europe in Arabic literature. Specifically, it discusses the emergence of an Arabic literature of forced or precarious migration to Europe written from the perspectives of refugees, asylum seekers, undocumented migrants, and others who are situated outside of normatively defined citizenship, as well as emergent modes of writing migration and exile. Drawing on conversations that are ongoing in border studies, it asks the following questions: how are literary narratives that use nonrealist and defamiliarising modes of writing contributing to broader questions and conversations about the liminal spaces produced by contemporary border policing and forced migration? In what ways has the emergence of these new approaches to writing about forced migration transformed the tropes and narrative styles associated with twentieth-century Arabic literary narratives of exile, travel and migration to Europe, which are anchored in colonial and postcolonial settings and relations? What are the aesthetic and political stakes of contemporary Arabic migration literature? How does Arabic literature of forced migration ask audiences to rethink belonging outside of the received notions about borders and citizenship?

The literary narratives explored in the book include novels, short stories and plays set on migratory routes and in contemporary Arab diasporas in Europe. These include northern Europe settings, such as Sweden, Germany and Denmark, and the routes of undocumented migration across the Mediterranean, Turkey and eastern Europe. This study also takes note of how literature of migration is being transformed in cities such as Paris and London, which have long histories of representations in Arabic literature. Most of the literary narratives discussed in the book are written by writers from Iraq, Syria, Algeria and Morocco, reflecting recent patterns of migration and trends in Arabic migration literature. Like 'The Arctic Refugee', the texts analysed in this book often depart from literary realism and from the assumption that narratives that deal with forced migration should be ethnographic or autobiographical.[7] Their approaches to writing migration often differ significantly from 'cultural encounter' frameworks, 'political commitment' and modernist understandings of exile, all of which were dominant in different genres of twentieth-century Arabic literary narratives of travel to and exile in Europe. Instead, many stage the liminal space of the border and the outside spaces that borders can produce.

Arabic Exile Literature in Europe argues that since the 1990s, there has been a marked shift in Arabic literature of travel and migration to Europe with the rise of a prominent literature of forced migration. As will be discussed in the next chapter, these texts represent a continuation of long-standing genres of writing exile, travel and migration to Europe in

Arabic literature, but draw on new aesthetics, styles and genres to render aspects of more recent forms of forced migration. Although these texts do not represent all the many different perspectives, aesthetics and concerns of Arabic diasporic writing in Europe, which encompasses a broad range of literary styles and explores a broad range of issues and types of mobility, the literary narratives explored in this book call for a comparative and sustained analysis of how literary, political and aesthetic categories are being rethought in response to contemporary contexts of forced migration.

On a related note, I use the term 'Arabic literature' in this book because the majority of texts discussed in the book are written in Arabic and respond to shared tropes and ways of writing exile that belong to an Arabic literary history. In this literary context, the term 'Arab' has for the most part been used in conjunction with specific national literatures written in local majority languages (Arab American, Arab Brazilian, Arab British). At the same time, and while recognising the inter-permeability of these categories, I broaden the definition of Arabic literature to include some narratives written in French, English, German and Swedish by authors whose belonging include ties to the Arabic-speaking region. I do this in order to show how the themes of the literature exceed the corpus of texts written in Arabic and to highlight the multilinguistic dimensions of migration literature, both in theme and in contexts of creation and circulation.

This study situates these approaches to writing migration within a recent flourishing of fantasy, science fiction, dystopian and future writing in Arabic literature, that are creating spaces to explore the unknown, imagine alternate worlds, and think outside of contemporary political impasses. Rather than explore one particular genre, a central query in this study is thus why nonrealist and defamiliarising modes of writing are such an important part of contemporary Arabic migration literature. To be sure, the analysis of specific speculative genres within Arabic literature is an important endeavour. Alexandra Chreiteh, for example, has shown that magical realism in modern Arabic literature has served to create heterotopia within the realist space of the nation. Magical realism, she argues, can create spaces of inquiry, especially for those (such as ethnic minorities) who do not align with the nation's dominant narratives.[8] This study, however, centres on how literary texts are stagings of forced migration and uses a broader definition of the speculative, identifying texts that employ a range of speculative fiction genres and defamiliarising modes of writing to render and reimagine the liminal spaces of forced migration.

In some narratives, such as Nadhir al-Zuʿbi's 2016 novel *Yuru* (Euro), which is discussed in the conclusion, the entire narrative is fantasy as it writes mobility from the perspective of a conscious Euro coin that crossed borders and forms new coin communities at the hands of humans. In other stories, realism and the fantastic alternate, and in some, elements of science fiction enter narratives unexpectedly. Several texts discussed in this book use metaphors of the wild and the wilderness both to imagine alternate forms of hospitality and to evoke spaces that are outside of citizenship. Settings such as forests, the Arctic space in Ahmad's aforementioned story, and different imaginings of wilderness as well as narratives that include animals that can cross borders with fewer restrictions invite imaginings of the pre-political (or perhaps post-political) and extend an invitation to see borders and citizenship in nonhabitual ways. By focusing on a range of nonrealist modes of writing liminal and unaccounted-for spaces, *Arabic Exile Literature in Europe* highlights the capacity of literature to conjure the 'outside' of citizenship, the spaces between citizenships, and states of existing *on* the border, states that are being produced for more and more people even as our frameworks for citizenship are often unable to account for them.

This variety of genres notwithstanding, I draw on Darko Suvin's broad understanding of science fiction as a literature of 'cognitive estrangement' to think through the role of the speculative in contemporary Arabic migration literature (even if its speculative qualities do not necessarily fall squarely under the genre of science fiction). Suvin's clear distinction between science fiction versus genres such as fantasy and the fairy tale in European literatures does not accurately reflect Arabic literary debates or those of other non-European literatures. As many have noted,[9] the classifications of different speculative fictions emerge out of particular European and Western histories that respond to advancements in science, notions of progress, as well as colonial expansion and domination.

Nonetheless, by placing cognitive estrangement (in Suvin's analysis, 'cognitive' stands for science or ways of knowing and 'estrangement' for fiction) at the centre of the selection and analysis of texts, I emphasise the ways that literature offers a space for thinking migration, borders and citizenship *differently*. Suvin writes that science fiction differs from fantasy because it is

> simultaneously perceived as *not impossible* within the cognitive (cosmological and anthropological) norms of the author's epoch. Basically, science fiction is a developed oxymoron, a realistic irreality, with humanized nonhumans, this-worldly Other Worlds, and so forth. Which means that it is – potentially – the space of potent *estrangement*, validated by the pathos and prestige of the basic cognitive norms of our times.[10]

The literary narratives of migration analysed in this book are immersed in the major questions and debates surrounding citizenship and migration of our time even as they elaborate on parallel worlds with and against current understandings of borders, one of the central 'cognitive norms of our time'. Literary texts have the capacity to transport us from the social structures, modes of belonging, and frameworks for understanding mobility and displacement that are often taken as givens or inevitable. Through defamiliarisation, they create spaces for imagining citizenship and migration in ways that can be dystopian, playful or mournful – powerful precisely because they are nonhabitual and invite us to imagine belonging differently. These nonrealist modes of writing, the book argues, open up productive ways of engaging with encounters with borders and with space and citizenship in their external and internal constitutive exclusions.

While the 'speculative' in speculative fiction refers to genres of fiction where narrative is unbound from the constraints of existing social structures or the scientific understandings of the world, the act of speculating or opening up inquiry into what might be otherwise is also inherent to its meaning. Human geographer Yi-Fu Tuan's distinction between 'space' and 'place' is useful for thinking about the relationship between speculation and belonging, especially in relation to literary narratives of migration. Tuan famously theorised place as geographical location endowed with meaning, familiarity and established significance, and space as geographical location that has yet to be endowed with meaning and whose affective resonances range from freedom to fear. His assertion 'Place is security, place is freedom: we are attached to the one and long for the other',[11] in his 1977 *Place and Place, The Perspective of Experience* points to the more circumscribed aspects of place and the more open-ended understanding of space. The unknowable dimensions of our future lives are amplified in times of mobility. In its most basic sense, migration might be understood as a speculation on a different future and calls for an exploration of space and the liminal.[12]

Of course, migration can be written through any number of literary genres and styles. My intention in this book is to explore how and why speculative modes of writing and a broad range of defamiliarising techniques are deployed in contemporary Arabic literary narratives of forced migration. One function of speculative genres is to render place, understood here as location endowed with established meaning and value, in ways that take on aspects of space, understood as a more open horizon of possibility, including the function of imagining differently and an acknowledgment of the real danger that many who migrate are exposed to. Speculative genres write outside of given conditions even as their inquiries often remain anchored in the social and political queries of their time. The narratives explored in the book defamiliarise borders as hegemonic concepts and speculate about different possible belongings. The two projects are inextricably linked. In the literary narratives explored in the chapters ahead we see the collapse of boundaries between human bodies, beings crossing between human and animal species, inversions of hierarchies between originals and translation, and new approaches to theorising national identities. In a time where borders and national identities are often dehistoricised and reified and where fixed narratives of forced migration proliferate (both from humanitarian discourses that tend to emphasise victimhood and political scripts that emphasise threat) nonrealist modes of writing migration remain anchored in real-world predicaments even as they transport readers to spaces that defamiliarise them.

The term 'forced migration' and the passive linguistic construction in Arabic – *tahjīr* – may conjure a lack of agency that is in line with the many images and discourses that represent the refugee or forced migrant as a passive victim. In line with Peter Nyers's *Rethinking Refugees: Beyond States of Emergency*, this book considers instead the creative ways that people are actively theorising conditions that emerge from contemporary forms of mobility and displacement and how these are central to questions about what it means to be human in a rapidly globalising system. In his poem 'The Sweetness of Being a Refugee', Agustin Nsanzinesa Gus exposes the many contradictions and tensions simmering withing the idea of the 'refugee' as a definable category.

> ... a refugee is a citizenshipless citizen
> A heartless human being
> A consciousless conscience
> An unbearable burden
> A society dirty and toy
> A spier and a spoiler
> And what not ...
>
> We all belong to the family of Humans
> Did I say humans?
> No, sorry
> The world of potential refugees
> Or better than that
> The world of refugees to be[13]

Far from the discourses of 'burden' and 'consciousless conscience' that Gus's words challenge, new literary forms and themes are being forged to contemplate what displacement and mobility can mean in the twenty-first century, which has both been a time of increased displacement and mobility and a period of intensified policing of borders and national identities.

There is some understandable resistance to the idea of refugee literature existing as a genre or a generalisable category, perhaps in the field of Arabic literature in particular. This reluctance, which will be discussed further in the chapters of this book, can be traced to the way that stories of forced migration circulate in the news media and the way that publishers and other cultural actors often market and frame literary narratives that stage forced migration of various kinds. Migration studies scholar Elana Fiddian-Qasmieh, leading the project Refugee Hosts: Local Community Experiences of Displacement from Syria: Views from Lebanon, Jordan and Turkey summarises three key tendencies in the representation of refugees. These include:

1. The persistent tendency of representing refugees as suffering victims and passive recipients of aid and the related tendency of the singling out of individual refugees as truly exceptional and worthy of aid.
2. The idea that international organisations as well as more economically privileged citizens and states are always the main providers of aid and support to refugee communities, thus obscuring the ways that displaced people support each other and how many people who become refugees have previous experiences with hosting or supporting displaced individuals and families.
3. The idea that the arrival of refugees in an area will inevitably lead to tensions and conflict.[14]

Pervasive narratives such as these simplify and flatten lives and agency of refugees and other migrants and, I believe, underly the resistance to thinking about some of the shared features and creative modes of writing about forced migration in Arabic literature. While there is sometimes a tension between presentation of Arabic migration literature as 'timely' or a humanising element amidst hostility to migrants and refugees, in particular for narratives published in European languages and translations, as a whole the narratives explored here are far from reducible to dominant narratives such as these. That said, many narratives do engage in a type of 'writing back' practice, reshaping and responding to implicit assumptions through literary means. Chapter 1 discusses in detail how expanding the scope of exile literature to encompass forced migration narratives requires a transition from the models of modernist exile literature and cultural encounter frameworks that were dominant in the twentieth century and makes a case for putting the literature in dialogue with critical border studies frameworks.

While this book emphasises new ways of writing migration many of its central queries have been posed for a long time by those who have theorised forced migration on a large scale. Hannah Arendt noted in her important 1943 essay 'We Refugees', 'A man who wants to lose his self discovers, indeed, the possibilities of human existence, which are infinite, as infinite as is creation.'[15] Writing as the modern notion of the refugee was being formulated, Arendt suggested that those who have lived statelessness understand the constructed nature of citizenship and experience a condition that is both painful and generative of creativity. *Arabic Exile Literature in Europe* takes Arendt's insight as a starting point for thinking about the link between literary stagings of these outside and in-between spaces to narrative modes that suggest new possibilities or the not yet possible.

Even though we live in a period of rapid globalisation, mobility and displacement, an 'Age of Migration',[16] rights continue to exist within the framework of the nation state and citizenship, spaces that largely remain unaccounted for when it comes to legal frameworks, rights and belonging. *Arabic Exile Literature in Europe* considers how questions about subjectivity born in contexts of forced migration become the subject of literary practices and how these literary practices reimagine both citizenships and subjectivities. My understanding of subjectivity is shaped by cultural studies approaches that see literature as both embedded in and irreducible to cultural and political contexts. Subjectivity encompasses both the recognition that humans are constructed by/subjected to material, linguistic and discursive forces that are beyond the self and place us in particular positions, on the one hand, and the idea that people are able to creatively articulate and reimagine these subject positions, on the other.

A few disclaimers are worth noting. By focusing on subjectivities, I do not mean that I am reading literature as a window into particular individual and collective psyches. The literary narratives discussed in this book are not memoirs, nor do they purport to document migration or necessarily reflect the author's personal experience of forced migration; rather, they engage ways of being and encountering borders that are becoming increasingly common experiences among people who are mobile and displaced. Though the book invokes rather broad categories of analysis such as 'Arabic literature', 'Europe' and 'citizenship', it carefully unpacks the inherent complexities and regional and conceptual differences within each. Rather, its broad comparative approach aims to highlight shared concerns and themes that are emerging in contemporary Arabic literary narratives of migration and how they imagine citizenship and its outside.

While the scope of the book is broad, it is not a comprehensive survey of the vast number of contemporary Arabic literary narratives that engage notions of migration, diaspora and displacement. Such a survey would include myriad genres, themes and literary approaches that are not in the purview of this study. And more importantly, a survey approach would preclude the close readings that are at the centre of this book. Rather than aiming to be comprehensive, I have selected literary narratives that in my view explore borders, citizenship and migration in innovative ways and present shared themes and approaches that represent both a continuation and transformation of previous genres and modes of writing migration to Europe in modern Arabic literature.

Chapter Outlines

In Arabic literature of forced or precarious migration to Europe we see a variety of narrative and thematic approaches to writing citizenship, rendering the spaces that lie outside of it and staging the liminality of the border. We also enter into the aesthetics and politics of writing Arab diasporas in Europe that are relatively recent, where the meanings of exile are being remade through the dynamics and questions of forced migration. Each chapter of the book analyses a particular approach and context and contributes to a sense of how Arabic literary narratives are reshaping the meaning of exile literature. The different modes of defamiliarisation explored in each chapter invite a de-identification with current border practices and regimes on the one hand and mark a departure from both twentieth-century Arabic exile literature and expectations of refugee literature, on the other. Indeed, while the liberating aspects of losing the self or exploring transindividual being are present, the narratives are often haunted by the violence that is constitutive of border-building practices, especially in the spaces outside citizenship.

The introduction, 'Speculative Belongings in Contemporary Arabic Migration Literature', introduces the major themes, settings and modes of writing migration that will be discussed in this book. It shows that the rise of different forms of creative defamiliarisation in Arabic migration literature, including but not limited to speculative genres such as fantasy and science fiction, serves to unsettle received understandings of borders and citizenship. On the one hand, this trend represents a subversion of expectations that literature of forced migration, often billed as a 'timely' literature, should be read through an ethnographic or autobiographical lens. The introduction makes a case for a broad understanding of defamiliarisation and speculative fiction, one that goes beyond any one particular genre (and the more general idea of defamiliarisation as a central feature of poetic language) to examine a wide range of approaches to writing precarious and forced migration. The introduction argues that these modes of writing have become an important feature of migration literature because they aim to transport us from the many social structures, modes of belonging, and frameworks for understanding mobility and displacement that are often taken as givens or inevitable, but also create the condition for violence in borderlands. Such defamiliarisation and speculation create spaces for imagining citizenship and migration in ways that can be dystopian, playful or mournful – powerful precisely because they are nonhabitual and because they invite us to imagine belonging differently. The nonrealist modes of writing that we see in some migration literature, the introduction argues, open up productive ways of engaging with encounters with borders and with space and citizenship in their external and internal constitutive exclusions.

Chapter 1, 'Shifting Frameworks for Studying Contemporary Arabic Literature of Migration to Europe: A Case for Border Studies', discusses literary and critical frameworks for understanding the emergence of a corpus of Arabic literary narratives that stage the experiences of refugees, asylum seekers, and others who find themselves outside of normative citizenship. In this twenty-first-century Arabic literature of migration, earlier modernist and postcolonial discourses on exile and migration are giving way to writings that grapple with subjectivities born of mass migration and the encounter with borders and borderlands. This chapter includes a historical overview of some of the themes and frameworks of twentieth-century Arabic travel and migration literature and its critical frameworks and a discussion of how contemporary literature both continues and departs from its literary predecessors. This chapter connects the questions of the speculative explored in the book's introduction to borderland and migration studies. It suggests that the most urgent antihegemonic critiques in contemporary migration literature pertain to borders, citizenship and belonging within the kinds of precarity created in contemporary contexts of migration. I make a case for reading recent Arabic literature of forced or precarious migration in dialogue with contemporary border studies, where we find multiple approaches to querying borders and borderlands: as barriers that uphold global inequalities, sites of transformations and as liminal spaces from which meanings can be reimagined. The close readings in the chapters that follow draw on the idea that borders are what Etienne Balibar calls 'transindividual' spaces where individual and communal relationships to the world are negotiated. Literature offers what Tarek el-Ariss has called a 'stage of confrontation' that exposes ideologies of belonging, in this case from the vantage point of precarity and in the encounter with borders, borderlands and new diasporas. Indeed, the kinds of creative rethinking of borders and borderlands that we see in the literature itself offer an invitation to imagine the very foundations of mobility and community differently.

Chapter 2, '*Harraga*: Mediterranean Crossings in Arabic Migration Literature', argues that the emergence of North African *harraga* literature in the early 1990s was a harbinger of the broader shifts in Arabic literary narratives on migration to Europe explored in this book. The chapter analyses two novels by Moroccan authors, Mahi Binebine's *Cannibales* (*Welcome to Paradise*) (1999) and Youssef Fadel's *Hashish* (2000) and Eritrean novelist Abu Bakr Khaal's *Taytanikat Ifriqiyya* (*African Titanics*) (2008) and outlines the contours of a veritable literary genre staging Mediterranean crossings. To this end, in addition to the novels it focuses on (selected because they engage with the fantastic and with myth), it also covers the plot structure and themes in novels that had broad international circulation, *Partir* (*Leaving Tangiers*) (2006) by Tahar Ben Jelloun, *Les Clandestins* (The Clandestines) (2000) and *Hope and Other Dangerous Pursuits* (2005) by Laila Lalami. On the one hand, these novels testify to the painful human toll of deaths in what Hakim Abderezzak has termed the 'seametery'[17] of the Mediterranean, that is, to the fact there are 'grievable lives'[18] behind anonymous statistics. In the novels that the chapter analyses closely, the liminal spaces outside citizenship that the characters enter align with storytelling and nonrealist literary modes. *Welcome to*

Paradise and *Hashish* evoke these spaces through tropes of wildness, such as nightmares of cannibalism, devouring seas and other forms of violence to migrants' bodies. In *African Titanics,* the *jurthuma,* or migration 'bug' that the narrator diagnoses as source of migration, intertextually conjures one of the central metaphors in Tayeb Salih's 1966 *Season of Migration to the North,* where the germ of colonialism and contact continues to resurrect cycles of violence. The main narrator, Abdar, initially posits that storytelling and literature can cure those affected/infected by the 'bug', but the role of literature in the novel gradually shifts to grieving, memorialising and mythologising lost lives. The three narratives thus call attention to different functions of storytelling and defamiliarise dominant narratives on undocumented Mediterranean migration.

Chapter 3, 'The Subversion of Borders and "Nightmare Realism" in Iraqi Migration Literature', probes the idea of 'nightmare realism', a term coined by Finland-based Iraqi writer Hassan Blasim to speak of the dystopian (ir)reality of his writing. Blasim's short stories, which are widely circulated and translated, have become emblematic of Arabic migration literature in Europe. This chapter links Blasim's approach to writing migration to a broader trend in Arabic literature that, like Blasim's stories, explores interconnectivity and porousness of the human body and other animate beings within contexts of violence. It reads Hassan Blasim's literary narratives of undocumented migration in his short story collections *Majnun Sahat al-Huriyya* (*The Madman of Freedom Square*) (2009) and *Al-Masih al-ʿIraqi* (*The Iraqi Christ*) (2013) and his play *Luʿbat al-Qubbʿat al-Raqamiyya* (*The Digital Hats Game*) (2015) with other recent Iraqi literary works that stage violence and war through nightmares, horror and the Gothic. Blasim's texts often link the hacking and irregular crossing of national borders with themes such as networked connectivity, parasitic relationships that challenge the integrity of the individual, and the breaking down of boundaries between what is human and nonhuman. Blasim's migration narratives imagine more porous ways of conceiving of ourselves and of community. The utopian ideal of opening up borders is continuously haunted by an undoing of the borders of the individual and community, a theme that connects Blasim's fiction of migration dystopian (and nightmarish) literary renderings of war in Iraq.

Chapter 4, 'Mistranslation and the Subversion of the Citizen–Migrant Binary', foregrounds how themes of failed translation and mistranslation in literary narratives of forced migration are used to defamiliarise, subvert and reroute discourses of authenticity, both in relation to the notion of the Arab exile writer and the notion of the citizen in twenty-first-century Europe. It analyses Hawra al-Nadawi's 2010 novel, *Tahta Sama' Kubinhaghin* (Under the Copenhagen Sky), a coming-of-age story of a young Iraqi-Danish woman, along with Abbas Khider's 2008 German-language novel *Der falsche Inder* ('The counterfeit Indian', published in English as *The Village Indian*) and Jonas Hassen Khemiri's Swedish-language play *Invasion!*. Al-Nadawi's novel is written in Arabic; however, the protagonist, Huda, writes her story through an Iraqi translator who, she hopes, can transform her Danish narrative into an Arabic novel and thus transform her image of an Arabic exile writer. The eventual failure of both the project and her attempt to reposition herself as an authentic exile writer challenges the gendered hierarchies that translation theorists have argued govern the relationship between 'original' and 'translation' and forces her to rethink hierarchies underpinning her desire to transform herself from migrant to exile, on the one hand, and the notions of authenticity in ethnic-based nationalisms, on the other. The chapter compares the collapse of the translation project in al-Nadawi's Arabic-language novel to the theme of mistranslation and counterfeit identities in the novel *Der falsche Inder* and the play *Invasion!*. Here too, mistranslation is linked to an undoing of discourses of authenticity, but the target in these texts is instead media discourses that would seek to make the figure of the male migrant both generalisable and *other*. This comparative analysis demonstrates that the theme of failed translations and mistranslations cross linguistic boundaries but serve to defamiliarise categories of belonging that rely on authenticity across different genders, genres and audiences.

Chapter 5, 'Writing Against "Crisis": Defamiliarising the Refugee Narrative in Arabic Literature and Theatre in Berlin', discusses the emergent Arabic literary, theatre and arts scene in Berlin shaped by the arrival of over one million Syrians in 2015–6. It analyses several of Rasha Abbas's short stories and Ziad Adwan's play *Please, Repeat After Me*, texts and performances that are defamiliarising migration in ways that create generative openings for transformative reflection. In Rasha Abbas's 2016 collection, *Kayfa Tamma Ikhtira' al-Lugha al-Almaniyya*[19] (The Invention of the German Language) a newly arrived refugee grapples with the German language and Berlin hipster culture through parody and situational comedy. Many of the short stories in Abbas's 2018 collection, *Mulakhkhas Ma Jara* ('A summary of what happened' or, as in a forthcoming English translation by Alice Guthrie, 'The Gist of It')[20] render the Syrian war and migratory contexts through speculative modes of writing and altered states of consciousness. Both collections unsettle the discourses and vocabulary of contemporary forced migration, especially those that relay a prescriptive message or reproduce a discourse of 'crisis'. Ziad Adwan's experimental play, *Please, Repeat After Me* (performed in 2018 and 2019), explores the impact of performing mistakes on the power dynamic between audience and performers, especially when the actors are presumed to be Syrian refugees. The play confronts notions of authenticity and testimony and creates a space of productive discomfort and confusion that invites audience members to ask themselves what they are asking of the play. Both Abbas's short stories and Adwan's play creatively theorise exile created by forced migration yet ask how to reframe both categories. In their work, analysed in conjunction with examples from the emergent Arabic literary, theatre and arts scene in Berlin, we find a deep probing of subjectivity and choice that invites reader and audience members into the fashioning of new, perhaps yet unformulated, responses and imaginings of the meanings of mobility.

Chapter 6 is titled 'Decentring the Metropole: Forced Migration Literature in London and Paris'. While *Arabic Exile Literature in Europe* has foregrounded literary texts from more recent Arab diasporas, this chapter highlights forced migration literature in the historical centres of Arabic literature in Europe, namely Paris and London, and their attendant national spaces. Although as a whole, the literary geography of Arabic forced migration literature decentres these metropoles, they continue to be home to important publishing houses, institutions, established Arab diasporas born of colonial histories, and prominent writers, all of which are contributing to the shifts in the politics and aesthetics of Arabic migration literature discussed in this book. In the section on Paris, I briefly discuss representation of clandestine space in the 2006 novel *La géographie du danger* (The Geography of Danger) by Algerian writer Hamed Skif. I then turn to the prominent Paris-based authors Samar Yazbek and Hoda Barakat and how their most recent novels stage mobility and forced migration. The central character of Yazbek's 2017 novel *Al-Masha'a* (She Who Walks) is a potent metaphor of the constraints and forced mobility created. The novel, which takes place in the Syrian civil war, relates the tale of a girl whose legs are shackled because they strangely refuse to stop walking. Hoda Barakat's IPAF-winning epistolary novel *Barid al-Layl* (*Voices of the Lost* 2018) explores different effects of migration and displacement, each character a migrant, refugee or expatriate. The chapter then turns to recent literary narratives of migration in London and in England more broadly. While there are numerous well-known Arabic diasporic novels from the early 2000s (for example, Hanan al-Shaykh's *Innaha London ya Azizi* (*Only in London*) (2000) and Haifa Zangana's *Nisa' 'ala Safar* (*Women on a Journey*) (2001)), there is also a more recent thriving literature and theatre scene that is integrally connected to the themes of the book, from the staging of plays (such as the adaptation of Hassan Blasim's story 'The Nightmares of Carlos Fuentes' by Rashid Razaq) to the hosting of prominent film and literary festivals showcasing forced migration themes and the publishing of Arabic speculative fiction in translation (for example, the future writing collections published by Manchester-based Comma Press *Palestine + 100* and *Iraq + 100*). This final chapter revisits the questions raised in Chapter 1, which argued that the most urgent antihegemonic critiques in contemporary migration literature pertain to borders, citizenship and belonging and shows a number of ways in which traditional literary centres in Europe participate in such an inquiry and how they belong to a broad, highly connected and varied Arabic-European literary space.

The book's conclusion, 'Imagining Mobility', reflects on how the varied approaches to writing forced or precarious migration explored in each chapter constitute a new kind of Arabic exile writing. As a final gesture in this direction, the conclusion discusses Syrian writer Nadhir Zu'bi's 2016 *Yuru* (Euro), a fantasy novel told from the vantage point of a Greek Euro coin which travels to Europe on the whims of commerce, theft, collecting and chance. Though the coin can cross many borders without losing value or relevance, it deeply regrets its lack of agency over its mobility. Among the literary narratives discussed in the book, *Yuru* may go the furthest in its departure from literary realism. Nevertheless, it is part of a broad inquiry into how literature can imagine migration through themes and vantage points that are variously constituted as 'outside' in relation to our citizenship frameworks (translation, the animal, the forest, the database, capital, etc.).

Emphasising similarities across different contexts and modes of writing, the conclusion stresses a sustained literary engagement over the past two decades with the questions and contexts of forced or precarious migration that are so ubiquitous in our era. Different contexts notwithstanding, each chapter of the book probes how twenty-first-century Arabic literature of forced or precarious migration departs from twentieth-century modes of writing exile in Arabic literature by making the refugee, the asylum seeker and the undocumented migrant its central figures. Moving beyond the binaries of East versus West and that of the exile as a privileged yet pained voice of their time versus the refugee as the subject of large-scale politics and forces, the writing in these Arabic literary texts insists on the capacity of literature and art to create spaces where dominant understandings of borders and citizenship (and mobility across them) can be reconsidered from novel angles. The speculative and defamiliarising modes of writing discussed throughout the book do just this and furthermore, add to an ongoing discussion about genres of speculative writing in contemporary Arabic fiction more broadly.

Notes

1. Ahmed was one of the pioneers of the very short story in 1970s Iraq. Like several other Iraqi writers who came to Sweden in the early 1990s, he had previously lived in exile in the Eastern Bloc. Arriving from Hungary, he began publishing short stories that merged a style based on fantasy and dark humour with migration themes. The translation cited here is from Ibrahim Ahmad, 'The Arctic Refugee', in Shakir Mustafa (ed. and trans.), *Contemporary Iraqi Fiction: An Anthology* (Syracuse: Syracuse University Press, 2008). The implicit back story to the narrator's impossible situation is

the early efforts to harmonise EU migration policy. Specifically, the Dublin Convention, which was first penned in 1991, stipulates that asylum seekers must apply for asylum in the EU country of first entry.
2. Ibrahim Ahmed, *Baʿd Majiʾ al-Tayr: Qisas min al-Manfa* (Budapest: Sahari, 1994).
3. Ahmad, 'The Arctic', 192. In *Arabic Exile Literature in Europe*, unless otherwise noted, I cite from published English translations, when available. If the work has not been translated, the translations are my own.
4. Ahmad, 'The Arctic', 194.
5. Viktor Shklovsky, 'Art as Device', trans. Benjamin Sher, in Viktor Shklovsky, *The Theory of Prose* (Bloomington: Dalkey Archive Press, 1991).
6. Berthold Brecht, 'On Chinese Acting', trans. Eric Bentley, *The Tulane Drama Review* 6, no. 1 (September 1961): 130–6.
7. See Adrian Wanner, 'Moving Beyond the Russian-American Ghetto: The Fiction of Keith Gessen and Michael Idov', *Russian Review* 73, no. 2 (April 2014): 281–96, and Margaret Litvin and Johanna Sellman, 'An Icy Heaven: Arab Migration on Nordic Stages', *Theatre Research International* 34, no. 1 (2018): 45–62.
8. Alexandra Chreiteh, 'Fantastic Cohabitations: Magical Realism in Arabic and Hebrew and the Politics of Aesthetics', PhD dissertation, Yale University, 2016.
9. For example, Mona Kareem, 'To Translate Octavia Butler: Race, History, and Sci-Fi', Online Lecture, Princeton Institute for International and Regional Studies, 7 December 2020.
10. Darko Suvin, *Metamorphoses of Science Fiction: On the Poetics and History of a Literary Genre* (New Haven: Yale University Press, 1978), viii.
11. Yi-Fu Tuan, *Place and Place, The Perspective of Experience* (Minneapolis: University of Minnesota Press, 2011), 3.
12. Here speculation includes the idea of a risk-taking venture, though not necessarily conceived in terms of capital.
13. Augustin Nsanzinesa Gus, 'The Sweetness of Being a Refugee', cited in Peter Nyers, *Rethinking Refugees: Beyond States of Emergency* (New York: Routledge, 2006), 65.
14. Elena Fiddian-Qasmiyeh, 'Disrupting Humanitarian Narratives: Reflections from the Refugee Hosts Project', paper presented at *Refugee Hosts International Conference: Without Execution – the Politics and Poetics of Local Responses to Displacement*, University College London, 24–5 October

2019, https://www.youtube.com/watch?v=XflyWu7kVqs&feature=emb_logo (accessed 29 November 2020).

15. Hannah Arendt, 'We Refugees', in Marc Robinson (ed.), *Altogether Elsewhere: Writers on Exile* (Winchester: Faber and Faber, 1994), 117.
16. Stephen Castles and Mark J. Miller, *The Age of Migration*, 4th ed. (New York: Palgrave Macmillan, 2009).
17. Hakim Abderrezak, 'The Refugee Crisis and the Mediterranean "Seamentary"', Lecture at Ohio State University, Columbus, OH, 2 November 2018.
18. Judith Butler, *Frames of War: When is Life Grievable* (New York: Verso Books, 2010).
19. Rasha Abbas, *Kayfa Tamma Ikhtira' al-Lugha al-Almaniyya* (Beirut: Heinrich Boll Stiftung, 2016).
20. Rasha Abbas, *Mulakhkhas Ma Jara* (Milan: Manshurat al-Mutawassit, 2018).

1

Shifting Frameworks for Studying Contemporary Arabic Literature of Migration to Europe: A Case for Border Studies

Contemporary Arabic literature of migration in Europe is often labelled and marketed as exile literature (*adab al-manfa*). However, the valences of this term (and many of its cognates) are fluid and changing. In contemporary Arabic literature of forced migration to Europe, modernist and postcolonial discourses on exile and migration found in literary narratives that centered on topics such as political exile, students travelling abroad for study and labour immigration have been giving way to literature that explores the perspectives of refugees, asylum seekers and other migrants. This more recent writing grapples with subjectivities born of mass migration and encounters with borderlands,[1] and explores spaces located outside citizenship. Although terms such as 'exile' and 'migration' continue to be used to situate this literature, they are quite fluid. This spaciousness is vital and offers us a wide array of linkages and possibilities for situating and analysing these literary texts. While keeping the literature's contemporary contexts in mind, we can also attend to the ways that it is being reimagined with earlier literary texts and frameworks. One of the important questions to attend to is how to situate the postcolonial in these twenty-first-century literary texts of migration.

In an interesting juxtaposition, in a review of the 2004 novel *Aqmar 'Iraqiyya Sawda' fi al-Suwid* (Black Iraqi Moons in Sweden) by the Sweden-based Iraqi novelist 'Ali 'Abd al-'Al,[2] the reviewer places the book alongside classic colonial and postcolonial Arabic novels of migration to

Europe, Tawfiq al-Hakim's 1938 *'Usfur min al-Sharq* (*Bird of the East*),³ Yahya Haqqi's 1944 novella *Qandil Umm Hashim* (*The Lamp of Umm Hashim*)⁴ and Tayeb Salih's 1966 novel *Mawsim al-Hijra ila al-Shamal* (*Season of Migration to the North*).⁵ A recurring trope in *Aqmar* is that of the exile as a moon that has lost its orbit. Extending the metaphor of Salih's iconic postcolonial novel *Mawsim al-Hijra*, the reviewer notes that the characters in *Aqmar* are living a season of forced migration, *mawsim tahjīr*. This metaphor situates the novel within a distinct period of time that both flows from and marks a break with a form of migration and literary expression located in a particular postcolonial past. How do we describe this new season?

Since the 1990s, Arabic literature of migration to Europe has increasingly foregrounded the perspectives of refugees, asylum seekers and undocumented migrants. For example, numerous Arabic, francophone and anglophone *harraga* novels from the Maghreb, including those by writers such as Youssef Fadel, Tahar Ben Jelloun and Laila Lalami, feature undocumented Mediterranean crossings and tell stories of those who choose to embark on them.⁶ *Harraga*, meaning 'those who burn', refers to the practice of burning citizenship documents before the crossing, but also, figuratively, to burning pasts. These literary narratives centre on the violence that border-building practices enact on migrants' bodies and often draw on fantasy, different modalities of storytelling and metaphors of wilderness to stage spaces outside citizenship. This genre of writing about undocumented crossings extends beyond North African literature to sub-Saharan African literatures and other Arabic literatures. *Taytanikat Ifriqiyya* (*African Titanics*) (2008),⁷ by Ethiopian writer Abu Bakr Khaal, and *Der falsche Inder* (*The Village Indian*), by Iraqi writer Abbas Khider (2010),⁸ both draw on myth and popular storytelling motifs in crafting stories of undocumented migration. Furthermore, many short stories by Iraqi writer Hassan Blasim, now based in Finland, explore border crossings and the spaces of undocumented migration in settings such as Serbia, Turkey and eastern Europe. Through a kind of 'nightmare realism' Blasim's stories explore a variety of border subversions, linking the crossing of borders in undocumented spaces to ways of imagining belonging and interconnections beyond citizenship.

In addition to these numerous literary narratives of undocumented migration, many Arabic literary narratives explore the perspectives of asylum seekers or refugees in Europe. Although these narratives do not typically focus on journeys or crossings, they share a focus on writing borderlands: that is, spaces outside normative citizenship. These writings are often deeply engaged with rewriting the modernist notions of exile that were dominant in Arabic literature, especially in the latter half of the twentieth century. For example, in the 1990s and 2000s, literary narratives by leftist Iraqi writers such as Haifa Zangana, Iqbal al Qazwini and Mahmoud al-Bayaty grappled with the shift from being political exiles to becoming refugees in different European countries.[9] On a larger scale, numerous Arabic literary narratives explore asylum processes as well as the dynamics of mass migration. For example, in al-Nadawi's (2010) novel *Tahta Sama' Kubinhaghin* (Under the Copenhagen Sky),[10] discussed in Chapter 4, the young protagonist, Huda, considers what it would take for her to transform herself into an exile writer. A daughter of Iraqi refugees who arrived in Denmark as a young child, she struggles to match her own experiences to discourses about exile and the exile writer. Why, she wonders, does exile feel so stifling and how can she, as a second-generation refugee in Denmark, draw on some of the creative agency assigned to the figure of the exile?

The subtext of many of her reflections is that the exilic condition, though painful, is supposed to be freeing and engender the possibility of individual detachment. The novel poetically explores the changing meanings of exile as well as citizenship in contexts of mass migration. Rasha Abbas, a Syrian writer now based in Berlin and whose writings are discussed in Chapter 5,[11] has staged border crossings and the war in Syria through speculative writing that draws on the absurd and elements of science fiction and fantasy. In her 2018 short story collection *Mulakhkhas Ma Jara* ('The Gist of It') and humorous accounts of learning German in her *Die Erfindung der deutschen Grammatik* (The Invention of German Grammar), which was translated from Arabic and first published in German, she explores alternate meanings of the words and discourses used to shape the public image of the refugee, especially the Syrian refugee after the so-called refugee crisis of 2015–16.

Arabic Exile Literature in Europe contributes to recent scholarly texts on Arabic literature of diaspora and migration, adding to them a discussion of the themes and forms of writing present in forced migration literature. Other recent studies on Arabic exile and migration literature have engaged topics such as Orientalism, gender, trauma and loss, and I build on their insights when appropriate, while maintaining a focus on a distinct group of texts. For example, Hanadi al-Samman's excellent 2015 book, *Anxiety of Erasure: Trauma, Authorship, and the Diaspora in Arab Women's Writing*,[12] examines women's diasporic writing from a trauma-informed perspective, showing how literary texts written in diasporic settings can create the potential for witnessing and healing collective and individual traumas. Her book centres on writers who engage deeply with the trauma of their homelands from diasporic and global perspectives, examining how they draw on figures such as the *mawʾūda* (the buried infant girl) and Shahrazad to write against bodily and discursive erasure. The engagement with the homeland and nation in these texts and approaches are distinct from the focus on migratory routes and borderland spaces in *Arabic Exile Literature in Europe*, yet the current study is indebted to the exploration of how diasporic texts have the capacity to make traumas visible, reimagined within the scope and capacity of the literary.

Though many different genres of Arabic literature are flourishing in Europe, including some that reimagine diaspora and mobility in different ways from those discussed in this book, this chapter will focus specifically on Arabic literature of forced or precarious migration and on how we might adapt some of our critical frameworks and comparative paradigms to better engage with it. Throughout, I use the terms 'forced' or 'precarious' migration to denote the broader material conditions that interact with the literature. The International Organization for Migration (IOM 2011) defines forced migration as 'a migratory movement in which an element of coercion exists, including threats to life and livelihood, whether arising from natural or man-made causes'.[13] Whereas categories such as 'refugee' and 'asylum seeker' describe specific trajectories towards citizenship in a country of arrival, forced migration encompasses a wide range of legal statuses and the variable (and often overlapping) elements that impel people to cross borders. Here, precarious migration[14] draws on Judith Butler's definition of precarity as a 'politically induced condition in which certain populations suffer from failing social and economic networks of support and become differentially exposed to injury, violence, and death'[15] and refers to the ways that the conditions of migration often increase vulnerability for migrants, especially in spaces outside established networks of support and citizenship. An inquiry into the literature that focuses on forced or precarious migration aligns with 'border thinking',[16] which asks us to think from the border and centre the languages and forms of knowledge that have been marginalised by colonial languages and epistemologies.[17]

Given that these spaces and forms of migration are increasingly part of the global landscape, this chapter considers how we can make the shift to global or planetary[18] understandings of space and migration that are so critical to migration literature. Though I mostly use the term 'global' to refer to worldwide trends in migration and displacement, the context and content of this literature on migration and border spaces emphasise the divisions and inequalities that are part of our current moment of globalisation. I thus incorporate some of the planetary critiques of the way that the global often emphasises unity and cross-border movement, sometimes at the expense of attention to how borders create immobility and extra-legal spaces for the many who are on the move. The new aesthetics and politics of contemporary Arabic literature of migration are being created in the context of mobility and precarious migration and in a climate of heightened anxiety about state sovereignty, which animates border and wall regimes. Though I refer to specific novels and short stories throughout, this chapter emphasises approaches for reading this literature and its changing contexts, approaches that I will continue to develop within specific contexts in the subsequent chapters. I argue for extending the scope of the postcolonial in Arabic literary studies to include the concerns and contexts of contemporary forced and precarious migration and the border-building practices that states employ in an attempt to limit or manage mobility. Specifically, I suggest that we can productively draw on frameworks from border studies to analyse what the postcolonial means in contemporary migration literature. These include questions about how communities and subjectivities are created by borders and border-building practices. Such queries help us see how the literature itself is theorising these issues and, through its imaginative capacities, introducing new perspectives on this current 'season of migration'.

Contemporary Arabic Migration Literature: Beyond the Postcolonial?

In both migration studies and literary studies, references to the global are superseding the postcolonial. At the same time, global divisions of access, resources and mobility stem from postcolonial disparities. In his *Borderlands: Towards an Anthropology of the Cosmopolitan Condition* (2016), anthropologist Michel Agier writes:

> Reference to the planet in its global dimensions is increasingly replacing a postcolonial conception of spaces of international migration (when migrants from the South headed for their former metropolises), and migrants no longer see the country of reception as the only country for their establishment.[19]

Here, Agier juxtaposes an understanding of postcolonial migration that is premised on migrants travelling to and settling in former colonial powers to a global or planetary conception of mobility where migrants move towards a broader array of spaces and often continue beyond the first new country they arrive in. In this formulation, the shift from the postcolonial to the global pivots on an understanding of the postcolonial as an experience of continuing domination exerted by a former imperial nation on the one hand, and a conception of the global, where domination and inequities are more diffuse and migration patterns less clearly charted, defined as much by points of transit[20] as points of arrival.

Yet the conditions of contemporary mobility and border-building practices are both global and postcolonial. Postcolonial North–South disparities of access and resources profoundly shape migration. Borders often act as 'asymmetric membranes'[21] that allow free passage for global 'haves' while creating liminal spaces or 'borderlands' for other movers. Though the rise of economic nationalism and challenges to net neutrality in recent years interrogate the status quo, we are still largely living in an era of unprecedented global connectivity; while information, capital and goods move freely across borders for the most part, migration is increasingly policed. More border walls are being built than ever before.

In the twenty-first century, the geographies of Arabic literature of migration to Europe have been rerouted in ways that echo Agier's assertions about the global. Cities such as Berlin, Stockholm and Amsterdam have become important centres for Arab cultural production in Europe, displacing the primacy of London and Paris. Newer diasporas are reshaping the field of Arab and Arabic cultural production in Europe. Literary narratives themselves are shifting away from the themes and contexts of colonial and postcolonial Arabic exile literature and exploring new aesthetics and modes of representing migration in a global context. In Arabic literature, the 'cultural encounter' frameworks, 'political commitment', and modernist understandings of exile of the twentieth century have been giving way to new approaches to writing migration, including creative defamiliarisation, new forms of testimonial narratives, and ventures into speculative genres.

Literary scholar Waïl Hassan argues that the field of Arabic literary studies has much to gain from the kinds of antihegemonic critique found in postcolonial studies and critical theory, even as these fields have not been adequately co-theorised.[22] He notes that the postcolonial tends to both denote how experiences of colonisation and empire continue to shape global disparities and to indicate how literary studies, especially English, have defined a field of study.[23] Hassan refers to cultural critic and historian Robert Young, who argues that we should continue to use the idea of the postcolonial as long as the effects of colonialism continue to be present:

> Analysis of such phenomena requires shifting conceptualizations, but it does not necessarily require the regular production of new theoretical paradigms: the issue is rather to locate the hidden rhizomes of colonialism's historical reach, of what remains invisible, unseen, silent or unspoken.[24]

Hassan argues that the types of critique that are possible within the framework of postcolonial criticism are essential. However, there has been something of a disjuncture between the fields of postcolonial studies and

Arabic literary studies. Though Edward Said's *Orientalism*[25] was essential to creating postcolonial literary criticism, the field has largely been developed within English departments, and has tended to focus on anglophone texts as well as texts that 'write back' to empire. Thus, to do postcolonial studies in Arabic literature, Hassan argues, means moving beyond the contexts and areas of inquiry that have defined the field and attending to the changing meanings of the postcolonial:

> Rigorous historicization demands that a reading of Sudanese writers of the generation following Ṣāliḥ's, such as Jamal Mahjoub (a half-Sudanese, half-British Anglophone writer who revisits from another perspective the colonial history covered in Ṣāliḥ's novel), Leila Aboulela (an Anglophone Sudanese-Scottish immigrant concerned with Muslim minorities in Britain at the turn of the twenty-first century), or Amīr Tāj al-Sirr (an Arabophone novelist pre-occupied with contemporary Sudan with its hybridity, inner migrations, and history) should follow different protocols, and presumably different trajectories of comparison. Rigorous historicization would reveal that even when dealing directly with colonialism and its ongoing legacy, those novelists' concerns respond to realities that are significantly altered from those of the 1960s, realities that nevertheless call for anti-hegemonic critique.[26]

Turning to this study, the question of whether Arabic literary narratives of migration are 'beyond the postcolonial' largely depends on what we mean by the term. Contemporary Arabic migration literature that stages the migration of refugees and clandestine migrants necessarily evokes North–South axes of power such as unevenly distributed access to mobility and the economic realities shaping migration. Furthermore, its settings in European spaces or en route to Europe further strengthen the push to read them through North–South postcolonial geographies. Tarek el-Ariss, for example, has argued for reading literary texts as stages of confrontation between the material and its representations. Though the literary cannot be reduced to its sociological or political content, it is produced in interaction with them: 'The literary thus designates a space of slippage, irreducible to representation and to materiality yet arising in between them and from their interaction.'[27] El-Ariss figures literature as a space of confrontation between ideologies, genres and modes of writing and, in contemporary literature, between the virtual and printed page:

> It is the current state of disintegration, facing the archaic in all its forms, that accentuates the urgency to rethink the literary no longer as a representation but as a stage of confrontation, as a stage of cruelty that exposes the violence of belonging, exclusion, and violence.[28]

Read through these lenses, contemporary Arabic literature of migration creates spaces of confrontation with concepts of rights, identity and indeed, the human, which are laid bare in the transitory routes and settings of migration. In literature, are new forms of relationality distinct from the East–West discourses of previous Arabic literature about travel to Europe and far from the modernist understandings of exile as a form of detachment that offers, in the words of Caren Kaplan (1987), a 'view from afar'?[29] Seeing citizenship, for example, in spaces of transition, from the outside or on the border, allows for contrasting ways of imagining the self and community in relation to the world. Literature thus offers an important space for retelling migration narratives, not necessarily as a testimony to personal experiences, but as an engagement with contemporary predicaments such as the meanings of borders and citizenship and the questions and imaginaries elicited by them.

To situate contemporary Arabic literature of forced or precarious migration in relation to previous postcolonial articulations, the following section surveys some trends in the postcolonial Arabic literature of travel to Europe as well as its adjacent literary critical frameworks. Awareness of these helps us situate the contemporary literature of forced migration in relation to literary and historical contexts.

Postcolonial Arabic Literature of Migration: Themes and Frameworks

In one of the broadest surveys of Arabic literature of travel to the 'West', *Arab Representations of the Occident: East–West Encounters in Arabic Fiction* (2006),[30] Rasheed El-Enany emphasises how the categories of East and West that originated in European Orientalist thought were adopted by Arab intellectuals and came to permeate the literary enterprise of writing

Europe after Napoleon's 1798 invasion of Egypt until the early 2000s. El-Enany's book offers a very useful periodisation of the literature: the precolonial period ('Enchanted Encounters'), the colonial interwar years ('Encounters under Duress'), the early postcolonial and nationalist period ('Proud Encounters') and the post–1967 period ('Humbled Encounters'). El-Enany shows that discourses on the 'West', whether hostile, ambivalent or desiring, have for a long time been deeply embedded in structures of power and domination. Similarly, the 'West' has signified differently in literary narratives through different historical moments and in relation to various ideological and aesthetic positionings. The dual face of Europe as representing economic, political and cultural domination, and promising progress and human rights is inscribed into the literary genre.

It will be helpful to briefly summarise some of the major trends of this colonial and postcolonial genre of writing the West in Arabic literature as outlined by El-Enany. Several of the now classic Arabic novels of travel to Europe were written during the interwar period when resistance to forms of European colonialism was articulated. In Egypt in particular, burgeoning nationalism, resistance to British control of Egyptian politics and economy, and the search for an independent national culture shaped the writing. Tawfiq al-Hakim's short novel, '*Usfur min al-Sharq* (*Bird of the East*) from 1938, depicts the young, idealistic student Muhsin's travel to Paris, reinforcing the familiar binary of a spiritually rich East and a materialist and morally bankrupt West. Similar romantic self-Orientalising occurs in Yahya Haqqi's classic 1944 novella, *Qandil Umm Hashim* (translated in 1984 as *The Lamp of Umm Hashim*). Unlike '*Usfur min al-Sharq*, instead of positing the East and its romantic spirituality as a source of Europe's progress and prosperity, it attempts to enact a synthesis between the two poles. As El-Enany shows, in the early postcolonial period of the 1950s and 1960s, a period of Arab nationalism and decolonisation, many literary narratives about the 'West', such as Yusuf Idriss's 1962 novella, *Al-Siyyida Fiyina* (Madam Vienna),[31] or Fathi Ghanim's 1960 novel, *Al-Sakhin wa-l-Barid* (The Hot and the Cold),[32] retain the East–West binaries but performatively diffuse or subvert them.

The one Arabic novel that has widely been incorporated into a world literature/postcolonial canon is Tayeb Salih's *Season of Migration to the*

North (1966), a forceful literary deconstruction of *Nahda* ideologies and East–West binaries.[33] The novel begins in 1956, at the time of Sudan's independence from Britain. The first-person account of a narrator who has just returned home following the completion of a doctorate in English poetry intersects with the narration of Mustafa Saeed, an outsider who has moved to the village, who confides the secrets of his former life to him. A prodigal child of the colonial school system, Mustafa had moved swiftly through its ranks, studying in Cairo, acquiring a doctorate in London, and becoming a well-known professor of colonial economics. In contrast to characters such as Muhsin from al-Hakim's *'Usfur min al-Sharq* or Ibrahim from Haqqi's *Qandil Umm Hashim*, Mustafa is cold and calculating. He creates an extravagantly Orientalised lair where he seduces women of all social classes, driving two of them to suicide and killing his wife. He thus performs an inversion of colonial violence, exposing the East–West binary as a 'lie', and, as discussed extensively by Waïl Hassan in *Tayeb Salih: Ideology and the Craft of Fiction*, dramatically refigures the East–West discourse of the genre to the North–South dynamics of postcolonialism.

The strong indictment of a colonial and postcolonial elite makes *Season of Migration to the North* a prescient commentary on the 1967 *naksa*, or 'setback'. Just as the 1967 Arab defeat by Israel came to symbolically mark the end of the *Nahda* project and the failure of secular postcolonial politics and thought, initiating an intellectual project of self-critical introspection, so 1967 marked a dramatic shift in Arabic literary narratives of travel to and exile in Europe. However, unlike *Season of Migration to the North*'s performative parodying and undoing of colonial East–West discourses, there is a re-emergence of pronounced East–West binaries in many post-1967 literary narratives of travel and migration to Europe. These are transformed though a focus on social and political oppression in the Arab world, operating alongside an idealisation of Europe. For example, Sulayman Fayyad's 1972 novel *Aswat* (Voices)[34] depicts the return of a successful Egyptian émigré to his home village in Egypt with his French wife, Simone, whose beauty, intelligence, curiosity and empathy are a counterpoint to village culture. Another narrative emblematic of the post–1967 discourse of crisis is Moroccan writer Mohamed Zafzaf's (1972)

Al-Mar'a wa-l-Warda (The Woman and the Flower),³⁵ a novel about the return to home in which the challenges are contrasted to European humanism, represented through the figure of a Danish woman. Here too, a sense of vitality and salvation is projected onto an idealised other.

A more pronounced exile literature emerged in the post-1967 period, which was shaped by the spirit of self-critique that dominated the intellectual production of this period. Although the idea of *manfa* (exile as a place of negation) and *ghurba* (a feeling of being estranged, or *gharib*, that also implicates a state of being in the West, or *gharb*) coincides with nostalgia and longing for home, exile and travel literature in this period tended to idealise European spaces and recentre the East–West categories that had long been part of this genre. Among the political exile novels from this period are Syrian writer Hanna Mina's ([1984] 1986) novel, *Al-Rabi' wa-l-Kharif* (Spring and Autumn),³⁶ which is set in the mid-1960s in communist Hungary, and Egyptian writer Baha' Tahir's (1995) novel *Al-Hubb fi al-Manfa (Love in Exile)*.³⁷

The idea of exile, *manfa*, which at once conjures displacement, alienation and estrangement, has a formidable lineage in modern Arabic prose and poetry; it is not surprising that literary narratives often continue to be framed as exile literature. In Arabic literature, as in other literatures, exile has often carried the resonances of modernism. For example, the modernist poetry of writers such as Iraqi Badr Shakir al-Sayyab and Abd al-Wahhab al-Bayati, who themselves were estranged from Iraqi postcolonial governments, made exile another lens through which to explore poetic experimentation and the alienating aspects of modernity. Palestinian poet and writer Hussein Barghouthi³⁸ has written extensively on exile as both physical displacement and an internal state of estrangement in both poetry and prose.

As for Arabic literature in Europe, Rasheed El-Enany's important study, *Arab Representations of the Occident: East–West Encounters in Arabic Fiction*,³⁹ shows that an ever-shifting 'Occidentalism', drawn from the East–West binaries of Orientalism, is very prevalent in the large corpus of Arabic textual engagements with the 'West' from the late nineteenth century through the twentieth century. Waïl Hassan's insightful 2011 study of Arab British and Arab American writing, *Immigrant*

Narratives: Orientalism and Cultural Translation in Arab American and Arab British Literature,[40] shows that Orientalism continues to be an operative lens through which many Arab English and Arab American literary texts navigate the critical terrain of identity and citizenship in the UK and the United States. Although Orientalism is a crucial discursive space for Arabic and Arab writing in Europe, the texts of forced migration explored in this book tend to move away from the well-established East–West notions of civilisational difference that have been so central to the history of writing Europe in Arabic literature, and focus instead on borders that create precarity and uphold global inequalities, defamiliarise them, thus opening up queries about how we might co-create them differently.

Modernist understandings of exile literature have tended to focus on the alienation and deracination of individual subjects over historical context and large-scale forces. One of the effects of this has been the creation of a hierarchy between the exile versus the refugee or forced migrant, rendering one the creator of art and original insight and the other the passive subject of history and politics. Anthropologist Liisa Malkki has noted that the term 'exile' has tended to align with modernist aesthetics and questions about the human condition whereas 'refugee' evokes mass displacement and the institutions that manage them. 'Exile', she writes, 'connotes a readily aestheticizable realm, whereas the label "refugees", connotes a bureaucratic and international humanitarian realm.'[41] Why is there this division between some types of mobility and displacement conceived as amenable to artistic representation, and other types to the logic of bureaucracy and politics? What are the reasons for (and consequences of) separating exile literature from the contexts that create and manage displacement, and artistic and cultural production of mass displacement from a broader literary or art world? These divisions have a lot to do with the privileging of art that maintains a sense of 'autonomy' from its political social and economic contexts. To insist on autonomy is often to stake a claim in hierarchies of prestige.

It is this elision that Edward Said critiques in his 1984 essay 'Reflections on Exile'. If the realities of exile include the painful and irretrievable loss of homeland and community, he asks, why do many literary critics insist on abstracting and idealising exile? Why do we dehistoricise it and detach it from the material and political conditions that produce it?

> If true exile is a condition of terminal loss, why has it been transformed so easily into a potent, even enriching, motif of modern culture? We have become accustomed to thinking of the modern period itself as spiritually orphaned and alienated, the age of anxiety and estrangement.[42]

Exile, he suggests, holds a privileged position in literary studies because it has come to signify the detachment that produces creativity and originality of vision. As Said notes, the problem with abstracting the exilic condition is that it dehistoricises exile, overwrites the real pain of displacement, and, importantly, obscures the structural conditions of mass displacement. He writes:

> You must first set aside Joyce and Nabokov and think instead of the uncountable masses for whom UN agencies have been created. You must think of the refugee-peasants with no prospect of ever returning home, armed only with a ration card and an agency number ... you must leave the modest refuge provided by subjectivity and resort instead to the abstractions of mass politics.[43]

Said's injunction that literary critics turn to the abstractions of mass politics has, in many ways, been realised with the subsequent turn to postcolonial and cultural studies approaches in comparative literature and in Arabic literary studies.

In her recent book *The Unmaking of the Arab Intellectual: Prophecy, Exile, and the Nation* (2017), Zeina Halabi shows some ways in which the post–1990s period has seen an unravelling of modernist understandings of exile and the intellectual in Arabic literature and other forms of art and cultural expression. She focuses especially on how, for many Arab intellectuals and writers, the 'exile' was something very distinct from the 'refugee', an imperative distinction for those who positioned themselves as catalysts of change.[44] As Halabi's book argues, the unravelling of modernist understandings of the exile and intellectual since the 1990s has coincided with the emergence of new conceptions of the political and of the status of the intellectual, writer or artist. Importantly, in contemporary literary texts and elsewhere, twentieth-century understandings of intellectuals and exiles as catalysts for change are being demystified and deromanticised. Indeed, the frameworks discussed above – the North–South analyses of postcolonial studies, the East–West discourses of Arabic travel and migration literature to Europe, and the concept of exile, *manfa* – are being transformed in the new contexts that contemporary migration literature stages.

Halabi's discussion of the undoing of the idea of the writer and intellectual as a vanguard and catalyst for change, a profoundly impactful idea in the mid-twentieth century, links to a central concern of the narratives discussed in *Arabic Exile Literature in Europe*: how to imagine new ways of writing exile in the wake of the loss that Halabi discusses, now in contexts of contemporary migration. While the contemporary literature of forced migration discussed in this book sometimes references twentieth-century understandings of exile, like some of the writers discussed by Halabi, it rewrites its meanings and assumptions. Distinct from the modernist idea of exile as a privileged but lonely site of meaning, contemporary migration literature searches for perspectives and narrative modes that can capture something about large-scale migration and the spaces that lie outside of normatively defined citizenship

Reading Arabic Literature of Migration at the Border

Literary texts exist in an ecology of critical and creative thought that is imagining what other models or ways of being might accommodate human mobility and the alternate and multiple belongings that movement so often creates. There is an alignment between the kinds of questions being posed in border studies and the way that Arabic literary narratives of forced migration are imagining the liminal spaces of borders and borderlands that many refugees, asylum seekers and migrants inhabit and pass through. As Michel Agier reminds us in *Borderlands*, borders are constructed and not natural. They are shifting, unstable, and must be continuously recreated through ritual and performance. They 'may still be "good for thinking" and "good for living"'[45] he suggests, if they become the basis of relationality and not enclosures that silence or exclude others. Recent work such as Amy L. Brandzel's 2016 *Against Citizenship: The Violence of the Normative*[46] and Sasha Roseneil's 2013 edited volume *Beyond Citizenship?: Feminism and the Transformation of Belonging*[47] critically assesses the ways that citizenship comes into being through the exclusion of others.

In 'At the Borders of Citizenship: A Democracy in Translation?', border studies scholar Etienne Balibar states that borders are constitutive of a 'transindividual relationship, or being in the world when it is predicated on a plurality of subjects'.[48] In the most general sense, borders help construct our relationships to the world and to each other; when we create borders, whether legal or social, we demarcate community and exclusion and create liminal border spaces. Secondly, Balibar posits that borders are spaces of paradox and internal contradictions, or 'antinomies'. For example, he argues, we can understand borders both through a 'paradigm of war' and a 'paradigm of translation'. On the one hand, the mechanisms of state sovereignty seek to manage and restrict mobility. On the other, borders are also constituted through collective and negotiable notions of identity and belonging, including creative practices. In this sense, borders can be understood as spaces of heterotopia. He writes that borders are 'both a place of exception where the conditions and the distinctions of normality and everyday life are "normally suspended" ... and a place where the antinomies are ... manifested and become an object of politics itself.'[49] Balibar suggests that the spaces of exception that are outside citizenship are simultaneously where border-building practices and the inequities that they uphold are most intensely made manifest.

In this sense of the transindividual, to write migration literature is to imagine a changing relationship to a world that is simultaneously individual and communally oriented. I suggest that the notion of the transindividual takes on a heightened significance in recent Arabic literature of forced migration because it so often stages individual narratives within and in relation to larger modes of legal and social belonging whose parameters are being constituted and undone by border-building practices. Furthermore, the contemporary literature of precarious and forced migration offers a space for imagining the transformations and paradoxes of the border. For instance, a focus on 'transindividual awareness' can entail an exploration of the antinomies of borders, such as the tension between individually felt subjectivities and an awareness of states' management of migration and restrictions on migration, or of asylum systems that make human trafficking the only available modes of transnational mobility for many. Hannah Arendt's (1951) assertion in *Origins of Totalitarianism*[50] that the 'right to have rights' is anchored in national citizenship remains pertinent even as more and more people find themselves in the extended and precarious borderlands outside full citizenship.

Arabic Exile Literature in Europe also puts Rossi Braidotti's rereading of biopolitics in dialogue with Arabic migration literature. In *Transpositions: On Nomadic Ethics* (2006),[51] Braidotti argues that cultivating a decentred view of the subject and the citizen that takes into account the forces that traverse us and our mutual interdependencies will better situate us to respond to the major ethical challenges that we face in the twenty-first century, including mass displacement and postnationalism. This mode of inquiry, 'a nomadic ethics', entails a disidentification with the naturalised link between citizen and nation.

One way that these outside spaces and borderlands are being imagined in Arabic literature of forced or precarious migration is through the semantic fields of wilderness and nature. For instance, a number of literary narratives use metaphors of nature and the wilderness to imagine alternate forms of hospitality in spaces that are outside citizenship: Farouq Yousef's (2007, 2011) poetic diaries that meditate on the Swedish forests as a site of infinite hospitality, for example, or Ibrahim Ahmad's (1994) short story 'Laji' 'ind al-Iskimu' ('The Arctic Refugee'). Furthermore, in many narratives, wilderness comes to denote states of exception where the conventions of law and human community cede and unmediated violence intrudes. In Abu Bakar Khaal's (2008) *Titanikat Ifriqiyya* (*African Titanics*), Mahi Binebine's (1999) *Cannibales* (*Welcome to Paradise*)[52] and Youssef Fadel's (2000) *Hashish*,[53] we find a variety of metaphors (cannibalism, beasts, sea monsters, and more) in the staging of these borderlands-turned-wilderness. In Hassan Blasim's (2009) stories of migration, wilderness often emerges in narratives that stage routes of human trafficking. In 'Shahinat Berlin' ('The Truck to Berlin'), published in *The Madman of Freedom Square*,[54] for example, a group of Iraqi men perish in a Serbian forest when a trafficker abandons a locked truck. To describe what takes place in the truck, the narrator returns to the idea that the boundaries between humans, animals and monsters have been dissolved. A scream arises that seems to belong to nobody and everybody:

> When they heard the scream, they tried to imagined the source of this voice, neither human nor animal, which had rocked the darkness of the truck ... It seems that the cruelty of man, the cruelty of animals and legendary monsters had condensed and together had started to play a hellish tune.[55]

In the story, a Serbian policeman later recalls a lone survivor – a wolf – escaping the truck and disappearing into the forest. Here, transmutation between humans, whose mobility is managed by states, and animals, whose mobility is less regulated, also becomes a powerful symbol. Examples recur in several of Blasim's short stories of the forced and precarious. Nature and wilderness at once come to signify states of exception and outside of conventional politics even as they become rich sites for exploring many different kinds of belonging and the role of storytelling in creating them.

Thus, many narratives of forced and precarious migration imagine novel forms of community and interbelonging. Such creative inquiries into how communities are and can be constituted, especially in an age of online connectivity and intensified globalisation, constitute a kind of transindividual awareness. At a moment when some theorists are rethinking the category of the citizen – our foundation for theorising political community – in light of the way that it is produced through exclusions,[56] literary narratives of migration are imagining other forms of community and connectivity. In contemporary Arabic literature of forced and precarious migration, this is a recurring theme that appears in multiple forms. For instance, the fantasy novel *Yuru* (Euro),[57] by Syrian writer Nadhir Zu'bi (2016), is narrated in the voice of a Greek Euro and then by a young man who slowly turns into steel, abandons his human relationships, and joins the parallel society to which Euro and all other metal objects belong. A fantasy reflection on mobility, the novel defamiliarises understandings of the relationship between border crossings, value and the boundaries of the human. Hassan Blasim's short stories also frequently accentuate and imagine the linkages, blending and networks that link community in ways that often subvert national borders and the integrity of the individual body and subject. Entities such as viruses, search engines and shared bodily fluids call attention to the ways that human beings are porous, networked and interconnected.

Such literary imaginings take us into the realm of the strange, unexpected and unfamiliar, and sometimes into literary genres such as fantasy and science fiction. Indeed, defamiliarisation has become an important component of writing borders and migration. Here too, the questions raised by the literature intersect with those of border studies, broadly conceived. For example, philosopher Rosi Braidotti's (2006) writings on a 'nomadic ethics' aim to capture the urgency of defamiliarising habitual and legally encoded modes of belonging. Philosopher Rosi Braidotti's (2006) writings on a 'nomadic ethics' aim to capture the urgency of defamiliarising habitual and legally encoded modes of belonging. Against a neoliberal understanding of a stable self amidst rapid changes in technology and information infrastructure she posits a 'non-unitary subjectivity' which 'here means a nomadic, dispersed, fragmented vision, which is nonetheless functional, coherent and accountable, mostly because it is embedded and embodied'. Far from relativism or emptiness, this non-unitary subjectivity is rooted in a commitment to sustainability, ethics, and in-depth transformation. Importantly, she notes that this understanding of subjectivity is perhaps most familiar to those who have experienced displacement. From this standpoint, a reimagining of multilocal belongings and interconnections such as those we see in literary narratives is an ethical practice.[58] A part of historicising this particular moment of the postcolonial in Arabic literature pertains not only to the inequalities that shape migration and border-building practices, but also to how the literature explores and imagines forms of connectivity, belonging and undoing in conversation with contemporary realities of forced and precarious migration. As suggested earlier, defamiliarisation is a central strategy in many literary narratives, a mode that departs significantly from the focus on cultural encounters and modernist exile in twentieth-century postcolonial narratives. The literature's venturing into speculative modes of depicting migration permits us to question the borders that create community and liminal spaces and imagine new ways to relate to the world.

Conclusion

This chapter has focused on theoretical and comparative paradigms for reading contemporary Arabic literature of forced migration or precarious migration to Europe. In so doing, it provides a general framework for the chapters that follow. Contemporary Arabic literature of migration is vast and varied and, certainly, different narratives call for different modes of reading and framing. My intention in this chapter and in this book is to situate this corpus of writing in a way that engages it as literature/art and as situated within contexts of border building and large-scale migration, thus challenging the modernist hierarchies between exile and refugee literature. We can be attentive to the aesthetics of writing precarious migration and large-scale migration without losing sight of how these intervene in the politics and history of our time. Contemporary Arabic migration literature is both postcolonial and global/planetary. I suggest that the most urgent antihegemonic critiques in contemporary migration literature pertain to borders, citizenship, belonging, and the biopolitical management of populations. In border studies, we find multiple approaches to querying borders and borderlands: as barriers that uphold global inequalities, as sites of transformation, and as liminal spaces from which meanings can be reimagined.

Perspectives from the border align with an emergent ethics and politics of a global age. We have yet to create the political frameworks and kinds of borders that account for the global challenges of our age and the mobility, displacements and changing subjectivities that emerge from them. To grapple with these emergent political frameworks, we should attend to the narratives and ideas that are emerging from the borderlands, including those being formulated in migration literature. The undoing and remaking of subjectivities that are staged in migration literature are an important part of this conversation. By locating literary texts as spaces of confrontation between representation and material reality, we can respond to the theorisation of borders, the meaning of the citizen and the human and the mobilities that occur within and beyond them. As our age of unprecedented mobility and its attendant anxieties (which are playing out in nativist politics all over the world) calls for creative and nonhabitual responses to the pulls between the state sovereignties and rights to mobility, we have a lot to gain by exploring the imaginative and defamiliarising capacities of literature such as those showcased in the following chapters.

Notes

1. See Gloria Andalzúa, *Borderlands/La Frontera: The New Mestiza* (San Francisco: Aunt Lute Books, 1987).
2. ʻAli ʻAbd al-ʻAl, *Aqmar ʻIraqiyya Sawda' fi al-Suwid* (Damascus: Dar al-Mada, 2004).
3. Tawfiq al-Hakim, *ʻUsfur Min al-Sharq* (Cairo: Dar al-Sharq, 1938).
4. Yahya Haqqi, *Qandil Umm Hashim* (Cairo: Dar al-Maʻarif, 1944); Yahya Haqqi, *The Lamp of Umm Hashim and Other Stories*, trans. Denys Johnson-Davies (Cairo: American University of Cairo Press, 2004).
5. Tayeb Salih *Season of Migration to the North*, trans. by Denys Johnson-Davies (New York: New York Review Books Classics, 2009).
6. For a discussion of contemporary North African movement and migration beyond established postcolonial routes and discourses, see Hakim Abderrezak, *Ex-Centric Migrations: Europe and the Maghreb in Mediterranean Cinema, Literature, and Music* (Bloomington: Indiana University Press, 2016) and Nahrain Al-Mousawi, *The Two-Edged Sea: Heterotopias of Contemporary Mediterranean Migrant Literature* (Piscataway: Gorgias Press, 2021).
7. Abu Bakr Khaal, *Taytanikat Ifriqiyya: Riwaya* (Beirut: Dar al-Saqi, 2008).
8. Abbas Khider, *The Village Indian*, trans. by Donal McLaughlin (New York: Seagull Books, 2013).
9. See Johanna Sellman, 'The Ghosts of Exilic Belongings: Mahmūd al-Bayyātī's *Raqs ʻalā Al- Maʼ: Ahlām Waʼrah* and Post-Soviet Themes in Arabic Exile Literature', *Journal of Arabic Literature* 47, no. 1–2 (2016): 111–37.
10. Hawra Al-Nadawi, *Tahta Samaʼ Kubinhaghin* (Beirut: Dar al-Saqi, 2010).
11. Rasha Abbas, *Die Erfindung der deutschen Grammatik: Geschichten*, trans. Sandra Hetzl (Berlin: Mikrotext, 2016); Rasha Abbas, *Mulakhkhas Ma Jara* (Milan: Manshurat al-Mutawassit, 2018).
12. Hanadi al-Samman, *Anxiety of Erasure: Trauma, Authorship, and the Diaspora in Arab Women's Writing* (Syracuse: Syracuse University Press, 2015).
13. 'Key Migration Terms', *International Organization for Migration (IOM)*, https://www.iom.int/key-migration-terms (accessed 21 October 2018).

14. See also Eleanor Paynter, 'Autobiographical Docudrama as Testimony: Jonas Carpignano's *Mediterranea*', *Auto/Biography Studies* 32, no. 3 (2017): 659; Vicki Squire, 'Researching Precarious Migrations: Qualitative Strategies Towards a Positive Transformation of the Politics of Migration', *The British Journal of Politics and International Relations* 20, no. 2 (2018): 441–58.
15. Judith Butler, *Frames of War: When is Life Grievable?* (London: Verso, 2009), 25.
16. Walter D. Mignolo and Madina V. Tlostanova, 'Theorizing from the Borders: Shifting to Geo- and Body-Politics of Knowledge', *European Journal of Social Theory* 9, no. 2 (2006): 205–21.
17. Mignolo and Madina, 'Theorizing', 207.
18. The notion of the planetary has come into being in conversation with the global. In general, it critiques the inequalities of globalisation and the totalising way that it has often been theorised. Like most perspectives on globalisation, writings on the planetary focus on the intensification of interconnections and relationality. However, they often emphasise ways that the global excludes and creates divisions (see Masao Miyoshi, 'Turn to the Planet: Literature, Diversity, and Totality', *Comparative Literature* 53, no. 4 (2001): 283–97) and how to theorise the areas that fall outside the often-rationalist categories of economy, media and profit (see Christian Moraru, '"World", "Globe", "Planet": Comparative Literature, Planetary Studies, and Cultural Debt after the "Global Turn"', *ACLA State of the Discipline Report*, 2015 https://stateofthediscipline.acla.org/entry/%E2%80%9Cworld%E2%80%9D-%E2%80%9Cglobe%E2%80%9D-%E2%80%9Cplanet%E2%80%9D-comparative-literature-planetary-studies-and-cultural-debt-after (accessed 25 June 2018)). Some have used the planetary as a starting point to theorise critique (see Mercedes Bunz, Birgit Mara Kaiser and Kathrin Thiele (eds), *Symptoms of the Planetary Condition: A Critical Vocabulary* (Lüneburg: Meson Press, 2017).
19. Michel Agier, *Borderlands*, trans. David Fernbach (Cambridge: Polity Press, 2016), 46.
20. Eleanor Paynter, 'The Liminal Lives of Europe's Transit Migrants', *Contexts* 17, no. 2 (2018): 40–5.
21. Ulf Hedetoft, *The Global Turn: National Encounters with the World* (Aarhus: Aalborg University Press, 2003), 146.
22. Waïl Hassan, 'Postcolonialism and Modern Arabic Literature: Twenty-First Century Horizons', *Interventions: The International Journal of Postcolonial Studies* 20, no. 2 (2018): 157–73; Waïl S. Hassan, 'Postcolonial Theory

and Modern Arabic Literature: Horizons of Application', *Journal of Arabic Literature* 33, no. 1 (2002): 45–64.
23. See Anna Bell and Karim Mattar, *The Edinburgh Companion to the Postcolonial Middle East* (Edinburgh: Edinburgh University Press, 2018).
24. Robert Young, 'Postcolonial Remains', *New Literary History* 43, no. 1 (2012): 20–1.
25. Edward Said, *Orientalism* (New York: Pantheon, 1978).
26. Hassan, 'Postcolonialism', 167.
27. Tarek El-Ariss, *Trials of Arab Modernity: Literary Affects and the New Political* (New York: Fordham University Press, 2013), 11.
28. Tarek El-Ariss, 'Return of the Beast: From Pre-Islamic Ode to Contemporary Novel', *Journal of Arabic Literature* 47, no. 1–2 (2016): 90.
29. Caren Kaplan, 13–14, cited in L. H. Malkki, 'Refugees and Exile: From "Refugee Studies" to the National Order of Things', *Annual Review of Anthropology* 24 (1995): 495–523.
30. Rasheed El-Enany, *Arab Representations of the Occident: East–West Encounters in Arabic Fiction* (London: Routledge, 2006).
31. Yusuf Idriss, 'Al-Sayyida Fiyinna', in *Al-'Askari al-Aswad wa Qisas Ukhra* (Cairo: Dar al-Maʿarifa, 1962).
32. Fathi Ghanim, *Al-Sakhin wa-l-Barid* (Cairo: Dar al-Jumhuriyya li-l-Sihafa, 1960).
33. See Waïl S. Hassan, *Tayeb Salih: Ideology and the Craft of Fiction* (Syracuse: Syracuse University Press, 2003).
34. Sulayman Fayyad, *Voices*, trans. Hosam Abou-Ela (New York: Marion Boyars, 1993).
35. Mohamed Zafzaf, *Al-Mar'a wa-l-Warda* (Beirut: Manshurat Galeri Wahid, 1972).
36. Hanna Minah, *Al-Rabiʿ wa-l-Kharif*, 2nd edn (Beirut: Dar al-Adab, 1986).
37. Baha' Tahir, *Al-Hubb fi-al-Manfa* (Cairo: Dar al-Hilal, 1995).
38. Hussein Barghouthi, *Al-Difa al-Thalitha li-Nahr al-Urdun: Riwaya* (Jersulalem: Dar al-Katib, 1984); Hussein Barghouthi, *Al-Daw al-Azraq* (Jerusalem: Bayt al-Maqdis li-l-Nashr wa-l-al-Tawziʿ, 2001).
39. El-Enany, *Arab Representations*.
40. Waïl Hassan, *Immigrant Narratives: Orientalism and Cultural Translation in Arab American and Arab British Literature* (Oxford: Oxford University Press, 2011).

41. Malkki, 'Refugees and Exile', 513.
42. Edward Said, *Reflections on Exile and Other Essays* (Cambridge, MA: Harvard University Press, 2002), 173.
43. Said, *Reflections*, 176.
44. Zeina Halabi, *The Unmaking of the Arab Intellectual: Prophecy Exile and the Nation* (Edinburgh: Edinburgh University Press, 2017), 83.
45. Agier, *Borderlands*, 15.
46. Amy L. Brandzel *Against Citizenship: The Violence of the Normative* (Champaign: University of Illinois Press, 2016).
47. Sasha Roseneil, *Beyond Citizenship?: Feminism and the Transformation of Belonging* (London: Palgrave Macmillan, 2003).
48. Etienne Balibar, 'At the Borders of Citizenship: A Democracy in Translation?', *European Journal of Social Theory* 13, no. 3 (2010): 316.
49. Balibar, 'At the Borders', 316.
50. Hannah Arendt, *The Origins of Totalitarianism* (New York: Harcourt, Brace and Co, 1951).
51. Rosi Braidotti, *Transpositions: On Nomadic Ethics* (Cambridge: Polity Press, 2006).
52. Mahi Binebine, *Cannibales* (Paris, Fayard, 1999); Mahi Binebine, *Welcome to Paradise*, trans. Lulu Norman (London: Granta Books, 2003).
53. Youssef Fadel, *Hashish* (Casablanca: Dar al-Fanak, 2000).
54. Hassan Blasim, *Majnun Sahat al-Huriyya* (Beirut: al-Mu'assasa al-'Arabiyya lil-Dirasat wa-l-Nashr, 2012); Hassan Blasim, *The Madman of Freedom Square*, trans. Jonathan Wright (Manchester: Comma Press, 2009).
55. Hassan Blasim, 'The Truck to Berlin', in *Madman of Freedom Square*, trans. Jonathan Wright (Manchester: Comma Press), 72.
56. See Judith Butler, *Notes toward a Performative Theory of Assembly* (Cambridge, MA: Harvard University Press, 2015) and Brandzel, *Against Citizenship*.
57. Nadhir Zu'bi, *Yuru* (Beirut: al-Dar al-'Arabiya li-l-'Ulum Nashirun, 2016).
58. Braidotti, *Transpositions*, 4.

2

Harraga: Mediterranean Crossings in Arabic Migration Literature

Moroccan artist and writer Mahi Binebine has moved between visual art and literary texts in creatively probing contemporary issues in Moroccan society, including questions of how to represent the lives of those who migrate across the Mediterranean Sea to Europe. Queried about the blank human figures that recur in his paintings, Binebine responded that the seeming absence of individuality creates 'excuses to tell stories about humans'.[1] In an untitled painting with figures similar to the ones seen on the cover of this book, we see two ghost-like bodies in a boat and a larger number of human figures suspended in the waters below. One of the figures in the boat reaches a lanky arm into the water in what could be a gesture of solidarity or one of resignation. The painting evokes the images of Mediterranean migration that often circulate in the media: unsafe boats filled to the brim with people seeking a life elsewhere. Yet here, the image is abstracted and resists categorisation. The human figures overlap and intersect, invoking a sense of a shared fate. As we make our sense of the abstract qualities of the work, we might also be reminded that we are projecting our own knowledge and assumptions about migration onto the canvas. Pondering Binebine's painting in relation to the texts explored in this book, it seems to offer a visceral representation of the transindividual, an awareness of how individual stories and subjectivities overlap with broader patterns, especially the ways in which border-building practices create precarious migration for some.

Mahi Binebine is one of many writers in North Africa and elsewhere who in their novels have 'told stories about humans' who cross the Mediterranean, the watery boundary that, for the past few decades, has been the deadliest border for migrants in the world. Although there are many official and vernacular ways of naming this migration, in North Africa, the term *harraga* has gained prominence. *Harraga*, which means 'those who burn' in Algerian Arabic, refers to the practice of burning citizenship documents before crossing the sea, but also, figuratively, to burning the past or burning paths, that is, insisting on mobility despite heavy border policing and the dangers of travelling on the sea and along the routes of human trafficking. The numerous literary texts in both Arabic and French about undocumented Mediterranean crossings are often referred to as *harraga* literature and typically centre on the violence that border-building practices enact on migrants' bodies, often drawing on fantasy, different modalities of storytelling, and metaphors of wilderness to stage spaces outside of citizenship.

Coalescing as a distinct group of literary texts in the 1990s, as more people began making undocumented Mediterranean crossings and as awareness of such crossings grew, *harraga* writing has been at the forefront of an Arabic literature of forced migration. Since the early examples of this literary genre in the 1990s, similar Arabic literary narratives of clandestine Mediterranean crossings have appeared outside the Maghreb, for example in Iraqi, Libyan and Eritrean literatures. Arabic, francophone and anglophone *harraga* novels by writers such as Tahar Ben Jelloun, Youssef Alemeddine and Laila Lalami from Morocco, Hamed Skif from Algeria, and Razan Naim Maghrebi from Libya join those of many others in staging undocumented Mediterranean crossings. Given the focus of this book, this chapter focuses on Arabic and North African francophone *harraga* literature; however, many African literatures have staged undocumented Mediterranean migrations beyond the Maghreb.

The emergence of *harraga* writing in the early 1990s was a harbinger of the broader shifts in Arabic literary narratives on migration to Europe explored in this book. As literary narratives increasingly explored forced migration, twentieth-century modes of writing exile and postcolonial migration started being reimagined in creative ways. The modernist basis of exile literature and the way that it positions the intellectual or writer has given way to narratives told from the perspectives of refugees, asylum seekers and undocumented migrants. As in other Arabic literary narratives of forced migration, the idealisation of Europe that is so common in post-1967 Arabic literature on Europe is subverted in *harraga* writing. In contrast to the relational East–West discourse in Arabic literature of travel and migration to Europe since the inception of the genre during the *Nahda*, the subject positions depicted in *harraga* literature teeter perilously at the edge of the citizen–state contract.

In this chapter, I focus on two novels by Moroccan authors, Mahi Binebine's *Cannibales* (*Welcome to Paradise*) (1999) and Youssef Fadel's *Hashish* (2000), and Eritrean novelist Abu Bakr Khaal's *Taytanikat Ifriqiyya* (*African Titanics*) (2008). In all three texts, the main characters are would-be migrants who attempt to cross the sea yet, owing to a variety of choices and circumstances, do not arrive at their European destinations. Though some characters survive, these novels testify to the painful human toll of deaths in what Hakim Abderezzak has termed the 'seametery' of the Mediterranean,[2] that is, to the fact there are 'grievable lives'[3] behind anonymous statistics.

The novels discussed in this chapter are not autobiographical; each author has his own personal history of mobility and migration, but it is distinct from those of their characters. Moroccan novelist and painter Mahi Binebine is from Marrakech. He lived in France in the 1990s, but after the rise of populist nationalism exemplified by Jean-Marie Le Pen, he returned to Morocco and dedicated himself to his writing and painting. He worked in New York in the late 1990s and returned to Morocco in 2002, becoming a leading figure in both the literature and arts scenes in his country. Through his literature and art, he has engaged with topics such as migration, the radicalisation of youth living in informal settlements and his own brother's experience in the infamous desert prison Tazmamart. Youssef Fadel, author of *Hashish*, was born in Casablanca in 1949 and is an acclaimed playwright, novelist and screenwriter. Fadel's work has long focused on the popular classes in Morocco and has not shied away from politically sensitive subject matter. At a young age, he was arrested following the 1974 publication of his play titled *Lguirra* (*War*), becoming one of many political prisoners in the Derb Moulay Chérif prison. After his release he continued publishing plays, screenplays and novels, often blending Moroccan Arabic and Modern Standard Arabic (MSA). In 2001, *Hashish* became one of the first Arabic-language novels to win the French embassy-sponsored Grand Atlas prize. *African Titanics* (2008) is Eritrean novelist Abu Bakr Khaal's third novel and perhaps the first Arabic novel to feature undocumented journeys across the Sahara Desert. An activist in the opposition group Eritrean Liberation Front, Khaal had lived and worked in Libya for some time when the 2011 Arab uprisings began, forcing him to leave. He was held at a refugee camp at the Libyan–Tunisian border and eventually received political asylum in Denmark, where he now resides.

The narrative structure and the different kinds of storytelling featured in the novels invite reflection on the liminal spaces outside the institutions and protections of citizenship. A narrative arc that recurs in many *harraga* narratives is created by a tension between fantasies about migration and the painful realities that the novels elicit. *Cannibales* and *Hashish* portray characters who dream of a transformative entry into a 'paradise' of sorts; however, the characters encounter spaces that are evoked through tropes of wildness, such as nightmares of cannibalism, devouring seas, and other forms of violence on migrants' bodies. In the liminal spaces that the characters find themselves in, storytelling and nonrealist literary modes take on particular significance. In *African Titanics*, the main character, Abdar, narrates his journey from Eritrea toward the Tunisian shores of the Mediterranean through a sustained reflection on the relationship between migration, storytelling and literature. The *jurthuma*, or migration 'bug', that the narrator diagnoses as source of the desire for migration, intertextually conjures one of the central metaphors in Tayeb Salih's 1966 *Season of Migration to the North*, where the germ of colonialism and contact continues to resurrect cycles of violence. Abdar initially posits that storytelling and literature can cure those affected/infected by the 'bug', but the role of literature in the novel gradually shifts to grieving and memorialising lost lives and connecting migrants across time and space. The three narratives thus highlight different functions of storytelling and literature that both call attention to the precarious position of migrant lives in the borderland and defamiliarise and reimagine dominant narratives about them.

The Stakes of Arabic Literature of Undocumented Mediterranean Migration

In her work on *harraga* literature, literary critic Nicoletta Pireddu suggests that the attempt to testify to the harsh realities of clandestine migration in *harraga* literature runs the risk of leading to literary approaches that are ethnographic in style and paternalist in intent.[4] The potential 'traps' are many. In addition to the Orientalist and ethnographic lenses through which 'ethnic' literature and Arabic literature in the West in particular is often read, literature that deals with 'timely' topics such as undocumented migration is sometimes written (and read) in ways that slide into testimony or a means to help readers make 'sense' of migration by providing individual stories that we can relate to in the place of numbers and statistics. *Harraga* literature thus runs the risk of creating space for a kind of voyeurism through which well-heeled readers and critics on both sides of the Mediterranean divide can comfortably contemplate the pain of those whose lives are at stake in these clandestine crossings.

While *harraga* literature does testify to painful realities that are at once social, political and individual, as literary narratives they are distinct from the *testimonio*, which anchors truth value in the author's or the narrator's subjectivity and lived experience. Although testimonies can be powerful and often abound in aesthetics and rhetoricity, the alternative tellings that we find in literary narratives of migration are often powerful precisely because they operate in a very different kind of truth economy. Though vested in exploring urgent questions and conditions they have a variety of aesthetic and narrative resources to draw on, including those that are nonrealist and including their intertextual dialogue with various other *kinds* of narratives about migration, literary and otherwise.

Literary and other expressive art forms are well placed to reframe dominant narratives of undocumented migration. Literary narratives allow us to see how complex lives exceed the categories ascribed to mobile humans, whether it is forced migrant, asylum seeker, undocumented migrant, economic migrant, or refugee. For instance, the play *Invasion!* by Swedish novelist and playwright Jonas Hassen Khemiri, which will be discussed in Chapter 4, playfully subverts the discourses that create the idea that European countries are being invaded by Middle Eastern Others. As explored in Khemiri's play, the idea of an immigrant 'invasion' from the Middle East and Africa permeates discourses on migration to Europe in ways that flatten the idea of the migrant. Instead of pointing toward the complexity and diversity of experiences and histories, they render migrants hypervisible and, by virtue of the erasure that such flattening entails, simultaneously invisible. A cursory Google search for images of undocumented Mediterranean migration brings up numerous photographs of boats filled with humans who, from a distance, appear indistinguishable from each other. Other photographs that often circulate are those taken during rescue efforts, showing migrants lined up wearing identical life vests distributed by humanitarian organisations.

Human rights groups that do the important work of tracking Mediterranean migration and deaths need to present such information through statistics and graphs that show trends of migration over time. Similarly, media reporting on refugees can be said to constitute a 'genre' in which norms of reporting override the particular voices or experiences of migrants.[5] A recent study, for instance, shows that reporting on asylum seekers in Great Britain has changed very little since the 1940s.[6] Of course, these images and types of reporting tell certain kinds of truths. Yet they are partial truths that reveal certain patterns and stories. Such stories can easily feed into preconceived archetypes of migrants, including that of the victim or threatening invader, and have the effect of obscuring experiences and narratives that do not fit these patterns.

Writing about Mediterranean migration and its representations in Italy, Teresa Fiore offers a persuasive reminder of the way that media reporting often erases long histories of contact and travel in the region, histories that, if more present, might better situate us to respond to movement across this border.

> Millennia of movements (peaceful as well as violent) of people, goods, and ideas shuttling in both north- and south-bound directions across this basin of water are compacted into a contemporary narrative of one-way voyages – except when refoulement practices are enacted – with the aim of reaching today's 'land of abundance', i.e. Europe …

> The Mediterranean is not occupied by invading migrants, as the media rhetoric and by extension a large spectrum of political groups and public discourses suggest, but it is instead pre-occupied by many other stories of movements and connections that remain untold or partially told.[7]

A view of the Mediterranean as 'pre-occupied' by previous histories of migration, movement and contact can provide a counter-narrative to flattening discourses of crisis that shape reporting on undocumented migration. Literature and art can (and often do) call attention to histories of contact, colonial and otherwise, and to the stories that are not being told. As such they can perhaps remind us of a shared social fabric, stretching beyond the immediacy of crisis.

Nahrain Al-Mousawi's incisive and wide-ranging study *The Two-Edged Sea: Heterotopias of Contemporary Mediterranean Migration Literature* discusses literary narratives of undocumented migration to reveal how the realities of the sea as a dangerous border and as a site of interchange exist side by side. She argues that literature of undocumented migration across the Mediterranean undoes and remakes the categories through which the Mediterranean as border and contact zone is understood. She writes,

> Even though the narratives appear intent on setting up an opposition between North and South, Africa and Europe, their intertextuality, scenes conveying multidirectional influence, a political and representational cultural ecology revealing a past and present of not only Europe in Africa, but Africa in Europe, are just as intent on deconstructing them as binaries. Thus, in a deconstructionist mode, they undermine the binaries of North and South, Africa and Europe, by demonstrating how one route of 'antithesis secretly adheres within the other'.[8]

As these studies show, it is not only by creating stories that assign cause, depth, agency and complexity to migrant lives and the Mediterranean as a zone of contact that literature introduces alternative lenses on undocumented Mediterranean migration. In other words, the stories of migrants' lives in *harraga* literature do not simply override the more dominant approaches to representing migration discussed above. Rather, the literature integrates an awareness and critique of how precarity, borders, and discourses on crisis are created.

In her study of *African Titanics* and *The Year of the Runaways,* Janet Wilson suggests a few different ways that literary narratives of migration can unsettle the layers of media narratives that sediment into lenses through which migration is interpreted. She writes,

> As narratives about the complexity of individual motive and hope, they challenge readers' habitual frames of perception, conditioned by affective documentary and media accounts of refugees. Their stress on the flow of experience at the expense of history, the strength of the impulse to survive in adversity, and the quizzical scepticism about ties of belonging, suggest fiction is meeting the new challenges of managing and adjudicating truth values in today's post-truth, globalised world.[9]

The 'quizzical scepticism about ties of belonging' is a critical component of how migration literature often rethinks some of the major categories through which we interpret ourselves and how we belong in the world, including citizenship and borders. Though individual perspectives featured in literature do not necessarily counter those of history, the interplay between them, the transindividual, opens up both for critical inquiry. They often bring to the light histories that media discourses of crisis erase and put the individual history in imaginative dialogue with the larger forces of border building that produce different kinds of belonging, including citizenship, precarity and illegality.

Arabic Exile Literature in Europe argues that Arabic literature of forced migration offers alternative and imaginative reinterpretations of dominant discourses on migration to Europe, especially those that portray migration as a threat, an aberration, or that do not see spaces outside citizenship as places of literary and artistic production. However, rather than refute the larger biopolitical project of managing populations that underpins contemporary migration politics and border policing, literary narratives often integrate an awareness of these larger forces into the individual stories that they tell. At the convergence of these macro- and micro-scales of narrating migration we often find the flourishing of the fantastic, the nightmarish, the rumour, and the mythical, modes of writing that invite us to imagine migration (and the categories that scaffold our knowledge of it) differently. We should resist reading works of fiction ethnographically, yet we can keep in mind this transindividual awareness that is cultivated in literature of forced migration, where individual stories are both shaped by and irreducible to their larger contexts.

At this intersection, we often find a departure from realist modes of writing. In fact, the fantastic, the nightmarish and the mythical take centre stage in these literary narratives of undocumented Mediterranean crossings. Migration in these narratives is often imagined as a form of wilderness, a space that the migrants encounter through the bare facts of the body. Such metaphors and modes of writing in *harraga* novels are numerous and include the idea that migration is a state that the migrant enters naked, vulnerable, or conceived of as non-human life. Storytellers, either characters who practice this art or the many who speak about migration or partake in rumour, are central to the narratives. In the novels, storytelling takes multiple forms; the Moroccan *halqa* (or public storytelling circle), anonymous collectives that circulate reflections and information on migration and characters who are storytellers (such as the Eritrean character Malouk in *African Titanics*) weave stories about migration that resemble myth and creation stories and thus add to the intertextual layering of narratives on migration in the novels.

There is a longstanding relationship in literary discourse between storytelling and survival. This is perhaps most famously showcased in the stories of the *1,001 Nights*, where the young woman Scheherazade sets out on a quest to save her life and those of other women by telling stories to the vengeance-bound king, a theme that permeates the stories in this ever-changing collection. While aware of the Orientalising impulses that often underpin references to the *Nights* in Western scholarship on Arabic literature, I still emphasise the idea that storytelling and literary narrative have life-giving qualities in how they can engage with dominant narratives about clandestine migration and point to modes of belonging beyond those that are upheld by the border regimes that create the very precarity that the narratives explore. Storytelling here is linked to both individual and collective practices of sustaining life even in the face of death, but also to the ability to imagine belonging in borderland spaces in ways that unsettle dominant narratives about contemporary migration in the Mediterranean.

Storytelling and the Liminal in Two Novels from Morocco

The opening paragraph of Mahi Binebine's *Welcome to Paradise* invokes a number of different storytelling practices, from the mythical to the popular and apocalyptic:

> Back in the village, the old people were always telling us about the sea, and each time in a different way. Some said it was like a vast sky, a sky of water foaming across infinite, impenetrable forests where ghosts and ferocious monsters lived. Others maintained that it stretched further than all the rivers, lakes, ponds and streams on earth put together. As for the wise old boys in the square, who spoke as one on the matter, they swore that God was storing up the water for Judgment Day when it would wash the earth clean of its sinners.[10]

The stories about the sea, we are reminded, are numerous and in constant transformation. Beginning with the tellings of village elders and continuing through renderings that figure it through wildness and finally divine wrath, the opening paragraph alerts the reader to attend to their own reading of the book as another storytelling event. Furthermore, the fantastic elements in the opening narrative foreshadow the characters' dreams and waking-life encounters with the sea later in the novel. As the characters come in contact with the sea and with Europe as undocumented migrants, these figurative renderings of the sea take on a new life.

Welcome to Paradise is told through a frame story. A group of seven would-be migrants from Morocco, Algeria and Mali huddle on a beach outside Tangiers overlooking the Strait of Gibraltar. Their destination, Spain, is seductively close despite the life-threatening journey that separates them. Aziz, the young narrator who, having received his schooling in a French Catholic mission seeks to be reunited with his teachers in France, recounts the stories of how his companions came to the decision to migrate. Among them are the Algerian Kacem Judi, who was a school teacher before his family was killed in the 1994 Blida massacre; Nuara, a young mother who, travelling with her infant, hopes to find her estranged husband in France; Yussef, a teenager who lost his family to accidental poisoning when his father stole grain that turned out to be rat poison; Reda, Aziz's hapless cousin who departed from his home village with his brother after their mother's suicide; Pafadnam, a Malian who fled drought and crossed several national borders before joining the group; and Yarcé, who worked as a masseur for a wealthy British expat in Marrakech. Through Aziz's telling of each character's story, we learn of the particular life experiences that brought them to this shore. All of the migrants harbour painful memories. Alienated from both state and family, they place their hopes in a high-stakes gamble for a better future. When the boat departs at the end of the novel, Aziz and his cousin, Reda, abandon it at the last moment. While the two cousins live to tell their stories, their co-migrants and the trafficker, they later discover, die on their journey.

Unlike *Welcome to Paradise*, which weaves together a number of different migrants' life stories, *Hashish* focuses on one would-be migrant while rendering anonymous the countless others who are present in the unnamed coastal town set somewhere between the Spanish enclave of Ceuta and the Moroccan city of Tangiers. The title *Hashish* conjures the illegal cross-border smuggling of drugs and goods that fuels the town's economy and, more luridly, the trafficking in humans that shapes the setting. The washing up of the bodies of drowned migrants on the shore punctuates the narrative, as do the laments of relatives arriving from all corners of Morocco to search for their missing kin. Fittingly, the use of hash defines many of the public settings frequented by the three brothers, Hassan, 'the Hajj' and 'the philosopher'. Drug-induced or otherwise, the quarrels between the three brothers return to their competing pursuits of Miriam, the young woman whose arrival in the town marks the beginning of the plot.

Miriam's desperate attempts to migrate to Spain, even as the three brothers and an elderly customs official each attempt to lure her to stay, direct the novel's energies toward the northern shores onto which, like a mirage, she projects her fantasies of paradise. Her encounter with Europe by proxy of the Spanish coastguard on her third attempt to leave Morocco, this time on her own, effectively shreds her dreams of migration to reveal a violent space outside citizenship. When she is raped by the Spanish men and sent off to sea to die, she becomes just one of the many unidentified bodies to reach the shores of the town.

The migrants in both novels enter a liminal state by separating themselves from family and home and by their resolution to burn the papers that link them to their nation. Therefore, the dominant settings of the novel – the beach in *Welcome to Paradise* and the unnamed border town in *Hashish* where the migrants await departure – are liminal sites. From this vantage point, the arrival in Europe is imagined as a transformation. However, while arrival in Europe is imagined as a transformation, or an entry into paradise, the liminal stage extends to encompass the passage across the sea and, correspondingly, shapes and ultimately overwhelms the encounter with Europe. Arrival in Europe does not herald the promised transformation but rather reveals itself as a precarious and prolonged state of being outside of the realm of rights and legal protection.

However, in these liminal spaces, storytelling, myth and fantasy take on particular significance. A similar idea about liminality is proposed in Victor Turner's *From Ritual to Theatre: The Human Seriousness of Play*,[11] where he suggests that liminal states, rather than always leading to reintegration (as often emphasised in structural-functionalist theory such as Van Gennep's writing on rites of passage) offer a wealth of performative possibilities. He suggests instead that liminal states can create 'the "subjunctive mood" of sociocultural action'.[12] Unpredictable in nature, the liminal offers a multitude of possible outcomes, many of which defy reintegration and, in fact, can be quite disintegrative.

Both novels begin by poetically conjuring a mood that invokes the liminal and permeates the setting before introducing their thematic take on migration. In *Hashish* the opening chapter immediately acquaints the reader with a setting defined by a pervasive – and shared – condition of frustrated renewal. Without yet introducing the main character Miriam, the short chapter poetically invokes her liminal condition by describing a brief spring that fails to deliver catharsis to a collective longing for rebirth:

> All of a sudden, spring arrived and even the trash heaps blossomed. Small white flowers to which nobody paid any heed spread through the cracks in the walls and under the wheels of the broken-down cars. The

spring did not last for more than a few days, as if it had been carried on a passing breeze for no other reason than to put on an unexpected performance. Or perhaps it just came to announce to the people that it was not the spring they had been waiting for, the spring that was supposed to come, were it not for those little flowers, orphaned and few, scattered here and there.[13]

Instead of a promised renewal, a yearly rebirth that offers hope, the fleeting spring launches the novel's setting into its long, ruthless summer. The little flowers that briefly adorn the trash heaps, crumbling walls, and stalled cars of the small town conjure an image of decay. Serving as a prelude to the rest of the novel and foreshadowing the metaphorical association of migration with burning, the first chapter introduces a setting that is permeated with signs of decomposition, thwarted rebirth, and unconsummated encounters. Such a condition shapes the novel in general and Miriam's fantasies of migration and transformation in particular.

Miriam's frequent and extended interior monologues stand in contrast to the silence and anonymity that the novel bestows on the many migrants who fill the unnamed Moroccan town. Unlike Miriam's, their presence is mostly made known through the reports of anonymous bodies washing up on the shore and the mourning relatives arriving in the town. At the same time, her interior monologues evoke the liminal condition that is at the heart of the novel's commentary on clandestine migration. Her desire to migrate to Spain rests on the idea that rebirth and renewal are only possible post-passage, in the form of the burning of identities that would take place in her passage to Spain. Having left her family and former life behind, Miriam already experiences her life as a liminal state and is awaiting a rebirth.

> I am twenty years old. And during these years I have not known any of those things that make life sweet. I am now walking the ledge between life and death, between a death that I inspect, that I carry, and a life that I await like a resurrection.[14]

Between her past life that she plans to throw overboard – figured as a burden and already dead – and her future life – conceived of as a resurrection – she dwells in the liminal space of the border town, searching for the boat that will transport her away from her former life, a boat that seems to herald both death and rebirth: '*Bghīt nkūn farḥāna ḥatā ana.*' Introducing her desire to be happy in Moroccan dialect ('I too want to be happy'), she continues, 'I have this past that I must carry with me and that I am waiting to throw overboard as soon as I am on the boat.'[15] If Miriam's dreams of resurrection are in a symbiotic relationship with the liminal condition described in the first chapter of the novel, there is already a prescience to her musings, a sense that the rebirth that she awaits may be destined to remain absent, a brief, counterfeit spring that fails to deliver.

Similarly, in *Welcome to Paradise*, the decision to burn identity papers and migrate is framed as a rebirth. To be reborn *elsewhere* after declaring the past dead – this is the shared desire of the Moroccan, Algerian and Malian migrants whose destinies are united by the human trafficking depicted in the novel. The narrator, Aziz, describes the moments preceding the boat's departure in very similar terms to Miriam:

> One hour left before throwing ourselves blindly into the great adventure, quietly slipping into a new life, donning its clothes, embracing its hours and days, so we could be born again somewhere else, change our skin, our air, our world, start everything again from scratch. One more hour and we could shrug off our cake-mud memories, drive the adobe hovels out of our minds, forget the barren fields, the life of struggle, poverty and distress. One hour, Lord, just one little hour, and, eyes closed, we'd be carried away on the tides of this forbidden dream.[16]

As in *Hashish*, Morocco is represented through the invocation of images of sterility and stagnation. The life stories of the seven migrants who await the boat's departure each in turn evoke a collective solidarity in the sense that the past cannot continue into an imagined future save for migration, figured as rebirth.

Aiming for Paradise

The characters in both novels invoke the concept of paradise (*paradis/ firdaws*) in speaking about their desire to migrate to Europe. When Aziz's cousin, Reda, in *Welcome to Paradise* mistakes the roaming lights of the Spanish coastguard for the Spanish coastline, the Algerian Kacem Judi jokes, '"If paradise were that close, son," ... "I'd have swum there by now."'[17] The irony in Kacem's remark is the way in which the state of exception that governs the sea is replicated in the novel's depiction of Paris, thus equalising the two spaces that are here set in contrast. In *Hashish* it is the Arabic word *firdaws* (paradise), or *firdaws arḍī* (earthly paradise)[18] that Miriam uses rather than the more religiously inflected *janna* (heaven) when imagining a life in Spain. In fact, Miriam invokes her desire to go to Spain, her earthly paradise, in direct defiance of the idea that she should wait for *al-ākhira* (the afterlife) to be happy. Like the migrants in *Welcome to Paradise*, her fantasy of paradise relies on the idea of rebirth on this earth, on the other side of a geopolitical border.

In both *Welcome to Paradise* and *Hashish* the fantasy of paradise relies on binaries of south and north, such as death/life, poverty/wealth, earthly drudgery/earthly bliss, sterility/possibility. In this construction of paradise, to migrate is not only to be transported into a different territory; it is also to move from one side of the binary to the other. As a fantasy of transformation, the paradise trope relies on the idea of paradise as a space with fortified enclosures, the crossing of which would enact a radical transformation. This conception of paradise is in concordance with its etymological lineage and historico-religious connotations. From the original conception of paradise, *paradayadam*, in ancient Persia, the term *pairidaēza* in Avestan Persian was constructed from two concepts: *pairi* signified 'encircling' or 'closing off' and *daēza*, 'to shape or mould'.[19] The idea of paradise that influenced the Abrahamic religions' understanding of an afterlife reflects this ancient concept of a space that is cordoned off and available only to the elect and deserving. Indeed, this etymology finds resonance in the construction of Europe as an earthly paradise in *Welcome to Paradise* and *Hashish*. For example, in Miriam's many meditations on her desired destination, her naive construction of Spain as a space of continuous bliss – an earthly paradise – relies on the idea that it is cordoned off and available only to a few.

By reversing this discourse and imagining Europe as a paradise-turned-wild space, both *Welcome to Paradise* and *Hashish* perform an act of 'writing back' that critiques the effect of biopolitical management of fracturing populations on the very border that delineates the Global South from the Global North. In this regard, *harraga* literature is part of a broader trend in postcolonial writing. The resurgence of paradise discourse in postcolonial literature in the past few decades reflects an effort to draw upon, revise and parody the kinds of paradise myths that emerged from European colonialism and which function discursively to replicate geopolitical boundaries. By mapping wildness onto Europe, *Welcome to Paradise* and *Hashish* perform the biopolitical construction of citizenship and its exclusionary processes even as they burn the boundaries (*ḥarq al-ḥudūd*) of a discourse that demarcates the Global North from the Global South.

Europe as Cannibal

In *Welcome to Paradise*, as the moment of crossing of the Strait of Gibraltar draws near, the trafficker summons the group of migrants and announces:

> 'All your papers. Passports, identity cards, birth certificates, address books: any document that could identify you. Got to be as good as naked there, on the other side.'
> 'Welcome to the *harraga*s!' said Kacem Judi.
> 'What's that mean?' Reda asked me.
> 'That by burning our identity papers, we're joining the ranks of the stateless.'[20]

When the trafficker calls on the migrants to rid themselves of any identifying papers, the papers that tie them to a legal regime of citizenship, he insists that they need to be *naked* upon arrival and, by extension, upon departure. As Aziz notes earlier in the novel, to learn how to be a refugee is to 'learn to keep in the background, to be nobody: another shadow, a stray dog, a lowly earthworm, or even a cockroach. That's it, yes, learn to be a cockroach.'[21] His reference to Kafka's *Metamorphosis* casts their future clandestine status as a dehumanising transformation – much in contrast to the kind of transformation that is desired.

The following readings treat the extended liminal state that, in the place of incorporation or paradise, appears along migratory routes and in the encounter with Europe. The metaphors of wildness and 'bare life' that appear in both novels perform the particular vulnerability that results from the suspension of the individual rights associated with citizenship.

In *Welcome to Paradise*, Morad, or 'Momo', serves an important role in the trafficking chain that brings the characters of the novel together. Thrice deported from France and having earned the ironic honorary title 'European Deportee', he recruits would-be migrants from his table in Café France in Marrakech's historic square *jami al-fna* through stories of his exploits in France. He is surrounded by intent listeners, who form a veritable *halqa*, or storytelling circle, of their own. But unlike the public storytelling circles in the adjacent square, which are celebrated and curated as authentic popular heritage, Morad's *halqa*, like the café in which it takes place, gazes outward.

The 'Madeleine' that sparks Aziz's memory of Momo's recurring Parisian nightmare is none other than the sight of Nuara's blood-stained mouth after she has gnawed off the paw of a stray dog that forced the group to hide under the boat. Emblematic of a bodily struggle for survival outside of the confines of society, Nuara's blood-stained lips serve as a narrative link to the metaphor of cannibalism, a metaphor that renders the encounter with Europe as a prolonged liminality figured as a reduction to bare life.

When living as an undocumented worker in France, working eleven-hour days at the restaurant Chez José, Momo experiences a recurring nightmare. In Momo's dream, his encounter with Europe is reduced to a few bare essentials. The dream begins with Momo and his boss, José, driving down an empty Champs-Élysées in a red convertible. Above them, the sky is eerily empty; beside them, the streets are abandoned. Momo and José sit down at a deserted street-side café to drink some almond liqueur. As José chatters incessantly, Momo begins to take note of the disturbing yet seductive nature of their exchange.

> Mr. José talks and talks. Momo can't hear him, all he can see is his outsize, open mouth where, instead of teeth, there's an infinite number of forks. The glittering, grinding stainless steel thrashes out a cascade of muddled words whose vague echo Momo begins to catch, just about; the voice is metallic yet soft, harsh and bewitching, irresistible. Momo lets

himself be swept along, opens his heart, swallows the words, absorbs their sense and inevitably, agrees with them.[22]

In the excerpt above, language is superseded by the mouth's capacity to devour. The scene is one of relationality through incorporation and digestion, not interaction or dialogue. José's terrifying yet sensual fork-filled mouth creates an atmosphere of seductive violence. At the same time that José's cannibalistic desire to consume Momo's flesh is elicited, Momo is swallowing, incorporating José's words. Bodily incorporation – of José's language for Momo, and of Momo's flesh for José – defines the scene.

The curious agreement that José and Momo make is emblematic of Momo's clandestine encounter with Europe. Here, as in the rest of the dream sequence, the brutal encounter is driven by desire on both sides. But the initially seductive dimension of the exchange – a desirous cannibalism – eventually gives way to its reductive properties. If only Momo will cede him a toe, a finger: 'Anyway, a finger, what's that? A little bit of nothing, a pathetic scrap of flesh and bone that sooner or later will end up food for worms, a complete waste.'[23] Momo's upward mobility – a cynical rendering of a social contract – will be based on giving up body parts in exchange for a sense of security and belonging. With each body part that Momo cedes to his boss's delectation, he moves up in the restaurant hierarchy. For two little toes he moves from dishwasher to server, and the rest of his toes, his thumbs, and a part of his buttocks buy him better living conditions. A salary increase costs an arm. Maybe he will even be able to get his papers in order with another bodily sacrifice. Finally, all that remains of Momo is his head.

Momo's reduction to the status of flesh that may be pillaged reflects the 'inclusive exclusion' that structures Giorgio Agamben's account of 'states of exception'. Included – indeed incorporated and devoured – into his Parisian setting through his body, he is excluded as a political being. The ironic rendering of a social contract in which Momo relinquishes his body in exchange for gradual recognition of personhood and small steps toward citizenship – first in the setting of the restaurant, where he is allowed to emerge from the dish room and appear in public and then through the promise of legal regularisation – serves to highlight the social and political exclusion at work.

The one time that Momo allows the dream to run its full course – the night before his arrest and deportation – he dreams that his head is perched on his pillow, overlooking the streets. He observes a garbage truck operated by two black men: 'Momo told himself that they obviously hadn't found anybody to snack on them, otherwise they'd be comfortably settled in the warmth on a pillow like him.'[24] The racial dimension of his peculiar and precarious social contract is made explicit just as it is about to come to an end. José appears behind him and whispers in his ear: 'I don't like heads. Calves' heads. Pigs' heads. None of them.'[25] When Momo pleads with José to just finish him off, José opens the window and, finding a garbage man urinating on the doorway to his restaurant, screams a host of racist epithets as he hurls Momo's severed head into the jaws of the garbage truck. Finally, this discarding is a harbinger of his deportation in waking life and as Sharae Deckard suggests, an allegorical rendering of the First World devouring the Third World.[26] Furthermore, with its invocation of cannibalism, the novel draws a parallel between Momo's precarious position in Paris and the fate of the migrants who drown in their attempt to cross the Strait of Gibraltar; both Europe and the sea are rendered as devourers of bodies.

The metaphor of cannibalism is also central to the depiction of the sea as a state of exception in *Hashish*. In Miriam's second attempt to migrate to Spain she, like Reda and Aziz in *Welcome to Paradise*, finds herself abandoning the boat at the last moment out of fear of the journey. On land, together with the boat's owner, Riki, she becomes a spectator to the boat's departure. Riki's prescient remark, 'The sea is anxious tonight. Too many people have entered it',[27] prefigures the continued personification of the sea, which is soon portrayed as a beast with arbitrary power over life and death. In the following scene, where the boat crashes against the rocks and sinks, the sea becomes a wild creature ready to devour the bodies that have entered it.

> Then they heard the first sound of wood cracking. The boat had not traveled out any further; it hadn't traveled at all. It was rocking back and forth,

but staying in place. Anchored to the water, it began to rotate and with it, so did the chanting of prayers. The water grew hands and fingers. The water grew nails. At times, the fore of the boat rose up as if it wanted to set sail but it would be grabbed and pulled down with a bestial strength by the water's ravenous nails. From the boat one could hear a sharp whistling sound. The chanting stopped when the wooden boards of the boat began to fly up into the air. One whirlpool to grind everyone: wood, water, and clay. Clay wailing, water laughing into a deep pit fashioned by the clawed fingers of the water. The moon beams that spread out across the water increased the moon's lustre. The boat became shreds. And for a short moment, the people, like feathers, were suspended in the air. Solemnly, the wooden boards crashed against the cliff one by one, striking the rock repeatedly as if they were seeking refuge in it. The two who had not attempted the crossing stood at the edge of the cliff peering down. The bodies, like children, were rocking on the water's surface. Sleeping children soothed by their dreams. The water rocked them as the moon guarded their small but impossible dreams. Then the surface of the water went blank; there was no trace of the boat, nor of the people. Riki stated: 'The sea has gone back to sleep now. The animal has eaten its fill and now it has gone back to sleep.' Then he descended to the shore. A light breeze ruffled the face of the water. And from below the rock a new boat emerged filled with more humans, who, in turn, were filled with more dreams of the same seductive slipperiness. After a moment Riki returned. He sat down next to Miriam and looked out upon the calm sea. Dusting off his clothes, he said: 'Tomorrow, the sea will spit out its drowned.'[28]

Once filled with hope, curiosity, and a desire for better circumstances, the migrants in this scene, like Momo in *Welcome to Paradise*, are reduced to bodies to be devoured by a watery cannibal.

The last section of *Hashish* features Miriam's final attempt to cross the Strait of Gibraltar, this time with the aid of the elderly customs official who, having overcome his obsession with her, furnishes her with a boat that she will ride alone. The conclusion of the novel completes the narrative arc in which the crushing of the fantasy of Europe as paradise reveals an extended liminal position, rendered as a wild space.

No, there was no reason for failure this time. All at once, the dark days had vanished. She stood at the stern and bade the dry land farewell. Without a trace of sadness nor regret she saw it fade away in the distance, out of her sight and out of her thoughts, shrinking in the distance. Soon, it would be all gone, not even a trace of its touch could be felt on her fingertips, no lingering image in her eyes, no ringing sound in her ears. Mustering all her senses, she prepared herself for the arrival of a new music. As for that piece of land to which she had said her farewells, it would remain where it was, introverted. Its people would continue to destroy each other. The big would continue to eat the small; the strong would continue to rapaciously devour the weak. People butcher (*yanḥar*) each other under all flags.

Is this the end? Is this the beginning?

She had gotten used to this kind of wavering, this going back and forth, this state of being suspended between freedom and slavery, imprisonment and release. The hours of the day were changing now; they were no longer the same as before. The sun no longer shone with its former intensity. Soon, the rays of hope from the other shore would reach her. A procession of small, white clouds slid across the sky. Perhaps they were driven by the same desire for migration and escape?[29]

The trope of cannibalism to describe her liminal position in Morocco recurs here even as she imagines her imminent arrival in Spain as a complete release from this condition, a fantasy of arrival as complete transformation, a transition from dark ('the dark days') to light ('rays of hope'). Nevertheless, if the novel resorts to a vocabulary of wildness to describe liminality and precarious subject positions, Miriam's final voyage reinforces the very liminal position that she hopes to escape.

Before describing the subsequent scene, it is worth noting how this particular scene echoes and parodies the well-known final scene of Tayeb Salih's 1966 *Season of Migration to the North*. At the end of that novel, as the narrator descends into the Nile and risks drowning in a desperate attempt to grasp at meaning, his identity crisis is figured through a liminal moment; he is suspended between the two shores of the river, between night and day, East and West, North and South, even between life and death. Whereas the ending of *Season* performs the postcolonial hybridity that plagues the narrator – a crisis of the intersection of his status as a European-educated intellectual and the needs of a newly independent Sudan – Miriam's liminal state of being suspended between two shores, life and death, relates to her precarious legal status and bodily vulnerability between the Global South and North. While arrival is imagined as a release from liminality, depicted in part as an endemic cannibalism at home, her body becomes the site of a violent encounter in the novel's final episode, when she is captured, raped, and sent to her death by three members of the Spanish coastguard.

Foreshadowing the ultimate loss of voice that this encounter entails, in the subsequent chapter the narration shifts from Miriam's interior monologue to third-person narration. Miriam wakes up in a daze to see three Spanish men from the coastguard in a boat next to hers. They help her over to their boat and though confused, Miriam assumes good intentions. When she is led to a bedroom, she notes that it will be a nice resting place. However, what follows is a violent episode in which she is raped and beaten by the three men. Like in *Welcome to Paradise*, Miriam's dehumanisation takes on an Orientalised/racialised character. After the first assault, the men force her to sprint naked to the stern and perform an Oriental dance for them.[30] The narration turns to this question of dehumanisation at this moment of violence: 'Miriam is not an insect. *I am human, I am human.* She screams at them, but no sound comes out.'[31] The line between the bare body figured as a violated human and that of a preyed-upon animal figured as an insect is at stake. When the boat containing her dead body washes up the next morning on the shore, she becomes simply another anonymous body to return to the town in this manner.

Both *Welcome to Paradise* and *Hashish* stage *harraga* migration as a liminal state. Tropes of wildness, wilderness and consumptive bodily encounters populate the narratives, especially in the liminal spaces where the desired transformations that the characters yearn for are indefinitely postponed. This is where storytelling of the fantastic often enters. These novels, I have suggested, unsettle dominant narratives on undocumented Mediterranean migration, especially those perpetuated by media and by discourses of crisis. By focusing on liminal sites and states, they centre a 'subjunctive mood of socio-cultural action', that is, spaces where unexpected shifts and the unsettling of the familiar may take place. The novels, too, open up lines of inquiry by defamiliarising migration through literary means.

In the following section, we turn to *African Titanics* by Abu Bakr Khaal, where the literary and nonrealist modes of retelling stories of migration also take centre stage. Importantly, this novel extends the geographical scope of *harraga* writing beyond the Maghreb by centring the dangerous desert crossing from Sudan to Libya, one of the routes that many undertake before arriving at the Mediterranean Sea. The novel thus highlights explorations of the liminal and of border policing that begin long before the sea crossings often featured in *harraga* literature. Written in Arabic, the novel features a multilingual milieu where migrants from various parts of the Middle East and Africa share routes, information networks, and stories that reimagine the journeys that are simultaneously underway. The theme of storytelling takes on an even more crucial role in *African Titanics* where it is self-consciously pitted against and in relation to a theorisation of the structural (and sometimes invisible) forces that underlie cross-Mediterranean migration and the journeys that surround it.

Storytelling and the Literary in *African Titanics*

In a mode similar to *Welcome to Paradise*, *African Titanics* introduces a mythical, even apocalyptic, rendering of water and migration told through a collective storytelling voice. In the opening lines of the novel, the narrator describes his exhaustion from moving between Khartoum and Omdurman (two cities separated only by the Nile River, which flows between them) looking for traffickers. Already a few legs into his journey northward from Eritrea, he is momentarily stalled in Sudan, assuming different nicknames and navigating rumours and networks of traffickers and migrants as he plans his next step. In this space, where the lives and journeys of so many are intersecting, he reflects on the phenomenon of migration:

> To some, migration seemed like an unruly wave or a fugitive waterfall that was difficult to comprehend. Nobody knew when or how it would end. Many were suspended in painful confusion as they watched the

madness unfold. 'Africa will be abandoned like a hollow pipe where the wind plays melodies of loss.'[32]

Here, the narrator situates himself with and in relation to the many others observing and experiencing the phenomenon of migration in Africa. By likening migration to powerful waters, the novel intertextually evokes the many discourses that figure migration as a flood, tide or wave. However, while 'waves' of migrants are most often imagined sweeping across and overwhelming receiving societies, the novel here recentres attention on so-called sending countries. Rather than imagining migrants themselves as waves, tides or floods, a practice that often serves dehumanising ends, the novel depicts water as draining the sending societies by conjuring loss and abandonment. He continues,

> Showing no mercy, the bell kept ringing, infecting our minds with the migration bug. As for me, I had managed to ignore it when I first heard its ringing five years earlier. It had seemed to me like any of the many noises in life that don't concern me, like the thunder of the Italian company De Ponti's dynamite blasting through Eritrea's mountains or the cries of the milk man 'milk, milk, milk' riding his donkey through the dark alleys of my village. But all those years of ignorance caught up with me. I discovered that the germ was firmly embedded in my blood and I scolded myself for my own foolishness in being unaware of it for so many years. From that moment, I was completely bound by its voice; it dragged my exhausted body behind it wherever it went.
>
> The bell snatched me, removing my body from my country. It dragged me across the border of Sudan into Libya in the dark of night. I was lost in the desert and then saved from a certain death. Then I slipped across the border into Tunisia. I felt like I had been fated for this journey and that there was no escape from my ceaseless roaming.[33]

Much like the flood metaphor, the evocation of migration as an infection draws on an oft-repeated and dehumanising notion. Here, it is the idea that migrants are contaminants, clouding the purity of nations, imagined as homogeneous and ahistorical entities. However, the site and effects of the infection are reimagined in this telling; rather than positioning the migrant as a contaminant, the body of the migrant becomes host and the site of the unfolding effects which, in the novel, are also directed toward the communities that the migrants are from and the communities that they form along their journeys. By rendering migration as a bug, or germ (*jurthuma* in Arabic), the novel suggests that the impetus to migrate is invisible and beyond the control of the infected person. Its ability to infiltrate minds and bodies relies on a very different logic than that of consent and autonomy. It does not respect the idea of individual sovereignty, but rather crosses both the porous boundaries of the body and between bodily hosts.

Intertextually, the metaphor of the germ, or *jurthuma* of migration, hearkens back to what is perhaps the most well-known Arabic and African novel of postcolonial migration, the 1966 *Season of Migration to the North*, by Sudanese writer Tayeb Salih. Set shortly after Sudanese independence, the novel explores the idea of contagion and infection in depth. Most centrally, one of the main characters, Mustafa Saeed, enters the British colonial school system as a young child and then travels to Cairo and London to complete his education and become a professor at the London School of Economics. His mission to turn the violence of colonialism back onto the metropole takes the form of parodying the Orientalist and anti-black stereotypes ascribed to him and instigating a number of his British lovers' suicides and killing his wife. In different scenes various characters and the narrator suggest that all of them, including Mustafa, are infected by a germ that stands in for colonialism as well as wanderlust and the violence that the kinds of cross-cultural contact explored in the book derive from. For instance, after Mustafa Saeed has disappeared, the narrator relates (or imagines) Mustafa's reflection at his own trial:

> In that court I hear the rattle of swords in Carthage and the clatter of the hooves of Allenby's horses desecrating the ground of Jerusalem. The ships at first sailed down the Nile carrying guns not bread, and the railways were originally set up to transport troops; the schools were started so as to teach us say 'yes' in their language. They imported to us the germ of the greatest European violence, as seen on the Somme and Verdun, the likes of which the world has never previously known, the germ of the deadly disease that struck them more than a thousand years

ago. Yes, my dear sirs, I came as an invader into your very homes, a drop of poison which you have injected into the veins of history. 'I am no Othello. Othello was a lie.'[34]

Season of Migration explores the idea of this germ spreading among the various characters as they come in contact with colonialism and its consequences. The germ's effects are invisible to the eye and experienced under the surface, in the psyches that shape the unfolding of the narrative.

In *African Titanics* too, the postcolonial is also an important context. Enduring postcolonial ties and uneven development are evoked in 'the Italian company De Ponti's dynamite blasting through Eritrea's mountains' and the 'dark alleys' that the milkman navigates. These sounds are framed as commonplace and mundane yet evoke the material equivalent of the bug that 'infects' the minds of would-be migrants.

The rendering of migration as a bug and an unruly wave that affects Africa (by infiltrating and sweeping away those who become migrants) and leaves loss in its wake evokes a sense of the forces of history that both overpower the individual and infiltrate the bodies and minds of the unsuspecting. The individual choices and narrative strategies that the characters create are in tension with these framing metaphors, which would have them unwittingly infected or swept away by force. This is the productive space of transindividual literary stagings of migration where individual narratives are shaped by, yet irreducible to, the greater forces that shape their journeys. The narrator, we find out, has tried to resist the migration bug by turning to the power of storytelling. We know, for example, that he has already been overcome/infected since he is already on his journey. Nevertheless, this framing tension between storytelling and the larger forces that shape our movement and choices infuses the novel with questions about the relationship between undocumented migration and the way that its stories are told.

Before recounting the details of his journey from Sudan into Libya and then Tunisia, Abdar briefly narrates a series of legends, stories and plays about people who face sorcery and are either overpowered by it or resist. One is a fairy-tale about a 'wicked wizard who lived in Europe long ago'. The wizard enchants a village's children with the sound of his bell, luring them into the forest, yet the mothers fight valiantly for their children. Unlike these children, the narrator notes, not everyone has people to protect them from sorcery and enchantment. It is the stories of Malouk, a Liberian storyteller that the narrator meets later in his journey, that really capture Abdar's imagination. Malouk presents him with a story collection titled *The Adventures of Kaji* wherein a storyteller named Kaji sets out to protect his nephew Bouwara against the migration bug by meeting him every night to tell him stories that will convince him to remain with his family. The narrator notes that 'this is the story in which Malouk allowed me to savour awe. It transported me to a world of imagination and amazement. He taught me the lesson that songs too can overcome sorcery.'[35]

African Titanics charts journeys that precede Mediterranean crossings, calling attention to how the boats that most often make headlines often represent one of many legs on migratory routes between Africa and Europe. The book opens in Khartoum, Sudan, where the Eritrean narrator Abdar lives among a community of migrants who are staying in and passing through the city. He joins a group of twenty-three Eritrean and Somali migrants who aim to reach Libya by crossing the desert in a truck. In conversations in the truck, travel across these arid lands is compared to the Mediterranean crossing. Like the sea border, the desert is also a space of extreme bodily vulnerability and exposure to violence. When the group is pursued by Hambata bandits, the driver, Naji, loses track of the route. Several men and women die of dehydration and exhaustion on the journey. A young Eritrean woman named Terhas steps up to the task of tending to and caring for the dying. She and the narrator form a bond and remain together for subsequent journeys. When they catch their first glimpse of 'civilization' (*'amrāniyya*)[36] in several days, people who recognise Naji's car rush out to provide food and care for the survivors. Once recuperated, Terhas and Abdar re-join friends who traversed the desert before them. They seize the opportunity to jump onto a truck filled with people a few days later and arrive at a smugglers' hideout where they stay until a police raid causes the residents and smugglers to disperse.

In Tripoli, the binary between 'sorcery' and storytelling that is set up at the beginning of the novel begins to break down. In the hideout,

Terhas and the narrator discover different kinds of writings left behind by migrants who have passed through earlier. Abdar finds love letters stored in a magazine, left by a previous occupant. On the walls, they find messages in multiple languages, registers, and effects.

> 'Where will you take me, oh fleeting hours?' read one of the beautifully written messages in Tigré, dated May, 1999, and signed 'Anonymous'.
> 'How can the journey from shore to shore be so very difficult? It seems so simple on the maps,' a French hand had written just a few days earlier.
> 'Forgive me my dear Hammoudi,' came another message in Arabic, which looked to be the work of a woman. When I translated it to Terhas, fresh tears welled in her eyes.
> 'Perhaps Hammoudi was her husband,' I suggested, 'or a lover? Or a friend?'
> 'Or maybe it was her son. Maybe it was a little baby that she left behind because she thought the journey was too difficult. What agony their lives must be!'
> Alongside the many melancholy messages there was also the odd amusing one. 'The date of his Majesty's sea voyage will shortly be announced!' read one of them in French, translated for us by one of the travellers from Morocco.[37]

The fate of these travellers remains unknown to Abdar and Terhas, and by extension the readers of the novel, and they are moved.

One night three buses arrive with migrants from Morocco, Algeria, Tunisia, Egypt, Iraqi Kurds, and Bangladesh. Later a second group arrives, among whom is Malouk the Liberian storyteller. Malouk, whose stories about the Kaji appear early in the novel, shows up at the smuggler's hideout carrying his guitar. The very source of the narrator's quest to overcome the migration bug/sorcery through song or storytelling has arrived, signalling also the shifting place of stories in the novel. Malouk too is on a journey northward, and his song and stories become both counterpoint to and part of the fabric of his continued journey, which merges with that of Abdar and Terhas. His goal of composing an epic song about the experience effectively merges migration and the power of song.

One of the first stories that Malouk tells the group is the story of his ancestor Malouk, a fisherman who dies at sea:

> Malouk's death enraged the sea. According to the storytellers, it stretched its watery arms to where the ship was anchored and carried it off as tenderly as a father might cradle a new-born baby. The ship was borne away over waters and Malouk's deep gentle voice rose from it, reciting poetry. To this day, fishermen and sailors still claim to see the ship far out at sea, with its ghostly sailors beneath their black sail.[38]

The story of Malouk the First and his demise foreshadows the stories that will circulate after Malouk's own death, linking the imagined past to imaginings in the future. Abdar mostly plays the role of a subjective narrator. In some instances, it is clear that he is narrating from memory after his journey, memorialising his own story and those whose path he crossed. In others, he narrates events that neither he (nor any survivor) witnessed, such as the sinking of the boat that Malouk was on board along with Malouk's and other passengers' tragic end.

The novel is written in Arabic and Abdar is a speaker of Arabic, but the spaces of the novel are multilingual and call attention to language. The title of the novel, for instance, derives from a naming practice that designates the boats that carry migrants to the sea as 'Titanics', a name that invokes strength but also the sinking of their famous namesake. In one conversation at the apartment where Abdar and Terhas stay in Tripoli before going to the smuggler's house, the residents frequently gather around the television to watch the weather reports and news in anticipation of their journeys. One Egyptian turns to address the Eritreans in the group:

> 'Isn't it you lot that called the boats "*Titanikaat*"?' he continued, mimicking our Arabic, 'As in *al-Titanik*?'
> 'Yes, that's us.'
> 'Damn you all! Who gave you the right to pluralise it as *Titanikaat* anyway? Are you the experts in Arabic grammar these days – or is the great grammarian Sibawayh travelling with you and personally advising you on new words?'
> 'What else should we call them?'

'Something optimistic. Noah's Ark perhaps. Or any other ship that never sank. Well? What d'you have to say for yourselves?'
'What can we say? The matter's closed. You are the all-knowing one.'
'Whatever! Just so long as you know that seventy percent of your *Titanikaat* sink – only around thirty out of a hundred survive! So I guess Titanic is an appropriate name for them after all. *Tita ... niiiiik,*' he said with force, heavily emphasizing the second syllable, transforming it into the Arabic word for 'fuck'.[39]

Chance plays a formative role in the narrative. One day, police storm the hideout. Abdar, Terhas and Malouk barely escape arrest. Later, after they have taken temporary residence with friends, smugglers return their money, awaiting another opportunity to leave. However, the group decides to head toward Tunis in order to shorten the sea route. The journey slows as they spend about four months in Tripoli, during which time they often gather in Malouk's room to hear his stories. Eventually they cross into Tunisia into the border town of Ben Gardane, where they find a driver who is willing to transport them to Tunis. When they enter Tunis, now on foot, they are confronted by a police officer. When he asks the group where they are from, Abdar, caught off-guard answers, Eritrea. The guard, however, mishears him as saying Mauretania, and thus holding the right to be in Tunisia.

Though they find their way to a hostel owned by a man who shows both kindness and solidarity with undocumented migrants in the city, conditions in Tunis are difficult. Malouk, who is increasingly dejected, delivers a story of Malouk the Second and an epic story of competing storytellers.

There is another raid and while Terhas and Abdar are arrested and held for several months, Malouk escapes and embarks on his crossing. He dies at sea. The story of his sea journey and the sinking of the boat is narrated in great detail even though the narrator is not present and there are no survivors. The narrator recounts how the boat's motor stops working and the boat gradually takes in water. There is hole in the boat left from tearing out a refrigerator to make space for more people. Many have already died when they encounter a ship they believe might save them. Instead of saving them, however, the passengers on the ship observe the sinking boat callously, arms crossed, and continue on their way. It is not clear whether the inhumanity of the tale that the narrator tells is from his imagination of the event or from some uncharacteristic omniscient knowing in his role as narrator. He and Terhas are eventually released from prison and deported back to Libya and then to Eritrea.

After his death, Malouk and his stories become the stuff of legend and myth. The narrator is haunted by dreams and memories of Malouk, which still come to him long after his return to Eritrea. 'Years later, I still dream of Malouk. I see him in a distant corner of a brightly-lit street, trying to strum his guitar even though its strings have been eroded by salt.'[40] It is not just the narrator who has been affected in this way. The legend of Malouk lives on in stories passed among people and shared in internet chat rooms. Addressing Malouk's memory, the narrator states, 'Your memory clouds all others, absorbing all of my relentless sorrows. I feel as if I crossed the desert just to meet you, so that your death would take me to the furthest limits of pain.'[41]

The stories, which are shared both in person and online, effectively imagine the moment of Malouk's death to re-inscribe life and dignity. One story, shared with the narrator in an internet chatroom, features Malouk standing on the sea, perfectly calm and dry. A ship arrives and he walks across the waves to board it. A similar story is shared with the narrator by a woman from India. In this story too, Malouk is standing in the Mediterranean Sea and is welcomed onto a ship that passes by. He is greeted enthusiastically by all those aboard and a celebration breaks out, 'pulsing with lively African music',[42] including one of Malouk's songs. This song becomes the final statement of Malouk, and the last words of the novel:

> To all the pounding hearts
> In feverish boats
> I will cut
> Through these paths
> With my own liberated heart
> And tell my soul
> To shout of your silenced deaths

And fill
Palms of dust with morning dew
And song

These stories, which recuperate and re-inscribe dignity and life in spaces where death is ever present, mourn and memorialise the dead even as they honour the living. The closing song, which is attributed to the now legendary Malouk, addresses migrants making precarious journeys across the Mediterranean. Their lives, 'hearts', are set in contrast to the 'silenced deaths', which the song shouts out in protest. In contrast to the torrents of water that are conjured in the narrator's vivid rendering of migration early in the novel, water is also recuperated as a metaphor for life. In contrast to the water that threatens the boats and the people in them, the image conjured is one that is gentle and life-giving, the morning dew that can give life to thirsty palms. Like *harraga* migration, which creates paths for mobility in the face of closed borders, the barrier of the sea, and border policing, the song sings of creating openings or 'windows' (*nawāfidh*; translated in *African Titatnics* as 'paths'). The song thus both mourns and memorialises deaths such as Malouk's and also sings of creating paths and openings. In a way, the song (like the stories that circulate about him) offers a form of extended life to Malouk, but its power is also in memorialising many others and opening up spaces.

The image of the window, an opening in a wall, links to the questions about literature and storytelling that the novel asks. Ultimately, in *African Titanics*, the song is not harnessed to overcome or defeat the migration bug, as the narrator imagines earlier in his journey. Rather, it is used to address those who are experiencing precarious migration. As Janet Wilson suggests, the use of song counters 'the inauthentic framework provided by the narrator, enabling the novel to fulfil one of the demands of testimony – that is, to overturn the perception that such lives will be forgotten because [they are] not "regarded" as materially grievable.'[43] In addition to centring attention on the grievability of lives that are too often represented as statistics, as threats, or through dehistoricised discourses of crisis, this novel, like so many other *harraga* novels, calls attention to *how* stories of migration are told.

Conclusion

Signifying multiple forms of 'burning', the term *harraga* evokes a liminal position, where the liminal is understood not only as a separation from birth communities but also as a departure from citizenship. *Harraga* literature explores a 'spectral condition'[44] of Mediterranean migration in which the migrant is suspended – literally and figuratively – between two shores even before making the crossing. This liminal position is not only that of being *in-between* citizenships (since the novels do not tend to portray a resolution or end to this state), but one that is situated outside of legal protection, subject to heavy surveillance, policing, and often, cruelty.

Teresa Fiore notes that like many earlier literatures of crossing and passage, contemporary art and literature of Mediterranean migration engage with the complex histories and representations that precede it and with the potential transformative visions and realities that migration can engender:

> As artists and activists take their own journey into this intricate network of old and new meanings of 'passage', their works challenge uncritical and over-simplified representations and instead search the reasons for the crossing itself, denounce its implications and hint at the possibilities it opens.[45]

Fiore's discussion focuses on art and literature of Mediterranean migration from the Mediterranean's European shores. *Harraga* literature, as literature written from the perspective of migrants seeking to make the journey north, has a slightly different emphasis, yet it shares the question of how mobility in the face of great obstacles can create new possibilities and how literary and artistic stagings of such journeys can create new ways of seeing or engaging with the liminal spaces or borderlands that migrants pass through. We should resist reading works of fiction ethnographically, yet we can keep in mind the transindividual awareness that is cultivated at the intersection of individual stories and the larger contexts they are both shaped by and irreducible to.

What possibilities do literary narratives of such borderlands open? As discussed earlier, migration literature can unsettle dominant discourses about undocumented migration. But it often goes further than that by defamiliarising the very categories that underpin modern conceptions of rights and belonging, such as citizenship and the nation. The capacity to imagine belonging and tell stories in borderland settings in unexpected ways is central to contemporary migration in the Mediterranean. In these literary narratives the fantastic, the nightmarish, the rumour, and the mythical flourish along with modes of writing that invite us to imagine migration differently. Such unsettling is necessary. Indeed, the routine realities of the past twenty to thirty years would do well to be defamiliarised. From either a historical or ethical perspective, the drowning of thousands of people in the Mediterranean Sea is in no way 'normal', nor is the flattening and dehistoricisation that a perpetual perception of crisis creates. The metaphor of the 'window' in the closing song in *African Titanics* is apt. The idea of creating a window, an opening in the wall, is linked not only to the way that *harraga* implies the 'burning' of paths and the insistence on mobility in the face of its criminalisation, but also to creating an opening to seeing or creating new vantage points on a seemingly familiar story.

The following chapter explores Finland-based Iraqi writer Hassan Blasim's more recent short stories of undocumented migration across Turkey, eastern Europe and northern Europe. The routes in these literary narratives are different, but the stories develop the theme of rendering liminal spaces through the fantastic and the speculative that we see in *harraga* literature and place them in contexts that are relevant to Iraqi history and displacement. From the novels that narrate the liminal and reflect in depth on storytelling and 'song' explored in this chapter, we move to meditations on mobility that link the movement across ostensibly closed borders to porosity of bodies and an opening of boundaries between humans and other life forms. From here, too, borderlands become a site where different modes of belonging can be imagined.

Notes

1. 'The Future Now: 10 African Artists to Watch', *ARTnews*, http://www.artnews.com/2018/07/18/future-now-10-african-artists-watch/ (accessed 29 November 2020).

2. Hassan Abderrezak, 'The Refugee Crisis and the Mediterranean "Seamentary"', Lecture, Ohio State University, Columbus, OH, 2 November 2018.
3. Judith Butler, *Frames of War: When is Life Grievable?* (New York: Verso Books, 2010).
4. Nicoletta Pireddu, 'A Moroccan Tale of Outlandish Europe: Ben Jelloun's Departures for a Double Exile', *Research in African Literatures* 40, no. 3 (2009): 29.
5. Terrence Wright, 'The Media and Representations of Refugees and Other Forced Migrants', in Elena Fiddian-Qasmiyeh, Gil Loescher, Katy Long and Nando Sigona (eds), *The Oxford Handbook of Refugee & Forced Migration Studies* (Oxford: Oxford University Press, 2016), 463.
6. R. Greenslade, *Seeking Scapegoats: The Coverage of Asylum in the UK Press* (London: Institute for Public Policy Research, 2005).
7. Teresa Fiore, 'From Crisis to Creative Critique: The Early Twenty-First Century Mediterranean Crossing on Stage and Screen in Works by Teatro delle Albe and Andrea Segre', *Journal of Modern Italian Studies* 23, no. 4 (2018): 522–42; 523.
8. Al-Mousawi, *The Two-Edged Sea*, 36. At the end of this quotation, al-Mousawi is citing Terry Eagleton, *Literary Theory* (Minneapolis: University of Minnesota Press, 1996), 11.
9. Janet Wilson, 'Novels of Flight and Arrival: Abu Bakr Khaal, *African Titanics* (2014 [2008]) and Sunjeev Sahota, *The Year of the Runaways* (2015)', *Postcolonial Text* 12, no. 3/4 (2017): 13.
10. Mahi Binebine, *Welcome to Paradise*, trans. Lulu Norman (London: Granta, 2003), 1.
11. Victor Turner, *From Ritual to Theatre: The Human Seriousness of Play* (New York: PAJ Publications, 1982).
12. Turner, *From Ritual to Theatre*, 84.
13. Youssef Fadel, *Hashish* (Casablanca: Dar al-Fanak, 2000), 5.
14. Fadel, *Hashish*, 7.
15. Fadel, *Hashish*, 35.
16. Fadel, *Hashish*, 108.
17. Binebine, *Welcome to Paradise*, 17.
18. Fadel, *Hashish*, 158.
19. Helga Ramsey-Kurz and Geetha Ganapathy-Doré, in 'Introduction: Some Uses of Paradise', in Helga Ramsey-Kurz and Geetha Ganapathy-Doré (eds),

Projections of Paradise. Ideal Elsewheres in Postcolonial Migrant Literature (Amsterdam: Rodopi, 2011), viii–xi, discuss the fact that the original meanings of the term 'paradise' were preserved as the concept spread from ancient Persia. For example, Xenophon's biography of the Persian ruler Cyrus the Great, *The Education of Cyrus*, recounts the young Cyrus's dissatisfaction with hunting in his grandfather's – the king's – enclosed garden (paradise) when the wilderness outside offers better game, thus prompting him to leave the enclosed space. The story appears to be a prototype of the biblical Garden of Eden and Fall. Indeed, the ideal of paradise as a space of cultivation and domination over nature runs throughout monotheistic religions and intellectual history.

20. Binebine, *Welcome to Paradise*, 166.
21. Binebine, *Welcome to Paradise*, 66.
22. Binebine, *Welcome to Paradise*, 96.
23. Binebine, *Welcome to Paradise*, 97.
24. Binebine, *Welcome to Paradise*, 102.
25. Binebine, *Welcome to Paradise*, 102.
26. Sharae Deckard, *Paradise Discourse, Imperialism, and Globalization* (New York: Routledge, 2010), 203.
27. Fadel, *Hashish*, 160.
28. Fadel, *Hashish*, 161–2.
29. Fadel, *Hashish*, 292.
30. The Orientalised/racialised and gendered claim to bare life is repeated in another *harraga* novel. In *Hope and Other Dangerous Pursuits*, by Laila Lalami, one of the protagonists, a young woman, avoids deportation from Spain by turning to sex work that builds on European fantasies about the idea of the harem.
31. Fadel, *Hashish*, 295.
32. (My translation) Khaal, *Taytanikat Ifriqiyya*, 8.
33. (My translation) Khaal, *Taytanikat Ifriqiyya*, 9.
34. Salih, *Season of Migration to the North*, 79.
35. Abu Bakr Khaal, *African Titanics*, trans. Charis Bredin (London: Darf Publishers, 2014), 16–17.
36. Khaal, *Afrian Titanics*, 39.
37. This and the following quotes are from the Charis Bredin translation of *African Titanics* (London: Darf Publishers, 2014), 47.
38. Khaal, *African Titanics*, 69.

39. Khaal, *African Titanics*, 60–1.
40. Khaal, *African Titanics*, 119–20.
41. Khaal, *African Titanics*, 120.
42. Khaal, *African Titanics*, 121.
43. Wilson, 'Novels of Flight', 8.
44. Pireddu, 'A Moroccan Tale', 29.
45. Fiore, 'From Crisis to Creative Critique', 525.

3

The Subversion of Borders and 'Nightmare Realism' in Iraqi Migration Literature

In Hassan Blasim's short story 'Kalimat Mutaqatʻia' ('Crosswords'), Marwan, a young crossword-puzzle writer, wakes up in a Baghdad hospital only to discover that his body now hosts the soul of another man: a police officer who died in the explosion that caused his own injuries. In the ensuing narrative, the two souls (Marwan and the police officer) are forced to coexist and intersect, much like the increasingly obscure words that are featured in Marwan's crossword puzzles. Marwan's sense of self is disrupted; no longer able to see himself as a singular or bounded entity, he becomes both a space of intersecting, open-ended signs and a space of claustrophobic and unwanted intrusion. The crossword puzzles and Marwan's perplexing predicament are both apt metaphors for the crossing and subversion of boundaries that are central to Hassan Blasim's literary narratives, especially those that explore migration, where similar metaphors of crossing and melding proliferate. Indeed, Blasim's many short stories of migration are tied to this broader project of exploring more open-ended subjectivities (and approaches to writing violence and war) and modes of interconnectivity that entail a subversion of boundaries and borders.

Finland-based Iraqi Hassan Blasim is a writer and filmmaker who has forged new directions in the twenty-first-century Arabic short story. His literary narratives stage recent conflicts in Iraq through the macabre, the fantastic and through experimental approaches to narrative. His stories of forced migration and human trafficking contribute to a rewriting of migration and exile in Arabic literature. As a public intellectual and activist,

Blasim often emphasises the liberating potential of opening up national borders and identities. He made the following remarks in a March 2016 interview in Helsinki, Finland:

> You're part of a dream. You're Finnish, and you're part of the world. Of the Earth, the planet. You're part of it all. It's all linked. But then people start talking about being *pure*, just this or that, like, 'You're Finnish', or 'You're Iraqi', or 'You're an engineer', and nothing else. That's so limited. You're everything. You're an engineer, an artist, a dead person, you're nothingness, you're a dream. This connectedness ... it helps you write better.[1]

Purity, of course, is a fiction. But as Blasim shows, fiction, especially in its speculative genres, is a fertile ground for exploring interconnectivity and the transgression of borders, whether they be national borders, the borders of the individual human subject, or the borders that separate species or literary genres. While the statement above emphasises the liberating dimensions of such subversions, his literary narratives often explore spaces that are highly ambivalent, where utopian and dystopian visions of interconnectedness alternate and coexist.

Blasim's short stories, which are widely circulated and translated, have become emblematic of Arabic migration literature in Europe. This chapter explores the convergence of migration and other forms of border crossings in Blasim's fiction by analysing short stories from the collections *Majnun Sahat al-Hurriya* (*The Madman of Freedom Square*)[2] and *Al-Masih al-'Iraqi* (*The Iraqi Christ*)[3] and the play *Lu'bat al-Qubba'at al-Raqamiyya* (*The Digital Hats Game*), which was performed in Tampere, Finland, and Tartu, Estonia, in the spring of 2016. Blasim has used the term 'nightmare realism', to speak of the dystopian (ir)reality of his writing. Indeed, the nightmare is an appropriate metaphor as it, like these literary texts, reshapes reality through the lens of individual and collective trauma and opens up the possibilities for blending and various kinds of border crossings. While borders and boundaries are omnipresent in Blasim's texts of migration, his writing creatively subverts these same boundaries, narrating, for example, the hacking of national borders, the blending together of human bodies, parasitic relationships that challenge the integrity of the individual and the breaking down of boundaries between the human and non-human. In other instances, entities such as viruses, search engines and shared blood banks call attention to the ways that human beings are porous, networked and interconnected. Far from writing a peaceful or harmonious unity between people and within a global community, it is precisely in the violent contexts of war, the irregular migratory routes between Iraq, Turkey and Europe, and the musings of perplexed characters that boundaries and interconnectivity are being reimagined.

This chapter links these literary approaches to broader trends in Iraqi and Arabic literature. The concept of 'nightmare realism' is closely linked to trends in post-2003 Iraqi literature, specifically its renderings of violence through an 'aesthetics of horror'[4] and an attention to heightened exposure to death and unaccountable violence through wars and occupation.[5] The nightmare is a repetitive symptom of post-traumatic stress. In literary texts, it is mobilised not as an individual diagnosis, but rather as one to witness, process, and reimagine collective trauma. In addition to its links to broader trends in Iraqi literature and other narratives of irregular migration explored in this book, the nightmarish qualities of Blasim's migration narratives can be productively compared to the dream-like magical realist renderings of Kurdish Syrian writer Salim Barakat, who has been based in Sweden for several decades. Salim Barakat's magical realist literary project has radically defamiliarised both northern European settings[6] and the Arabic language and imagined a world where everything – including the dead – are animate. While Barakat's magical realist corpus is linked (though not reducible to) to Kurdish histories and cosmologies, Blasim's nightmare realist narratives of migration take on the states of exception in borderlands outside of citizenship. The utopian ideal of opening up borders is continuously haunted by an undoing of the borders of the individual and community, a theme that connects Blasim's fiction of migration dystopian (and nightmarish) literary renderings of war in Syria and Iraq.

Blasim's writing is part of an emergent trend in Arabic migration literature in which modernist understandings of exile are giving way to perspectives that grapple with large-scale migration and the spaces outside of citizenship. An iconoclast seeking to move beyond given identities such as religion, ethnicity or nationality in favour of imaginative reconstellations of being that take us beyond many of our established categories, Blasim creates spaces in his writing where boundaries are unsettled and characters, like the rest of us, are grappling with uncharted territory. These themes link his fiction to the trends in forced migration literature discussed in this book as well as to literature that bears witness to large-scale traumas of war, most prominently in Iraq and Syria. In these ways, in Blasim's literary narratives, migration and the crossing of borders point toward more nuanced and porous ways of conceiving of ourselves and our belonging.

Writing Migration: Borderlands and Networks in Hassan Blasim's Writing

Hassan Blasim was born in 1973 in Baghdad. He spent most of his childhood in Kirkuk in northern Iraq before returning to the capital to study at the Academy of Cinematic Arts. While there, he received recognition for his films (his films *Gardenia* and *White Clay* both won the Academy Festival's Award), but the critical nature of his work also drew the attention of government informants in Saddam Hussein's Iraq. After several arrests, he left Baghdad in 1998 and moved to Sulaymaniyah in Iraqi Kurdistan. He continued to work as a filmmaker, now under the pseudonym Oazad Osman, and made a film titled *Wounded Camera*, a drama focusing on the displacement of millions of Kurds as a result of the Iraqi army's campaign of retaliation following the 1991 Kurdish uprisings. Blasim left Iraq in 1999. He worked in under-the-table jobs in Istanbul for several years and travelled clandestinely through Iran, Bulgaria and Hungary before arriving in Finland in 2004. He has since resided primarily in Helsinki and made several short films for Finnish national television.

It is worth noting that unlike many relatively recent Arab diasporas in Europe, such as in Sweden and Germany, there are rather few Arabic speakers in Finland. A country which often upholds a myth of cultural and linguistic homogeneity, Finland has a restrictive migration policy[7] and admits few asylum seekers. As a point of comparison, estimates of Arabic speakers in Sweden, a country with around double the population of Finland, range from 200,000–500,000;[8] in Finland there are around 15,000 Arabic speakers. Sweden hosts a mature Arabic language publishing and theatre scene, largely established by Iraqis in the 1990s but increasingly includes many Syrian cultural actors and artists of other national origins. Blasim's work has been studied and, to a large extent, celebrated in Finland, where it has a great deal of visibility, but he travels often to other European and North African countries for festivals and workshops.

Blasim's own experience with migration was nonlinear. Like many others, his journey was clandestine and took place along the routes of human trafficking. As he relayed in an interview with the Finnish Institute in London,

> Maybe you have heard my story. I came illegally, crossing the border from country to another. I had problems with the secret police in Iraq. They were [a] difficult four years: First, I had to walk to Kurdistan, because they wouldn't give me my passport in Iraq. I walked from Iran to Turkey. I worked in Turkey in many different places, through the black market. I tried to make money for smugglers. After Turkey, I tried to walk to Bulgaria four times, failed, and tried again. From Bulgaria I walked to Serbia.[9]

Blasim's literary renderings of migration are not autobiographical, yet they take place along the kinds of routes and conditions that he and so many others have experienced. The short stories of migration in *The Madman of Freedom Square* and *The Iraqi Christ* are set along migratory routes between Iraq, Turkey and Europe, taking place in forests, trucks, asylum-processing centres, and other sites of passage. Other stories are set in contexts of civil strife, political conflict and occupation in Iraq; yet others are set in Finland. As in the quote above, the migratory journeys in his stories often include twists, backtracking, reroutings and unaccountable traffickers. The violence of contemporary border-building practices provides the subtext for much of Blasim's writing on migration.

Gloria Anzaldúa theorised borderlands as spaces that come into being through the creative efforts of those who inhabit and cross borders and who mix and negotiate multiple languages and identities.[10] Michel Agier's 2016 book, *Borderlands*, adapts the idea of borderlands for contemporary migratory contexts, especially in Europe, examining the margins of nation states that have become temporary or long-term homes for a growing population that is not within the protections and structures offered by citizenship. Agier argues that the kinds of belonging that are forged in these spaces outside of citizenship represent a 'banal cosmopolitanism' that, in its increasing prevalence and intensity, can be used as a starting point for theorising global and mobile subjectivities.

Like many other post-1990s Arabic literary narratives of migration, Blasim's writing draws on tropes associated with the pre-political (nature, the body, wilderness) to represent spaces outside of citizenship. In reading Blasim's fiction, I draw on feminist philosopher Rosi Braidotti's re-evaluation of the biopolitical. She makes life forms and networks that have traditionally been excluded from the realm of full citizenship (the feminine, racialised bodies and non-human elements that sustain life) central to her theorisation of the ethical challenges we face in the twenty-first century, including innovations in biotechnology, rapidly evolving networks and information technology, environmental destruction and mass displacements and migration. In place of the centred and bounded subject emphasised in liberal conceptions of citizenship, she calls for viewing subjectivity as decentred and shaped by our mutual dependencies and the forces that traverse us. Such a conception, she argues, can better situate us to respond to the challenges of the twenty-first century.

To Braidotti, the transnational and postnational condition associated with displacement and migration is one of the central ethical questions of our current age. The process of disidentification with national and bounded notions of identity, she argues, is a necessary process for facing a rapidly globalising world and being able to see it through our interconnections rather than through what separates us. This disidentification and the shift toward embracing multiple, complex and shifting belongings, she suggests, is both a painful and life-affirming process, one that is intimately familiar to migrants and exiles, but that will also become increasingly imperative for those who have not experienced the physical dislocation that migration entails firsthand.[11] This invitation to see subjectivity as 'an assemblage that includes non-human agents'[12] and disidentify with bounded and unchanging categories parallels the playful and often dystopian exploration of porous subjectivities in Blasim's writing.

Rita Sakr's article 'The More-Than-Human Refugee Journey: Hassan Blasim's Short Stories'[13] reads Blasim's stories from an ecocritical and biopolitical framework, anchoring their theorisation of rights to mobility and possibilities of community in the environment and in non-human species rather than the nation. She explores the imaginative possibilities within the liminal spaces that Blasim's fiction so often imagines and specifically, how his stories offer an invitation to consider how the construction of the category of human is complicit in creating the precarity that many migrants face, even as precarity is one of the conditions that humans share with non-human beings.[14] Blasim's stories, she argues, 'confront the reader with a heightened and sustained sense of a crisis of representation urging the need to create imaginative responses'.[15]

These questions of disidentification are linked to how we view the entanglements of our globalised and interconnected world. Kathrin Thiele suggests that as an alternative to neoliberalism, which takes entanglement and interconnectivity for granted while also imagining a self-sufficient, rational individual actor who can separate their sense of self from this condition, we can allow entanglement to inform an ethics of how we engage with and interpret the world, when we understand the 'I' or 'we' to be always already co-created through relations and entanglement.[16] Sarah Nutall suggests that 'a focus on entanglement in part speaks to the need for a utopian horizon, while always being profoundly mindful of what is actually going on'.[17] Seeing ourselves and the world through our interconnectivity is at once a kind of realism and an opportunity to imagine differently. In Blasim's work, these potential worlds can be utopian, dystopian, and otherwise playful, but they tend to link back to a distancing and subversion of borders that are selectively upheld.

One way that such subversions take place in Blasim's writing is through online and networked spaces. Blasim began to publish in a digital environment, making his debut as a short-story writer on the website iraqstory.com. Though most of his writing has moved from an online environment to print, his work has continued to engage the digital in both form and content. In form, his writings draw on the interactive and open qualities of online creative culture. Characters that appear in one text might reappear in another. His short story 'The Gardens of Babylon' in the future-writing collection *Iraq+100* imagines a future Babylon as a hub of innovation in information technology, virtual reality and gaming through a narrative structure that resembles a video game.

As sociologist Manuel Castells writes, 'Humans create meaning by interacting with their natural and social environment, by networking their neural networks with the networks of nature and with social networks.'[18] Castells' writing emphasises the potential for collective agency and resistance through and in relation to digital networks. In Blasim's project, too, we see glimpses of new possibilities of being in the world (and narrating our world), but in a much more ambivalent way. In his public statements and his literary texts, Blasim theorises ways that both destructive and creative online practices such as gaming, programming and hacking are reshaping the literary texts of today and the future.[19] Blasim's narratives frequently make use of metaphors, themes and modes of writing drawn from the digital realm. In his stories, networked information environments are spaces where boundaries of individual sovereignty are undone and refigured.

Blasim's oeuvre has troubled the hierarchies between original and translation as well as print and digital. Finnish literary critic Olli Löytti, who studies Blasim's work through the networks and power dynamics of 'world literature', has noted that Blasim's work is both 'born digital' and 'born translated'.[20] Indeed, like many other contemporary writers, Blasim often publishes his work on the internet before it appears in print. His earliest stories appeared in Arabic on the website IraqStory. com, which he co-founded. In print, translations of his work have often preceded the Arabic originals, expertly translated by Jonathan Wright. His first short story in print, 'The Reality and the Record', was featured in the English-language collection *Madinah: City Stories from the Middle East* (2008), edited by Lebanese author and activist Joumana Haddad. Blasim received international acclaim as a writer following the 2009 publication of his short story collection *The Madman of Freedom Square*, which was translated by Jonathan Wright. An edited version of the Arabic original, *Majnun Sahat al-Huriyya*, was published in Beirut in 2012 by the Arab Institute for Research and Publishing. It was subsequently banned in Jordan and Kuwait. The first uncensored Arabic version of the collection was published in 2014 in Milan by al-Mutawassitt Press. Blasim published a second collection of stories, *The Iraqi Christ*, translated by Jonathan Wright, in 2013. The following year, it became the first Arabic literary narrative to win the Independent Foreign Fiction Prize. US-based publisher Penguin selected stories from both collections and published *The Corpse Exhibition* in 2014. Al-Mutawassitt Press published Blasim's prose poetry collection *Al-Tifl al-Shi'i al-Musum* (The Shi'a's Poisoned Child) in Arabic in 2016.

The following section explores the subversion of borders such as clandestine migration, parasitic relationships, and digitally networked activism and consciousness in Hassan Blasim's literary narratives. In Blasim's fiction of migration, liminal borderlands are often spaces of dissolution theorised through modes of interconnectivity, porosity, and digital networks. These modes of writing invite us to see beyond the category of the human in order to grapple with pressing questions relating to mobility and displacement in a global age that is at once profoundly interconnected and invested in building walls.

Iraqi War Literature, Iraqi Refugee Literature

Blasim's 'nightmare realism' is embedded in a broader Arabic and post-2003 Iraqi literary and historical context. The US-led occupation and the ensuing conflict unleashed pervasive and unpredictable violence, often directed at civilians. Estimates of casualties from the US-led occupation and the subsequent internal conflicts range from around 100,000 to over a million,[21] with countless others experiencing traumas related to living in an active conflict zone, losing loved ones, or being displaced from their homes, either within Iraq or in diasporas in the region, Europe and the United States. A number of Iraqi writers have responded to this violence by writing narratives infused with nightmarish and monstrous qualities, writing the irreality of the real by reimagining violence in speculative or interiorised psychic forms. Another result of the collapse of Saddam Hussein's Baathist regime is that authors were able to write and publish on previous conflicts, such as the 1980–8 Iran–Iraq war and 1991 Gulf War, and some of these narratives share a similar approach and aesthetics.

Yasmeen Hanoosh has written on the various ways that Iraqi writers have responded to the changing realities ensuing the 2003 occupation, regime ouster, and civil conflict. Some Iraqi writers in the post-2003 period, she notes, sought to recuperate the social realist styles of important authors associated with the pre-Baathist era of the 1960s and 1970s, like Gha'ib Tu'umah Farman, Mahdi 'Isa al-Saqr and Fu'ad al-Takarli. Some enlisted literary realism to challenge the Hussein-regime's efforts to re-write Iraqi history through a Baathist nationalist lens.[22] Many writers in exile, forced to flee Iraq in the 1980s and 1990s, had already been writing in ways that departed from the national vision upheld by Iraq's Baathist regime, including upending taboos on writing the self and exploring minority identities.[23] Another important trend, and one that is particularly relevant to this book, is that of the turn toward nonrealist writing to evoke the traumas and irreality of Iraqi's conflicts. Hanoosh writes,

> More strikingly, however, this past decade has witnessed multiple serious departures from these mimetic norms that characterized the dominant narratological models of the twentieth century, most notably in the minimalist, impressionistic short stories of Luay Hamza Abbas, and Hassan Blasim's at once peremptory and incredulous accounts of human violence.[24]

Haytham Bahoora has examined the particular nonrealist aesthetics of violence that have emerged in Iraqi literature in the post-2003 era. In 'Writing the Dismembered Nation: The Aesthetics of Horror in Iraqi Narratives of War' he analyses the role that the monstrous and the metaphysical plays in post-2003 Iraqi literary narratives that centre the violence of occupation and war. In analysing the writings of Ahmad Saa'dawi, Hassan Blasim and Luay Hamza 'Abbas, Bahoora shows how nightmares, the supernatural, and the unconscious enter literary narratives to stage violence that seems unspeakable, even unreal. This crisis of verisimilitude is anchored in the idea that violence of the occupation and civil war has nightmarish qualities and exceeds the capabilities of language and realistic representation. Bahoora draws on theories of the postcolonial gothic that stress the return of the repressed and buried histories[25] to align these narrative and aesthetic choices with unaccountable violence of the occupation and the ensuing violence.

Ikram Masmoudi has probed the question of how Iraqi literature has been reshaped by the violence of past decades in her 2015 book *War and Occupation in Iraqi Fiction*. This study of literary narratives of the Iran–Iraq war, the US-led occupation, and post-2003 conflicts focuses on how literary narratives explore 'the continued devaluation of human life throughout the past three decades in Iraqi history'.[26] She draws on Giorgio Agamben's concept of 'bare life' developed in *Homo Sacer: Sovereign Power and Bare Life*[27] to consider literary representations of those whose lives have been most intensely exposed to violence in these conflicts. To this end, she considers literary stagings of the following categories: the war deserter, the soldier, the suicide bomber and the camp detainee. She notes the centrality of figures whose lives can be extinguished with impunity in a context where rights are suspended (either in the context of the global 'War on Terror' or in the chaos of civil war).

The fiction of Hassan Blasim demonstrates a continuity between the themes and aesthetics of Iraqi war/occupation literature and the writing of migration. Blasim's nightmare realism is part of both his literary narratives of migration and those of war. The intertwined contexts and themes make links between the unspeakable violence that is produced both by war and on irregular migratory routes. The irregular migrant, like the categories enumerated and explored in Masmoudi's work, is also one that is at increased risk of death and unaccountable violence (either direct or through neglect). Nightmare realism bridges and blurs reality and fantasy; in a way, it opens the border between the two, rendering it porous like so many other borders in his work. Porosity is part of the kind of vulnerability that we see in Masmoudi's discussion of necropolitics, that of bare life. But in addition to critiquing the conditions that create this vulnerability, it also reaches for the sites of connectivity a recognition of porosity gives rise to.

Hacking National Borders: *Digital Hats Game* and 'The Truck to Berlin'

In Hassan Blasim's play *Digital Hats Game* (*Lu'bat al-Qubb'at al-Raqamiyya*), which was performed in Tampere, Finland, and Tartu, Estonia, in the spring of 2016, a group of 'white hat' (activists not seeking profit) hackers target drones and create a 'borders game' to hack into border surveillance systems to open up borders to migrants attempting to cross them. In the play, the hackers target a world order that allows for the free passage of the materials of clandestine warfare while policing human mobility. In the short story 'The Truck to Berlin' ('Shahinat Berlin') featured in *The Madman of Freedom Square* and also recounted in *Digital Hats Game*, a group of Iraqi men perish in a Serbian forest after a trafficker abandons them in a locked truck. Read together, hacking, understood both in its literal sense and as a metaphor for infiltration and subversion of borders, structures the representation of clandestine migration. As in several of Blasim's texts, the opening of borders creates a sense of possibility for creating new relationships with the world and calling attention to the ways that we are networked and connected across borders. However, in both of these texts, national borders are upheld and the porousness and vulnerability of individual bodies and communities are exposed to the violence of border-building practices. In *The Digital Hats Game*, the hackers are themselves hacked when they play the borders game and their community is subsequently dissolved. In 'The Truck to Berlin' the bodies of the Berlin-bound migrants are violently blended together and the non-human intrudes in ominous ways. In these texts, Braidotti's ethical injunction that we recognise our porosity, the non-human forms that sustain and traverse us, and our inherent interconnectedness plays out in dystopian ways. The policing of borders instead becomes directly linked to the exposure of bodies and communities to violence.

In reading the hacking of borders in Blasim's fiction, I draw on Tarek el-Ariss's article 'Hacking the Modern: Arabic Writing in the Virtual Age'.[28] El-Ariss uses the metaphor of hacking to describe the changing practices of a generation of Arab writers who draw on online writing cultures to reshape their relationship to a literary and political establishment. In contrast to modernist writing that centres on the nation and the politically committed author responsible for the edification of the masses, this newer generation's fiction, he argues, is fragmented, decentred and interactive, like the globalised world around us. Reading Egyptian writer Ahmed Alaidy's novel *Being Abbas al Abd*, he argues that hacking 'operates as a literary bricolage that opens up the novel to new forms of writing and cultural production'.²⁹ As a metaphor, hacking includes both destructive and creative practices that target a unified system through infiltration. Similarly, opening the literary text to other areas of cultural production, especially online writing culture, wreaks havoc on certain aesthetic forms and indexes a search for alternatives to the idea of a unified system, be it in the political or aesthetic realm. As el-Ariss notes, Alaidy's novel both transliterates the English word 'to hack' into Arabic and refers to it as *ikhtiraq al-nizam*, or 'infiltrating the system', where *nizam* also implicates the idea of political 'regime'.³⁰ In contrast, *Digital Hats Game* uses the term *qarsana* (piracy) or *qarsanat al-net* (piracy of the net) to refer to hacking. This formulation, in contrast to *ikhtiraq al-nizam*, does not have a singular aim (such as the system, *al-nizam*); its scope is more diffuse and global – and implicates the notions of making claims that are either figured as illegal or outside of current legal orders.

Blasim wrote *The Digital Hats Game* in Arabic and it was translated into English by Jonathan Wright and into Finnish by Sampsa Peltonen. The performance (in Finnish and Estonian) was a co-production between the Tampere-based Telakka Theater and the Estonian Artu Theater and presented a radically reworked version of the themes in the script.³¹ *The Digital Hats Game* is a memory play; in its near-future frame story, the character Jennifer State tells her daughter about the white hat hacker community that she was part of in her youth and how it eventually dissolved. Her reflections on the past (our present) are tinged with disappointment that their activism failed to have the desired effect. The play turns to this past. Jennifer is a hacker and a performance artist. She meets and falls in love with a young hacker named Mohamed whose alias is 'The Prophet'. He is European, but his hacking targets censorship in the Arab world. He approaches Jennifer after seeing her performance piece 'The Rape' by hacking into her computer. In the script, the performance piece is a collage of violent episodes where actors alternate between different roles from the 'war on terror as victims of perpetrators': civilians, US soldiers and Islamic State fighters, for example. Mohamed joins Jennifer's white hat hacker community and begins to co-create performance art pieces on themes such as the war on terror, media, and different violence-driven ideologies.

In Blasim's script, Jennifer and Mohamed's performances intersperse the scenes where the audience learns about the hackers' activism and personal stories. The hackers, Jennifer State, Mohamed ('The Prophet'), Carlos ('Cool Frog'), Isabelle ('The Chef') and Anti ('Little Fish'), are working to acquire technology from 'black hat' hackers, hackers who perform work for hire and profit. The black hats are developing a technology that can bring down passenger planes in order to sell it to terrorist organisations. The white hat hackers are trying to buy this technology so that they can use it to take down drones. The white hat hackers see their work as an 'open war' on the open-ended and lawless wars of our time. Their hacking is, of course, literal; their activism is based on an infiltration of information networks. However, it is also implicated in projects affecting the distribution of mobility and the subversion of borders. They aim to reverse a logic of mobility wherein the 'elastic sovereignty'[32] of the war on terror era allows drones – but not people – to freely cross borders.

A woman who calls herself 'the woman in the red hat' introduces herself to the community. A developer of 'black games' – illegal virtual games – she seeks the group's assistance in developing a game called 'The Borders Game'. In this game, hackers would join forces to dismantle border-surveillance systems and earn points based on how many refugees safely cross national borders without the aid of traffickers. Making use of existing networks of activists, hackers and aid organisations, they would first develop the land-borders game, and then create a sea-borders game. However, while playing with other hackers around the world, they discover that migrants are being arrested at the borders of Mexico, Hungary, China, Indonesia, Greece, Bulgaria and Spain. The woman in the red hat is an agent of the international police; she has used the game as a ploy to infiltrate the network of hackers seeking to dismantle border controls.

An intimate infiltration has also taken place. Jennifer learns that Mohamed has slept with the woman in the red hat. This betrayal causes a rift between Mohamed and Jennifer, who is pregnant with their daughter. Mohamed, torn between a desire to maintain his political and ethical commitments or to pursue more direct, violent actions,[33] disappears, first creating a hostage situation at a factory that produces weapons and then disappearing to work with various resistance and terrorist organisations.

His location and the question of whether he chose to follow either of his two muses remain ambiguous. His absence continues to affect his daughter, Sarah. The play ends when Sarah detonates a cyber bomb. Like the activism of her mother's community, the question of whether this act of destruction will create an opening for new possibilities remains unresolved.

The play is more didactic than Blasim's other fiction. The characters often read as mouthpieces for an open-borders activism. For example, in a press conference scene where the white hat actors answer questions clad in Anonymous masks, a conversation unfolds as follows:

> **Mohamed**: What moral law allows us to roam across the world while others cannot enter our selfish fortified castle?
> **Journalist**: Are you a hacker or a philosopher?
> **Mohamed**: Someone who develops ethical viruses, as you call them.[34]

The ethical practice that the play invites the audience to think about runs counter to current legal and extra-legal regimes of border control and warfare. Activism here relies on creating viruses and other means of infiltrating barriers, borders and security, that is, forcing open borders that are selectively closed. It was Blasim's intention to create activist theatre that could contribute to conversations about activism, smuggling and borders that were raging at the time of the play's performance. While the characters are unabashedly idealist, the practices that they undertake end up exposing their own vulnerability. The global community that is formed in the process of playing the borders game, for example, gains both its power and its vulnerability from its horizontally networked and open structure.

While not a presence on stage, the figure of the migrant haunts the play as it calls attention to the ways that undocumented and clandestine border-crossing runs parallel to the ethical viruses and infiltrations performed by the hackers. The anonymity of the migrants in the play, represented as points that hackers score as they secure a border crossing, resembles the anonymity of the hacker community. Hacking comes to resemble the practices of the migrant who seeks safety and new possibilities in spite of closed borders. In the play, the exposure and arrest of migrants globally coincides with an infiltration and dissolving of the hacker community. It is no coincidence that it is Blasim's story 'The Truck to Berlin' that appears as an intertextual interlude in the play.[35] In the script, it is read as the woman in the red hat discusses the plans for the Borders Game with the group. The stage directions state, 'The theatre goes dark and turns into a dark truck.'[36] In the version of the play performed in Tampere, the excerpt from the short story was recited to the audience before we took our seats. When the doors to the theatre opened, the audience was ushered into a small, dark area guarded by actors in Anonymous masks. The audience hears the story, and thus experiences a form of liminal passage as they cross the threshold between the outside world and the world of the play.

First appearing in print in the collection *The Madman of Freedom Square*, 'The Truck to Berlin' stages a similar dynamic in its chronicling of the journey and tragic demise of a group of Iraqi migrants travelling from Turkey toward Germany. A group of young men attempting to cross borders that are not legally open to them perish in a way that erases the boundaries both between them and between the human and the non-human. While the 'filtering' function of national borders is upheld, the narration, intertextual references and themes of the story call them into question, shifting the focus to an open-ended question of responsibility.

Like *The Digital Hats Game* and many of Blasim's short stories, 'The Truck to Berlin' is recounted through a frame story. Narrated by a young Iraqi man working at a bar in Istanbul to save enough to pay a smuggler to take him to Europe, the framing narration betrays an anxiety about locating the boundaries between humans and their animal and monstrous Others that is more fully developed in his story. Fleeing from Iraq, he notes, was like being 'on the run from myself and other monsters'. Years of Saddam Hussein's rule had 'brought to the surface a savagery which had been buried beneath a man's simple daily needs. In those years a vile and bestial cruelty prevailed, driven by fear of dying from starvation. I felt I was in danger of turning into a rat.'[37] In his view, the whole world is characterised by inhumanity and fragility: 'All it needs is a little shake for its hideous nature and its primeval fangs to emerge.'[38]

In Istanbul, stories about migration across forests and seas circulate between traffickers, illegal residents and would-be migrants through layers of hearsay and reporting. The narrator relates the story of the Berlin truck group recounted to him by 'Ali the Afghan', an Afghan man living in Istanbul without papers. In Ali's story, thirty-five young Iraqi men are locked in a truck bound for Berlin after paying traffickers a hefty sum. Every evening, they make a short stop to refill water supplies and take care of bodily needs. Everything seems to be going according to plan until the third day, when the truck suddenly stops and changes direction. In the claustrophobic darkness of the truck's interior, the men are unable to discern where they are headed. The truck stops and it soon becomes clear that they have been abandoned. The story then chronicles the migrants' progression from attempts to remain calm and offer comforting words and distractions, to panic. To describe what takes place in the truck, the narrator returns to the idea that the boundaries between humans, animals and monsters have dissolved. A scream arises that seems to belong to nobody and everybody:

> When they heard the scream, they tried to imagine the source of this voice, neither human nor animal, which had rocked the darkness of the truck ... It seems that the cruelty of man, the cruelty of animals and legendary monsters had condensed and together had started to play a hellish tune.[39]

After a few days, the truck, now silent, is discovered in the forest by the Serbian authorities. Upon finding the mass of dead bodies within, they conjecture that the men had been torn apart by the talons of eagles and the teeth of crocodiles. No longer thirty-five discrete entities, the bodies have dissolved and blended together into a 'large soggy mass'.[40]

'The Truck to Berlin' reads as a retelling of Ghassan Kanafani's well-known 1963 novella, *Rijal fi-l-Shams* (*Men in the Sun*), which tells the story of three Palestinian men who suffocate in a water tank while being smuggled from Basra to Kuwait in search of better futures. As in 'The Truck to Berlin', the liminal space of wilderness in *Men in the Sun* (in this case the desert) is both a rat-eat-rat world[41] and a space onto which the characters project their hopes and fears. In *Men in the Sun*, the desert is a space that resonates with the characters' emotions, seemingly echoing their heartbeats. Unlike *Men in the Sun*, which can be read as an allegory of Palestinian suffering and the failures of both Palestinian and

Arab leadership, the responsibility for the death of the migrants in 'The Truck to Berlin' is more dispersed. When the smuggler Abu Khayzuran calls out at the end of the *Men in the Sun*, 'Why didn't they knock on the side of the tank?' his question implicates both the perceived lack of resistance among Palestinians and the inaction of Arab leadership.[42] In contrast, although the men in 'The Truck to Berlin' pound on the side of the truck, there is nobody there to hear them. Who should have heard them? Who is responsible for their fate? The story suggests a wide web of responsibility encompassing border regimes, trafficking networks, and the vast range of conditions that drive the types of migration described in the story. Considered together, 'The Truck to Berlin' and *Men in the Sun* highlight the shift in Arabic literature from a national cause to a critique of an international borders regime that is diffuse and pervasive. The traffickers in 'The Truck to Berlin' are largely anonymous, and finally, absent, their individual identities irrelevant. They seem to appear because migrants' creative navigations of current border regimes necessitate them. If *Men in the Sun* condemns an Arab leadership for its failure to secure and protect a Palestinian nation, 'The Truck to Berlin' invokes an anonymous international community that 'lets die' at its borders. The responsibility for creating spaces such as the Serbian forest where the truck stops is both diffuse and shared. Similarly, located in a legal no-man's land, the now tangled and dissolving bodies – each indistinguishable from the next – signify a shared condition. They also point to a shared responsibility for the border-building practices that cause death at the gates of Europe and beyond.

'The Truck to Berlin' leaves us with a lingering sense that the boundary between 'civilisation' and wilderness is thin and unstable. The ever-present non-human reference points in the story serve multiple functions. On one level, they can be understood as representing the radical lack of empathy born of repressive politics and the state of exception surrounding the migrant's undocumented status. The narrator's cynical reading of the world as a space where monstrosity lurks just under the surface assumes new dimensions in the stories of clandestine migration that are circulating around him. The location of the tragedy – the forest – mirrors the wildness that unfolds in the truck. However, the forest would also be a safe refuge if they only could escape the truck. This dual representation of wilderness as a state of exception and as a refuge from the border-building practiced by humans is a recurring theme in contemporary Arabic migration literature.

In the story, one of the Serbian policemen who find the truck tells his wife that he saw a young man covered in blood escape the vehicle. He swears that the man turned into a wolf as he disappeared into the forest. In the end, it is a human-turned-wolf that hacks the borders by taking on the very wilderness that is ever-present in the story. Predator, escapee, survivor, fantastic vision, the wolf merges into the forested surroundings, only to appear intertextually, haunting Blasim's project of writing migration.

The Wolf that Escapes, the Wolf that Appears

Is the wolf that escapes a figment of the Serbian policeman's imagination or is it a marker that moves the story into the realm of the fantastic? The wolf subverts borders by surviving and taking on an animal form that is not subject to the same kinds of policing as the human migrants. However, it does so in a way that is ethically ambiguous. Does its survival and mobility hinge on extracting life from the Berlin truck men? In an intertextual move, a wolf appears in Blasim's collection *The Iraqi Christ* in a story titled 'A Wolf' (The two Arabic versions are titled 'Dhi'b' (Wolf) and ''Adat al-Taʿarri al-Sayyi'a' (The Bad Habit of Getting Naked), respectively). In the story, a wolf appears in the apartment of Salman, an Iraqi refugee in Finland. The framing device features Salman recounting his story to Hassan Blasim in a bar. His frequent exclamations, expletives and meanderings between topics give the narrative the feel of oral storytelling.

The story references several kinds of discourses on wilderness indexed by the Arabic root *wa-ha-sha* (وحش). Salman's loneliness, *waḥsha*, and social isolation are central to the story. An Iraqi refugee living in an unnamed Finnish city, he has recently returned to an urban environment after a period of living in the forest. Salman now spends his days cruising the marginal spaces of the city. He gambles, drinks beer and talks to strangers. Each day, he suggests, should include some 'human touch, however small. You know.'[43] He is positioned as an outsider to human community in a kind of urban wilderness, which is also shaped by his memories of living in the Finnish forest and, perhaps, by the unspoken experiences of his journey to Finland. The beast, or *waḥsh*, that appears one day in his apartment is a wolf. In the story, Salman is forced to confront various levels of wilderness. On the one hand, wilderness can signify the outside spaces that he has inhabited both in the forest and the city. On the other, if we read intertextually, the intrusion of the wolf can signify a confrontation with himself as a survivor, a part that he might relate to as ethically ambiguous. Much like the wolf, whose domesticated counterparts inhabit cities and homes, some parts of the main character of the story seem to linger in different kinds of wilderness. Salman resides in what Michel Agier calls the 'borderlands', where liminality extends in time and space.

The linkage between the border and the wilderness is a rich topic in contemporary Arabic migration literature; in 'A Wolf' it is also a space where border crossings are coupled with reflections on various kinds of unbounded subjectivities. As Salman recounts the fateful day when the wolf appeared in his apartment, his musings keep returning to imagined scenarios where individual consciousness and bodily fluids – elements associated with a bounded, individual mind and body – become networked, blended, and shared across a population of humans. Within these musings, borders between individuals dissolve in time and space in ways that parallel global databases and networks. For example, he proposes a theory of networked dreams organised by a searchable database:

> Imagine there's an Indian painter in Delhi working on some subject that's also taking shape in the dream of a man who's asleep in Texas. Okay, fuck that. But would you agree with me that all art comes together in this way? Perhaps love and unhappiness too. If, for example, a poet wrote about loneliness in Finland, then his poem could be the dream of someone asleep in some other part of the world. If there was a special search engine for dreams, like Google, all dreamers would find their dreams in a work of art. The dreamer would put a word, or several words, from his dream into the Dream Search Engine, and thousands of results would appear. The more the search is narrowed down, the closer he gets to his dream and eventually he finds out it's a painting or a piece of music or a sentence in a play. He would also find out which country his dream was in. Yes, you know, maybe life ... okay, fuck that.[44]

In these musings, dreams become discrete entities that circulate freely across borders like bits of data uncoupled from the original dreamer. These kinds of reflections provide openings for imagining different kinds of boundaries between humans and their Others.

The loneliness that Salman typically experiences in his apartment is periodically interrupted by visits from the Jehovah's Witnesses, and he uses these visits to fantasise about and experiment with different possible realities. In one conversation, he voices questions about the impermissibility of blood transfusions in their creed. Blood shortages, he solemnly explains, will be at the core of future wars. A plague could easily cause a blood shortage and such a war, a 'clean war', would demand new rules of engagement. Fighters would wear helmets and padding like American football players to avoid bloodshed and the object of the war would be to capture as many enemies as possible and redistribute their blood through a network of blood transfusion centres. In this scenario, blood is redistributed and shared. Like the Google search engine for dreams, this war relies on cross-border movement and the undoing of boundaries between humans. Unlike the search engine, however, which treats dreams as discrete objects that circulate without barriers, the network of blood banks creates a mixing and dissolution of individual bodily fluids. Both the dream and blood bank visions share a utopian yearning for open borders and the dissolution of boundaries between humans. However, Salman's own recent experiences of blood extraction contrast vividly with his stories of networked and open sharing. Remembering his own struggles in the city, he relates,

> I was happy in my seclusion, with the gifts of the forests, oblivious to the world of humans. I would drink red wine, in moderation. But the disaster was that none of the creams with which I covered my face and body deterred the mosquito attacks. And how can I relax when a swarm of them was hovering over my head all day long like Christ's halo in old paintings? At night the female ones got through the sheets like armoured vehicles and sucked my blood greedily.[45]

Like the captured enemy combatants of his story, his blood is being drawn and circulated. But in his lived version, the process is uncomfortable and intrusive. The metaphors of contemporary warfare, in particular, contrast with the futuristic image of a clean war. The future of such sharing and opening has not arrived.

The wolf does arrive, however, one day after Salman returns to his apartment. Salman quickly locks himself into the bathroom. The wolf, which has intruded into his most private space and into a most intimate condition (as one of the Arabic titles indicates, Salman's habit is to undress completely upon returning home) raises many questions. Salman wonders, did it come from the zoo or maybe from the forest? Did it fly and enter through the balcony? Do all of his neighbours have wolves now? Why does he always have to undress when he comes home? Is the wolf even real? It seems as though the various levels of wilderness – his *waḥsha*, the Finnish forest, his wilderness of contemporary migration – have become embodied in a wolf and are challenging him to a confrontation. Salman spends two days in the bathroom, occasionally peeking out of the keyhole to behold the wolf, which mostly sits silently or sniffs his clothes. Delirious with hunger, Salman finally decides to face the wolf. As the wolf leaps toward him, Salman faints. The wolf is gone when he awakens.

At the end of the story, Salman tells the author,

> I decided to go back to the forest and try to stand up to the mosquitoes, instead of seeing them as crocodiles. Fuck that. This is the last glass I'll drink with you. You are a strange man – perhaps you are rather like me.[46]

The interlocutor then introduces himself as Hassan Blasim. The likeness between the narrator Salman and the interlocutor with the name of the author should not be taken as a call to read the story autobiographically, but rather as an invitation to consider the implications of the diffuse networks that connect them, and by extension, all of us, though we may be positioned differently. The many discourses and questions on wilderness and open-ended subjectivities explored in 'A Wolf' are intertwined with Blasim's broader project of writing migration and, even more broadly, with trends and issues in contemporary Arabic literature of migration. The many spaces of wilderness that the story references – the forest, the spaces outside of community, and the intertextual linkages to other stories such as 'The Truck to Berlin' through the wolf – connect to a variety of ways of imagining networked and open subjectivities as well as the shared complicity the border-building practices that provide the backstory for contemporary literature of forced migration.

Conclusion

Like other texts explored in this book, Blasim's literary narratives ask and reimagine foundational questions about the nature of citizenship, rights, and even the category of the human through speculative and defamiliarising modes of writing. Though speculative genres often defy the natural laws and contexts with which we are intimately familiar, they are usually anchored in contemporary issues and frameworks. In Blasim's fiction, the project of writing border subversions and porosity in contexts of migration, I suggest, represents an experimentation with modes of perceiving that take entanglement as a starting point. The texts inquire into the not-yet-possible as much as they narrate the impossible.

The subversion of borders in Hassan Blasim's literary narratives of migration shifts our attention to different ways of perceiving the world. They seem to ask us to see ourselves and the world through our interconnectivity, indeed, to see the world as entangled on multiple levels, such as the porous body, the opened border and the online network. As suggested, metaphors of these entanglements include characters whose bodies intersect, hacking, viruses, networked consciousness and shared bodily fluids. They also find formal resonance in open narrative structures, intertextuality between stories, and the global print and online circulation and translation of Blasim's work. The focus on entanglement represents both an attention to what is already present in our world (though perhaps unnoticed or outside of our familiar ways of perceiving) and an attention to what is possible. With modes of writing that range from the reassuringly connective to the distressingly intrusive, there is space for both horror and beauty in these imagined possibilities and literary borderlands.

Notes

1. Hassan Blasim, 'Hassan Blasim', interview by Margaret Litvin and Johanna Sellman, *Tank Magazine* 8, no. 9 (2016): 238.
2. Hassan Blasim, *The Madman of Freedom Square*, trans. Jonathan Wright (Manchester: Comma Press, 2009).

3. Hassan Blasim, *The Iraqi Christ*, trans. Jonathan Wright (Manchester: Comma Press, 2009).
4. Haytham Bahoora, 'Writing the Dismembered Nation: The Aesthetics of Horror in Iraqi Narratives of War', *Arab Studies Journal* 23, no. 1 (2015).
5. Ikram Masmoudi, *War and Occupation in Iraqi Fiction* (Edinburgh: Edinburgh University Press, 2015).
6. Jonathan Morén, 'Inverting the Stranger: Salīm Barakāt in the Land of the Living Dead', in *Arabic Literature in a Posthuman World. Proceedings of the 12th Conference of the European Association for Modern Arabic Literature (EURAMAL), May 2016, Oslo* (Wiesbaden: Harrassowitz, 2019), 119–27.
7. For emigration and immigration statistics (tracking all kinds of migration), see *Statistics Finland*, https://www.stat.fi/til/muutl/2018/muutl_2018_2019-06-17_tie_001_en.html (accessed 4 February 2020).
8. Sara Malm, 'Arabic Overtakes Finnish to Become the Second Most Common Language in Sweden after Migrant Influx', *Daily Mail*, 7 April 2016, http://www.dailymail.co.uk/news/article-3528381/Arabic-overtakes-Finnish-second-common-language-Sweden-migrant-influx.html (accessed 25 April 2018); Conversation with Arabiska Teatern, August 2018.
9. Hassan Blasim, 'In Conversation with Hassan Blasim', *Finnish Institute*, http://www.finnish-institute.org.uk/en/articles/1511-in-conversation-with-hassan-blasim (accessed 29 November 2020).
10. Andalzúa, *Borderlands/La Frontera*.
11. Rosi Braidotti, *Transpositions: On Nomadic Ethics* (Malden: Polity Press, 2006), 84.
12. Rosi Braidotti, *The Posthuman* (Malden: Polity Press, 2013), 82.
13. Rita Sakr, 'The More-than-human Refugee Journey: Hassan Blasim's Short Stories', *Journal of Postcolonial Writing* 54, no. 6 (2018), 766–80.
14. Butler, *Frames of War*, 13.
15. Sakr, 'The More-than human', 778.
16. Kathrin Thiele, 'Entanglement', in Mercedes Bunz, Birgit Mara Kaiser and Kathrin Thiele (eds), *Symptoms of the Planetary Condition: A Critical Vocabulary* (Lüneburg: Meson Press, 2017).
17. Sarah Nutall, *Entanglement: Literary and Cultural Reflections on Post-Apartheid* (Johannesburg: Wits University Press, 2009), 11.
18. Manuel Castells, *Networks of Outrage and Hope: Social Movements in the Internet Age* (Cambridge: Polity Press, 2012), 5–6.

19. Hassan Blasim, interviewed by Margaret Litvin and Johanna Sellman in Helsinki on 25 March 2016.
20. Olli Löytti, 'Follow the Translations! The Translational Circulation of Hassan Blasim's Short Stories', in Heidi Grönstrand, Markus Huss and Ralf Kauranen (eds), *The Aesthetics and Politics of Linguistic Borders: Multilingualism in Northern European Literature* (New York: Routledge, 2019), 33.
21. See, for example, the *Iraq Body Count*, https://www.iraqbodycount.org/ (accessed 29 November 2020).
22. See Yasmeen Hanoosh, 'Unnatural Narratives and Transgressing the Normative Discourses of Iraqi History: Translating Murtada Gzar's Al-Sayyid Asghar Akbar', *Journal of Arabic Literature* 44 (2013): 145–80.
23. Hanoosh, 'Unnatural Narratives', 147.
24. Yasmine Hanoosh, 'Beyond the Trauma of War: Iraqi Literature Today', *Words Without Borders*, https://www.wordswithoutborders.org/article/beyond-the-trauma-of-war-iraqi-literature-today (accessed 29 November 2020).
25. Bahoora, 'Writing the Dismembered Nation', 188.
26. Masmoudi, *War and Occupation*, 21.
27. Giorgio Agamben, *Homo Sacer: Sovereign Power and Bare Life*, trans. Daniel Heller-Roazen (Stanford: Stanford University Press, 1998).
28. Tarek El-Ariss, 'Hacking the Modern: Arabic Writing in the Virtual Age', *Comparative Literature Studies* 47, no. 4 (2010): 533–48.
29. El-Ariss, 'Hacking', 543.
30. El-Ariss, 'Hacking', 543.
31. For a discussion of the adaptation in the context of Arab Nordic theatre, see Margaret Litvin and Johanna Sellman, 'An Icy Heaven: Arab Migration on Nordic Stages', *Theatre Research International* 43, no. 1 (2018): 45–62. The current discussion focuses on Blasim's script.
32. Lisa Bhungalia, 'Elastic Sovereignty: A Global Geography of US Terrorism Law', Yi-Fu Tuan Lecture Series Talk, Department of Geography, University of Wisconsin-Madison, WI, February, 2018.
33. In the script, the dilemma is staged as a conversation between an angel and devil luring Mohamed in opposite directions. In the staged version of the play, actors write '*Hubb*' (love) and '*Mawt*' (death) on the on-stage screen.
34. Hassan Blasim, *The Digital Hats Game*, trans. Jonathan Wright (unpublished manuscript), 64.
35. The script cites a part of the story toward the end of the play.
36. Blasim, *Digital Hats*, 50.

37. Blasim, 'Truck to Berlin', 67.
38. Blasim, 'Truck to Berlin', 68.
39. Blasim, 'Truck to Berlin', 72.
40. Blasim, 'Truck to Berlin', 73.
41. On his first attempt to cross the desert Asʿad is abandoned by the smuggler and then saved by foreigners: 'oh this desert is full of rats, what on earth do they eat? ... oh, rats smaller than them'; Ghassan Kanafani, *Men in the Sun and Other Palestinian Stories*, trans. Hillary Kirpatrick (Boulder: Lynne Rienner Publishers, 1999), 61.
42. See, for example, Barbara Harlow, in Ferial Jabouri Ghazoul and Barbara Harlow (eds), *The View from Within: Writers and Critics on Contemporary Arabic Literature* (Cairo: AUC Press, 1994), 161.
43. Blasim, 'A Wolf', in *The Iraqi Christ*, 45.
44. Blasim, 'A Wolf', 45–6.
45. Blasim, 'A Wolf', 50.
46. Blasim, 'A Wolf', 53.

4

Mistranslation and the Subversion of the Citizen–Migrant Binary

This chapter foregrounds how themes of failed translation, mistranslation and translations with missing originals are used in contemporary migration literature to defamiliarise, subvert and reroute discourses of authenticity, both in relation to the notion of the Arab exile writer and the way that the category of the migrant is constructed in opposition to the citizen. It analyses Hawra al-Nadawi's 2010 novel, *Tahta Sama' Kubinhaghin* (Under the Copenhagen Sky), a coming-of-age story of a young Iraqi-Danish woman, along with Abbas Khider's 2008 German-language novel *Der falsche Inder* ('The counterfeit Indian', published in English as *The Village Indian*) and Jonas Hassen Khemiri's Swedish-language play *Invasion!*. Under the Copenhagen Sky is written in Arabic; however, the protagonist, Huda, writes her story in Danish and enlists an Iraqi translator who, she hopes, can transform her Danish narrative into an Arabic novel and thus transform her into her image of an Arabic exile writer. The eventual failure of both the project and her attempt to reposition herself as an authentic Arabic-language exile writer challenges the gendered hierarchies that translation theorists have argued govern the relationship between 'original' and 'translation' and forces her to rethink hierarchies underpinning her desire to transform herself from migrant to exile, on the one hand and the notions of authenticity in ethnic-based national belonging, on the other. The chapter compares the collapse of the translation project in al-Nadawi's Arabic-language novel to the way that failed translation of various sorts become productive sites of new meanings in Abbas Khider's novel *The Village Indian* and Jonas Hassen Khemiri's play *Invasion!*. In these texts too, mistranslation is linked to an undoing of discourses of authenticity, but the target in these texts is not Arabic exile literature but rather media discourses that would seek to make the figure of the male migrant both generalisable and constructed in opposition to the citizen. This comparative analysis demonstrates that themes of failed translations, mistranslations and translations with missing originals serve to defamiliarise categories of belonging that rely on authenticity across different gender, genres and audiences.

Conventional understandings of translation often operate through a discourse of authenticity, which posits a binary and hierarchical relationship between an original text and its translation. The theme of mistranslation and missing originals in the literary texts explored in this chapter serve to question a politics of authenticity that posits certain identities as original and others as derivative and diluted, particularly in discourses on migration and diaspora. To analyse these literary texts and the interventions that they offer, we can productively draw on perspectives from critical translation studies that rethink the binaries that relegate us to thinking about translation in opposition to an original and therefore less authentic, on the one hand, or as a transparent medium of rendering meaning, on the other. Instead, these ideas can redirect our attention to what happens *in* translation, *when* translating, as well as to the politics and economics of translation in a global publishing market.

In her 2006 book *The Translation Zone*, Emily Apter posits that translation can act as a process of repositioning subjectivity. She writes,

> Cast as an act of love, and as an act of disruption, translation becomes a means of repositioning the subject in the world and in history; a means of rendering self-knowledge foreign to itself; a way of denaturalizing citizens, taking them out of the comfort zones of national space, daily ritual, and pre-given domestic arrangements.[1]

An act of disruption, a repositioning of subjectivity, and a process that renders the familiar foreign, translation is an apt metaphor for migration and writing the self with and against existing categories in new diasporic spaces. Migration of all kinds involves a repositioning of one's self in the world that amounts to a kind of self-translation. Those who have crossed borders to find new homes may find themselves translators, positioned with and between multiple languages, practices and belongings. Moira Inghilleri delves into the many ways that translation and migration intersect in her 2017 book *Translation and Migration*. She argues that translation offers crucial spaces for navigating the transformations and transitions that migration entails.

> Migration has never been a simple matter of reproduction in a single direction: it has always involved a combination of diffusion, appropriation, assimilation, resistance, and enduring ambivalence; and translation, as a particular form of interaction, functions as and within crucial discursive spaces where alternative modes of perception are negotiated, challenged, and configured. Acts of translation are simultaneously reflective and directive; they contribute to both strengthening and weakening of prior understandings.[2]

Inghilleri's assertion that translation can either strengthen or weaken prior understanding, depending on how it is wielded, is clearly present in Under the Copenhagen Sky, where translation creates a space where notions of both citizenship and the exile writer are put into focus and then defamiliarised. Translation, in the novel, initially serves to reinforce the very categories of authenticity that have created Huda's marginalisation, thus 'strengthening ... prior understandings'. However, the movement that translation allows for (between languages, modes of being, concepts) eventually creates space for reconfiguring her understanding of self as an exile and member of the Iraqi diaspora. Apter's assertion that translation 'denaturaliz[es] citizens' functions here not to make citizenship irrelevant, but rather by exposing the ways that citizenship is constructed in opposition to an imagined migrant, alternately construed as an outsider-within or a potential intruder. In the three narratives explored in this chapter, failed translation projects, mistranslation and missing originals align with an act of claiming creative agency to denaturalise received modes of belonging and reposition subjectivity.

In *Tahta Sama'* the theme of translation serves as a way to explore binary identity categories such as exile versus forced migrant and citizen versus immigrant; Huda's failed translation project forces an impasse of these binary logics and gives rise to more fluid understandings of being in the world. In *The Village Indian* and *Invasion!* missing originals and mistranslation becomes another way to unsettle 'pre-given' identities assigned to migrants. The main character in the *The Village Indian* embraces counterfeit identities already assigned to him in Iraq (where his father claims that his mother is Roma and many around him mistake him for South Asian) as a source of creativity. The absence of the Arabic original that results from the narrator retelling the story in German and his insistence on retelling the same migration story over and over again – each time in new ways – aligns the departure from original texts and belongings with a process of creative transformation. In the play *Invasion!* a group of teenagers take the name Abulkasem from a play they attend on a school field trip and begin resignifying its meaning. It eventually morphs into an all-purpose slang word and from there, becomes an alternate identity for several of the characters. At the same time as its playful invocation signifies malleability and transformation in the realm of translation it also begins to play a more insidious role. Panels of experts appear to seek to define Abulkasem, now a stand-in term for a migrant who, as the title would suggest, is 'invading' the country. Eventually the term lands on an asylum seeker whose testimony is purposefully mistranslated by his interpreter. The three texts analysed here are clearly positioned differently with regards to audience and language, yet they all stage the theme of translation as an ethical intervention into hardened notions of belonging in the context of forced migration between the Arabic-speaking region and Europe.

Under the Copenhagen Sky

What would it mean to rely on a translator in order to write your own story? This is one of the many questions explored in Hawra al-Nadawi's 2010 debut novel, *Tahta Sama' Kubinhaghin* (Under the Copenhagen Sky). The novel is the coming-of-age story of Huda, a young woman whose Iraqi parents came to the Scandinavian country as refugees. Though the novel is set in a post-migration diaspora, it deeply engages with the question under discussion in this book: that is, how Arabic literature is rewriting the borderlands outside of normative citizenship in contemporary contexts of forced and precarious migration. Al-Nadawi, in her twenties when the novel was published in 2010 and longlisted for the 2012 International Prize for Arabic Fiction (IPAF)[3] has stated that writing the novel was an exercise in exploring the psychological dimensions of being an outsider.[4] In reading this novel, I explore this 'outside' in reference to rigid culturalist and ethnic conceptions of citizenship that shape the novel and that have been on the rise in Europe in recent years. The novel's protagonist, Huda, holds Danish citizenship and thus has access to the rights and legal belonging that such status entails. At the same time, she experiences marginalisation in Denmark and within her smaller Iraqi Danish community. This marginalisation in a post-migration diaspora gives rise to a longing and desire for a positionality that is recognised as a site of social intelligibility and intellectual production and exchange. By writing her story, she aspires to both create space for experiences like hers, which she knows are common but not widely recognised, and at the same time make claims on a recognised – even celebrated – category: the exile writer. Huda's aspirations to become someone who is recognised by a broader Arab community and diaspora are impelled by a sense of lack. Like many other literary narratives discussed in *Arabic Exile Literature in Europe*, Huda's exilic position is negotiated in conversation with modernist conceptions of the exile writer, which no longer seem to fit her predicament.

Tahta Sama' is written from the point of view of two characters, Huda and Rafid. It is entirely written in Arabic, a language whose written expression the novel's protagonist Huda does not master.[5] The transaction that structures the novel is as follows: Huda writes in Danish and emails her narrative to Rafid, an Iraqi ten years her senior, who then translates it into Arabic. The novel is thus mediated by translation and haunted by the absence of the 'original' Danish text. As readers, we only access Huda's texts through their Arabic translations. The chapters written from Huda and Rafid's point of view alternate and when Rafid abandons the translation project about halfway through, the novel is left in an incomplete state. In the chapters that he does translate, Huda tells the story of her childhood and adolescence. Her narrative accentuates moments in which her exclusion from different social spaces is made apparent. These social spaces are numerous and include Danish mainstream culture; the Iraqi

Muslim community her mother is striving to join; and the Iraqi identity that her older brother, arriving from Iraq when Huda is ten, chastises her for betraying. Despite Huda's bilingualism and her multiple and transnational belongings, she experiences her world as an increasingly claustrophobic space. In his chapters, Rafid reflects on his more recent migration from Iraq, his life in Copenhagen with his Iraqi Danish wife, and his uneasiness about his role as a translator and intermediary in the production of Huda's novel.

Huda's insistence on writing in Arabic translation and thus transforming her Danish coming-of-age story into an Arabic novel is structured by existing discourses on belonging that pertain both to citizenship and to her experience of post-migration diaspora. She recounts how she fell in love with Rafid from a distance prior to asking him to be her translator and we gradually come to understand that her desire for him is inextricably tied to her hopes of transformation through writing and translation. This translated version of her writing – and this translated version of herself, Huda imagines – offers her both an escape from her predicament and an opportunity to redefine the parameters of her otherness. Rafid also has his own interests in this transaction: he seeks to transform himself from translator into writer and assert a sense of ownership over the text. Huda and Rafid's desire to reposition themselves through translation intertwines with an ill-timed intimacy between them in ways that both build upon and complicate the hierarchy governing the relationship between conceptions of 'original' and 'translation', in which the translated or 'derivative' text is often gendered feminine and assigned a secondary role.[6] In this novel, both author and translator position translation as a recuperative act,[7] that is, one that offers the possibility of restoring a sense of fullness to belongings that are felt to be incomplete and located in a receding past, especially when external recognition does not correspond to one's inner and perceived orientations and past. However, these translational aspirations and the translational structure of the novel end up unravelling this binary and defamiliarising assumptions about belonging and citizenship. This process, I will argue, implicates shifting conceptions of exile in twenty-first-century Arabic literature, where exile has begun to be theorised in relation to a community or a 'body politic' shaped by forced migration.

Proving One's Existence

In her first chapter, Huda introduces herself, directly addressing her imagined Arab readers. 'This is me ... Huda Mohamad Al ...'[8] She will not share her last name, she writes, not because her family would object to her writing a novel about her life, but rather because she feels it is irrelevant to her story and her sense of self. The belonging, or rather disjuncture, that she wants to explore is in the relationship between her – the Iraqi Danish writer – and her imagined Arab audience. In this first exploratory venture into this dialectic relationship, she addresses her audience directly: 'My belonging to you is limited to my first and last name.'[9] On the other hand, she writes, her personality, thinking and culture are afflicted with 'something distorted and impure'.[10] In this binary between the 'me' that she is defining and the 'you' that she is addressing, there is an implied distinction between belongings that are secure and recognised and those that are in question and muddled. After she has defined this conflicted narrative *I* of her novel, she defines the audience.

> So ... who are you?
> Who am I addressing?
> To put it simply ... you are all the people who are not like me. As for those who are like me, I am sure that they will be narrating their stories through mine. Perhaps you don't know what it means to be like me, but I promise you that you will.[11]

The 'us' in this passage is defined as those, who like her, have been displaced to northern Europe.

In this first chapter narrated by Huda, she chastises her prospective Arab readers for writing her out of their narrative of exile and diaspora. The way that diaspora has been imagined, she emphasises, has centred on the postcolonial metropoles of London and Paris. These outdated internal maps have now created a felt sense of invisibility among the now many who live elsewhere in Europe. She writes,

> I was born in Copenhagen.
> Do you know Copenhagen?
> It is the city of youth and folly, as they say.

I am surprised by your previous lack of attention to this city. Maybe you've never even given it a second thought until today. You have probably never been enthralled by its name or let the city enter your mind like other well-known cities. In truth, I have always been amazed by how little the Arabs know about Denmark. When they think of Europe, they think of London and ignore the other cities. It's as if all of Europe could be reduced to London and Paris and other cities are viewed with little interest and even condescension. …

What do the Arabs know about Denmark other than the fact that it is a producer of dairy products and that commercial for Lurpak Butter? You know, the one where men with red jackets (and even redder faces) gather around a cow, pampering it so that it will produce its 'opulent butter from Denmark'.

That commercial! I used to be so happy when it came on. For one, it relieved the boredom that I usually felt when my older brother Emad came to visit and insisted on watching the Arabic satellite channels. I would be so happy when it came on. It was as if the commercial wasn't merely advertising butter. It felt as if it were advertising me … my presence in this country.

It was as if I were in the place of the cow. As if the men were swinging me back and forth and letting me fly through the air and then milking me. This is how I am advertised. Huda Mohamed, an Iraqi from Denmark. Or a Dane from Iraq. I really don't know the correct order.

I find your distance odd.

Neither your artists nor your radio and satellite channels have made our presence here known. We, the ones who emigrated to northern Europe. We ended up here in this country of heavy shades of grey.

Did you ever consider the number of your brethren who are here?

Did the reasons for our migration ever spark your interest?

I feel cheated by your distance.

Do you think that this feeling of being cheated would have blossomed within me if I had lived in America or in Britain or any of the important countries? That is, the ones that you show an interest in?

I don't know.

I do know that I live in this country in northern Europe, a country that has been hidden away from the world. And I also know that I too have been made invisible to my own roots to the degree that a mere commercial about a Danish product delights me as if it proved my very existence![12]

The expression that Huda uses to refer to her prospect of being made visible by virtue of her writing – *ithbāt kaynūnatī* – is noteworthy. In *ithbāt*, proving or making something stable, there is the idea that the Arab readers that she addresses are positioned to provide the visibility and acknowledgement that she desires, making her existence stable. In this formulation, it is her very existence or beingness, *kaynūnatī*, that is at stake. Her chastising here is gentle by virtue of the absurdity of the scene in which the young Huda feels the need to identify with a commercial (and a cow!) in order to feel like she occupies a place in the world. Nevertheless, it is the wound that her restorative translation project seeks to address. Later in the novel, Huda will introduce a similar turn of phrase *i'lān kaynūnatī*, when describing the prospect of Rafid noticing her. *I'lān* signifies at once announcement, proclamation and advertising. The act of writing is a declaration of self in a space whose parameters are set by the politics of diaspora and the received knowledge surrounding both Arab diasporas and Arabic diasporic writing in Europe. The declaration is necessary because the field has been defined by postcolonial migratory geographies that no longer fit the parameters of the communities that Huda identifies with. When used later in the novel, *i'lān*, which also refers to advertisement, posits Huda in relation to the exaggerated and stereotyped representation of Denmark that she encountered on satellite television as a child. In this later usage, it signals the prospect of Rafid noticing her, thus aligning her desire for recognition from Rafid and her desire to be made visible to her imagined Arab readers.

Huda's insistence on writing in translation, her desire to transform her exilic subjectivity from invisibility to visibility and recognition, is intertwined with a sense of being wounded and overlooked by a larger diasporic Arab community, invisible to her own roots, as she puts it. Translation becomes a reinvention of self, and a way to become visible. This visibility, she imagines, will allow her to connect with a transnational public, to reimagine herself as an Arab exile writer and, in the process, her relationship with her multiple homelands and potential readers.

Exile in Community

Huda is part of a number of national and transnational networks; she is Danish, Muslim, Shi'i, Iraqi, Arab, Scandinavian, a foreigner and one of the many residents 'under the Copenhagen sky'. However, the exclusionary discourses within the communities around her produce less a sense of hybridity and multiple belongings than a sense of alterity, a sense of being a perpetual foreigner in all spaces. Huda uses several terms when reflecting on her sense of being out of place, including *manfa* (exile), *ightirāb* (estrangement/alienation) and *ghurba* (exile/estrangement). All of these, but especially *manfa*, are terms that evoke a long and complex lineage of literary discourses in Arabic literature, conjuring political commitment, nostalgia for the homeland, and literary innovation. In contrast, Huda's understanding of her own exile is conditioned by the idea that although exile *can* offer such liberation and transformative possibilities for the individual, it mostly offers constraints when experienced in community. She writes,

> Many years had gone by before I realized that my estrangement [*ightirābī*] was considered an inborn disability that I gotten used to without ever having known the pleasure of living without it.
>
> I was not normal. But I also was not aware of the fact that I was not normal ... I was like a person who, having been born blind, was unaware that there was such a thing as sight and only learned about it when people began to prepare her to act in a way that was unique to those like her.
>
> They prepared me as well, everyone did ... my home, my school, the street, Danish people, the foreign community, the Arab community, the Iraqi community ... everybody taught me to act according to my disability. And I learned quickly.
>
> But I still didn't know what it would mean to see the world without the disability of exile [*ghurba*].[13]

Huda's experience of exile as a form of disability is best understood when we consider disability as an effect of the conditions that *produce* limitations and enclosures that are unequally distributed among populations.[14]

The idea of *seeing* the world through the disability of exile directly engages that centrality of sight in modernist understandings of the exilic gaze, detached yet empowered to yield insight and transformation. In contrast, at several points in the novel, Huda reflects on the 'narrowness'[15] of exile. She uses the metaphor of a shell (in Arabic, *qawqaʿa* and *ḥalazūna*) to visualise the confines produced by her exile. In an extended reflection, the figure of the shell evokes a singular accepted path that, when followed, circles inward into an ever-shrinking space for agency. She writes,

> A shell within a shell, a spiralling pattern like a television within a television within a television within a television within a television ...
>
> My isolation from my country is followed by my isolation from its people and then isolation from ideas, beliefs, and concepts. Everything in our exile is shielded from itself. Even my soul is shielded and separated from itself, each part unknown to the other.
>
> Perhaps exile (al-ghurba) gives you a lot if you are an individual but takes even more from you when you become a community.[16]

In contrast to the modernist understanding of exile as a condition that, though painful, can also be a source of creativity by virtue of the exile's detachment and distance from multiple communities, Huda posits a conception of exile that enforces simplified yet alienating and constricting notions of community. Pursuing the metaphor of the shell, she begins to enumerate the various categories that form each layer of her spiralling path, or *ḥalazūna*. Within the leftist/pious split within the Iraqi community in Copenhagen, she muses, she is automatically placed in the pious camp. This is not because of personal conviction or the way that her family has identified historically but rather because of her mother's recent attempts to align the family with the values and habits of their religious neighbours and thus experience a sense of belonging herself. The second layer of the shell is her identification as Shiʿi. Despite the obvious simplifications at work, the layers of this spiral, or *ḥalazūna*, have a deep effect on Huda. To step out of this rigid structure, she reflects, would be like ceasing to exist[17] and so it encircles her to the point of suffocation.

As the story of Huda's childhood and adolescence unfolds through the chapters that are being translated by Rafid, we notice that many of the chapters are centred on moments when Huda becomes aware of the contours of her exile, that is, moments when others – whether Danish or Iraqi – make it known that she does not belong. For example, one chapter in her narrative recounts how her childhood friend Klaus rejected her because she is, in his words, 'black', thus introducing her to the implicit racial and ethnic definitions of citizenship in Denmark that will continue to haunt her. This is a pivotal moment in Huda's reflection on her childhood. She notes, 'All of my ties to my neighbours and schoolmates were severed and I found myself on a wave that would thrust me onto an unknown path I had never intended to walk upon.' She compares this surrender to the circumstances of her world to the circumambulation (*ṭawāf*) around the Ka'ba Although the religious ritual performs the unity and thus the boundaries of belonging among believers, in Huda's formulation it refers to the exclusion created by the enforcement of similarity as a basis of community.

> As for me, I have not yet circled the Ka'ba, other than the Ka'ba of my exile, and this experience taught my feet to walk without any real directions from me. I was walking, but also unaware of how I was gradually acclimating to this tense climate filled with racism.[18]

A later chapter focuses on the impact that the arrival of new Iraqi neighbours has on her family. Unlike Huda's parents, this family spent years in Iran before coming to Denmark. Their Iraqi Arabic is inflected with Persian and they are religiously observant. Huda's mother befriends the family and begins to change her own lifestyle and that of her own family accordingly. Huda is encouraged to play with the family's daughter Fatima, though she does not enjoy her company. After Fatima's father sees the girls interacting with a woman who is sunbathing, he calls the two girls over and sends Huda home. After being dismissed, Huda overhears Fatima's parents saying that Huda and her family are nothing like them, *mu mithlina*. As she ponders why difference immediately becomes an accusation, she makes the link between this moment and Klaus's earlier rejection. The shell-like circuits that Huda is drawn into punish difference and, as she experiences them, create a path that seems to keep narrowing.

If difference is punished in Huda's narrative, similarity is stifling. When Huda begins high school, a classmate named Zeina immediately befriends her after finding out that she too is Iraqi. She notes, 'We became friends unintentionally. Without choosing. The friendships of immigrants – especially Iraqis – are not chosen. They are one of the many conditions that that exile [*ghurba*] imposes on us.'[19] Unlike Huda, Zeina seems to know most of the Iraqi families in Copenhagen and is well aware of the ins and outs of the Iraqi and Arab society in the city. Zeina, however, soon begins policing Huda's friendships and activities. Huda feels rather ambivalent about the friendship: while Huda values becoming more integrated into the Iraqi and Arab youth culture in Copenhagen, she resents Zeina's control over her social interactions and eventually, Zeina's romantic relationship with her brother, Emad. Zeina is inextricably part of the narrowing path that Huda treads in her adolescence. At the same time, when Huda first notices Rafid and (unbeknownst to him) becomes deeply enamoured, she is dependent on Zeina for information about him and his whereabouts.

Huda understands her coming of age within this experience of exile through these metaphors of a narrowing path. Even the celebration of Huda's eighteenth birthday, her entry into adulthood, is staged as a lengthy suffocation, as she wanders around her own party looking for air to breathe.[20] She notes, 'The empty circle that I have been walking around for the past eighteen years will not change. The only thing that is different is that I feel tired.'[21]

There is a transindividual awareness in these reflections, that is, an awareness of how the boundary-building practices that create and divide communities shape an individual narrative. Huda's narrative of self is shaped both by her diasporic community and the exclusionary processes that take place when citizenship is defined narrowly through ethnicity and cultural heritage. The impetus to write the book is deeply intertwined with a desire to find alternate paths, to reimagine what exile can mean within the communities that she is already a part of. How can she imagine a different body politic when, as she notes, exile may 'take from you' when you become a community? In order to connect with a transnational and Arab public and step outside of this spiralling path, Huda seeks to reimagine herself as an Arab exile writer who writes in Arabic. In seeking out a relationship with her desired audience, Huda implicates some of the meanings of migration that she feels have remained elusive to her, such as the perceived benefits that exile may bring to the individual, and especially to the exilic writer.

Translation and the Repositioning of Subjectivity

In the novel, translation is initially figured as a tool to create alternative versions of self, a means of restoring a more authentic and rooted version of self. In the first chapter, Rafid recounts how he first became aware of Huda after receiving an email from her asking him to translate her novel. Although Rafid has worked as a professional translator, he has not previously translated literary works and is thus surprised by the request. He is also struck by Huda's weak written Arabic; although she speaks Danish and Iraqi Arabic, she, unlike the author of the novel or her translator, does not write or fully comprehend formal or literary Arabic. Despite, or rather because of this, she seeks out expression in Arabic as a remedy to the narrowing *ḥalazūna*-like path that she has been treading.

Yet, both Huda and her translator, Rafid, fall back into dualistic, hierarchical and gendered models of theorising translation. Although they complicate the position of the author and the original text by reversing the prevalent hierarchies between original and translation, they end up reproducing its discourses on authenticity. The dynamic echoes the way that translation has often been theorised through gendered hierarchies that confer legitimacy and creativity on an author as father figure. Lori Chamberlain explored these issues in her seminal 1988 article, 'Gender and the Metaphorics of Translation'.[22] Chamberlain places the assumed hierarchies between original and translation, author and translator, within a historically gendered discourse of production and reproduction. Whereas the role of the author has historically been constructed as a paternal figure that bestows authority and legitimacy, the translated text has often been relegated to a secondary and feminised role. She references the French adage '*les belles infidèles*' which suggests that translation, like a woman, can either be beautiful or faithful. On the other hand, the fidelity, or paternity, of the original text is not held up to scrutiny. Therefore, she argues, when translators make claims of creativity and authorial intent, they often do so by 'usurping' the role of the author while simultaneously feminising the text as an entity that exists under their protection and tutelage.[23] She suggests that such gendered discourses on authorship in translated texts tap into 'an anxiety about the myths of paternity',[24] an anxiety about legitimate authorial voice.

The hierarchies and anxieties about translation in *Tahta Sama'* align with the politics of similarity that mean that belonging and inclusion is conditional on the extent to which one resembles the normative citizen. These posit a hierarchy between an original and a copy, a full citizen and her pale imitation. When, for instance, Huda remarks that she will not settle for being seen as a guest in Denmark, even though she has come to accept that she will continue to be considered a perpetual outsider, she is remarking on the hierarchies produced by a politics of similarity. In the realm of translation, even as Huda and Rafid reverse the hierarchies by refashioning the translated text as the more legitimate and authentic version of the novel, they cling to the binaries of original and translation that seem to offer the potential to shift both of their subjectivities. What is at stake is a kind of ownership; the transaction will allow Huda to position herself as an Arabic exile writer and Rafid to claim a type of ownership and authorship over her text.

Huda's infatuation with Rafid runs parallel to her quest for transformation through translation. She first spots Rafid at a café in central Copenhagen, where he is having lunch with a group of friends. Immediately enamoured, she begins to love him from a distance. In each chance encounter and in the space of her imagination she projects a sense of authenticity on him that is anchored in the Arabic language and what she perceives to be a secure sense of Iraqi identity, that is, in the very components of her own identity she feels are lacking. Not infrequently, Huda seeks out Rafid's presence by calling his phone and listening in silence as he repeats his greeting *na'am* (yes?) repeatedly. In these moments of listening in, she finds pleasure in his confidence that the caller will be speaking Arabic, not Danish. She cherishes his voice, which to her seems to bear all the traces of the country that her family left behind. 'A deep voice, the sound of Iraqi dates crashing into coarse earth ... a delicate voice in which you can hear the ringing of the church bells of my city.'[25] Similarly, the few times when she is in his vicinity, she notices his Arabic and his Arabic-speaking friends. This is in contrast to Huda's social world, where she mostly uses Danish, even with friends whose families are Iraqi or Arab. Rafid is both an object of desire and the means through which she can reach her desired goal. When Huda spots Rafid one day at the Central Station of Copenhagen she observes him at length, noting that although she is standing only a few feet away, 'there is a great obstacle between us/ Announcing my existence ...!'[26] The heretofore insurmountable obstacle to his attention is phrased as an obstacle to her existence being known, *'ilān kaynūnatī*. These are words that hark back to her earlier address to an imagined Arab readership whose acknowledgment would also 'prove' her existence, *ithbāt kaynūnatī*.

On Rafid's end, his infatuation with Huda, which only follows his invitation to translate her book, is also tied to questions of authenticity, authorship and translation. His positionality within the Iraqi Danish community is distinct from Huda's. He migrated to Denmark from Iraq after two of his brothers were executed under Saddam Hussein's rule. Arriving in Denmark as an adult, he married a woman who, like Huda, was born in Denmark into an Iraqi family. Rafid's anxieties about being in the position of the translator are processed from the very opening paragraphs of the novel. His writing process, he suggests, is characterised by a constant vacillation between a sense of authorship and ownership, on the one hand, and a sense of being in a secondary role as a producer of a derivative work, on the other. He remarks,

> Every time that I thought that I had succeeded in taming my pen I would once again be taken by surprise by the fact that I was not the real author of what I was writing. I would once again be overwhelmed by the sense of transience that was appropriate to my role as translator [*nāqil*]. By applying myself assiduously to the task before me I would gradually return to a sense of being a writer. ...
> No that is not it!
> I am the translator of her text.[27]

For Rafid, the process of translation is characterised by a struggle to achieve authority over the text, a struggle, as Chamberlain has suggested, against the author. When pitting the writer, *kātib*, against the translator, *nāqil*, he contrasts the creative role of the writer to the reproducing role of the translator. The choice of the term *nāqil* over the synonym *mutarjim* for translator signals a conception of translation as reproduction and literal transfer of meaning from one code to another (the verb *tarjama* aligns more closely with a conception of translation as interpretation and explanation). He muses – in the language of copyright – that he would like to 'arrive at an open space coloured by a freedom that is mine … with rights that are reserved only for me'.[28]

His quest for rights to the text is simultaneously articulated as a quest for paternal authority over Huda as he assumes the task of making her text both visible and legitimate to a potential Arab readership. In doing so, he posits himself as a father figure, who gives legitimacy to a feminised text. He notes,

> I have the right to consider myself a father. I am the father of this text … I am her father. Without me, how would she make herself known?
>
> Maybe I am an illegitimate father, since I am merely translating the text from one language to another. But her text would not see the light of day without me.[29]

Like Huda's, Rafid's relationship to the text is bound up in aspirations for self-transformation. However, as in his attempt to be a writer rather than a translator, the quest for paternity is incomplete and fraught with anxiety that he is 'merely' a translator.[30] Filiation, which becomes a source of anxiety for both Huda and Rafid, ties into the challenges of forging a sense of belonging in an adopted country.

Patching Shredded Desires

As the novel progresses, both Huda and Rafid's aspirations for transformation through their translational relationship break down and with it, the models of authenticity that underpin it. Both of their understandings of translation have been built on the models of citizenship and diaspora of spiralling similarity. The failure of translation (as it is initially understood) forces a reassessment of self.

Rafid's aspirations to occupy the role of the writer and take ownership of the text crumble when he realises that it is he who has been the object of Huda's desires. The realisation that he is the *beloved* and not the lover and that he has been translating himself as much as he has been translating Huda causes a shift in self-perception.

> I am the man who began to doubt his own facial features after being painted by a woman who rendered me as she pleased and loved me according to her desires. Her love for me filled me with both jealousy and pride ... I am the beloved, the conceited, the proud, the weak, the unaware, the lost and the deluded. I am the one whose heart is split in two.
>
> I cursed my soul repeatedly after discovering her love.[31]

His repetition of passive grammatical constructions and the alternation between positions of weakness and strength reflect the loss of the authoring role that he has been trying to maintain as a translator, as well as the gendered hierarchies on which they are based. They also introduce a split sense of self that comes from seeing himself, indeed having translated himself, through the eyes of another.

> I re-read the lines where I have translated her descriptions of me. I am astounded that I have both translated myself and with such ease become distanced from myself. Bounding from my chair I rush to the mirror to certify with my own eyes that it was actually me in those pages. I soon discover several disparities. My eyes are not black as she describes them. They are dark brown. But I hadn't noticed before the way that my lips slope down when I speak and laugh. How did Huda see things in me that I hadn't noticed myself?[32]

As for Huda, abandoning her translational aspirations means disentangling Rafid from the Arabic language.

On the morning after Rafid's wedding (whose date Zeina has informed her of), Huda sits in her parents' kitchen in an anguished state, hiding her tears from her mother. Here, her reckoning is not so much with Rafid as with the Arabic language – specifically its written form – and how it has underpinned her hopes for transformation and community. When her mother tunes the radio to a Qur'anic recitation of *Surat Āl-'Imran* (Family of Imran), Huda's frustration about not fully understanding the Qu'ranic Arabic soon implicates Rafid. Neither one will be hers. She states,

> I don't approve of languages where the noun precedes the adjective. The adjective startles me, exploding in my face as if it were balloon filled with water. *Rajul mutazawwij*. A man? What about this man? Oh, he's married! What a surprise! I don't like surprises.[33]

Like Rafid, the translation is not forthcoming. The only partially understood recitation leaves her in a state of limbo. She ponders, 'These words take advantage of my tears, leaving me half crying, half conscious, half woman, half girl.'[34]

In the end, Huda's hopes for transformation through translation and Rafid's tenuous claims of ownership over the text are both thwarted. Rafid abandons the translation project halfway through and Huda's Arabic novel is left incomplete even as she continues to email Rafid new chapters, chapters that will remain unread (and then, of course, are not part of the novel).

While Rafid chooses to distance himself from the project entirely, there are moments in the text where Huda begins to re-theorise desire and subjectivity with this sense of incompletion in mind, at least incompletion from the perspective of the politics of similarity that she is intimately familiar with. We glimpse this older Huda in the emails that she sends Rafid. In these, it appears as if Huda's reckoning with her inability to be transformed into the exilic author that she imagined through translation is tied to a transformation of the obsessive love for Rafid she has so long cultivated. In one email she addresses the way that her unrequited love has forced her to re-theorise her attachments through the lens of transformation and multiple possibilities. She writes, 'Love has many faces, hatred has only one',[35] and further into her message she adds,

> Not because I cannot possess you, but because I do not wish to. ... I don't want you to be mine because it pleases me that you are yours.

> I have gotten used to blessing your body every day. This has taught me to patch up my shredded desires.[36]

These desires, we can infer, refer not only to a love that will not be reciprocated, but also to the many desires she has attached to her translated story and translated self. Exploring a position of vulnerability, this passage also playfully imagines how the bond between them might have been different given, for example, different gender constellations. Musings such as *if I were a man* or *if you were a woman* reimagine the subjectivities upon which their relationship was built, but also seem to loosen the gendered aspirations behind their incomplete translation project.

In other moments in the novel, Huda seeks to read evidence of change and transformation in the landscapes of Copenhagen, at times mapping Copenhagen onto her own body. The ever-changing sky and the drastic shifts in climate from one season to another become signs of the capacity to change.

Defamiliarisation and the Vanishing Original

Throughout the novel, we access Huda's voice through Rafid's translation. Her voice is mediated by him and by the translation from Danish to Arabic, leaving the 'original' absent. Despite the fact that the structure of the novel is driven by a search for a more authentic voice, her voice is only heard in mediation.

In contexts of migration and exile, the home(s) of one's roots and the home of one's present can easily be rendered as oppositional binaries, with both perceived as more authentic than subjectivities born of migration. In *Anxiety of Erasure*, Hanadi al-Samman discusses Hanan al-Shaykh's 2001 novel *Innaha London Ya Azizi* (*Only in London*).[37] As she notes, several of the characters who move to London initially seek to fully embrace their European life at the expense of recognising the integral importance of their Arab heritage.

> They learn to negotiate the gains and losses of hyphenated identities, and to appreciate flexible citizenship, thereby forsaking homeland longings and engendering new belongings articulated through the 'dialogic' relationship between roots and routes.[38]

As al-Samman demonstrates, the characters in *Only in London* overcome the lure of becoming European at the expense of their other identities and reclaim their own hybridity, bodies and agency, and at the same time overcome a reliance on characters who act as intermediaries to this desired identity. Like these characters, Huda comes to understand how untenable the idea of an original and authentic identity is and in turn, she too, overcomes her reliance on an intermediary, Rafid. Though the processes are similar, the directionality is different. The vanishing original for Huda is the impossibility of return to an Iraqi identity perceived as original and her inability to refigure herself as an exile writer writing in Arabic within established diasporic centres of culture. Furthermore, for her to grapple with her transnational belongings means taking into account her relationship to self and to communities that have been created by forced migration.

In literary narratives of forced migration, translation plays a vital role in mediating multiple languages in multilingual and borderland spaces. As a device that shapes narration, it can also serve to subvert fixed notions of identity and authenticity and as a means to generate new narratives and perspectives. In Under the Copenhagen Sky and in the novel and play discussed in the next section, Abbas Khider's novel *Der falsche Inder* (*The Village Indian*) [2008 (2013)] and Jonas Hassen Khemiri's play *Invasion!* [2008 (2013)], mistranslation and translations whose originals are missing or unknowable can strategically intervene in flattened accounts of migrants or migration. This use of mistranslation or missing originals to unsettle ideas about the migrant or migration is equally salient in the two narratives discussed in the next section, though the dynamics are shifted slightly given that they are addressed to audiences reading in European languages. While *Tahta Sama'* mobilises translation as a way to explore longing for a more knowable and stable identity (and ultimately destabilises the binary categories that this desire is built on) and engages with tropes of the exile drawn from Arabic literature and intellectual history, the literary narratives discussed in the following section use mistranslation and missing originals to destabilise and reshape narratives and ideas about migration circulating in European contexts.

The Village Indian

Like *Tahta Sama'*, Abbas Khider's 2008 debut novel *Der falsche Inder* (*The Village Indian*) is told through the conceit of translation. And here too, the original text is conspicuously absent and translation aligns with a repositioning of subjectivity. The idea of an original, or a true story, takes a back seat to the variety of ways that it can be told and reimagined. The title itself *Der falsche Inder,* the 'false' or 'counterfeit' Indian, directly conjures the idea of an identity that is not what it seems. In the novel's frame story, a young Iraqi man residing in Munich notices an envelope on the seat next to him on a routine train ride between Berlin and Munich. A stranger then shoves the envelope in his lap as she clears a space to sit. The seeming congruence between the young Iraqi man and the Arabic letters on the envelope is enough for her to jump to conclusions about authorship. Opening the envelope, which has the Arabic word for 'memories' written on it, the narrator discovers the unpublished Arabic-language memoirs of a man named Rasul Hamid. The unpublished manuscript contains a series of retellings of Hamid's migratory journey from Iraq to Jordan, Libya, Turkey, Greece and Germany. Each telling of Rasul Hamid's irregular migratory journey emphasises different aspects and encounters that defined it. When the narrator has finished reading all of the narratives in the envelope, we find out that his name is also Rasul Hamid. His marvel that the author not only shares a name with him, but also the very same story/stories of migration points to both the transindividual and translational qualities of the narrative.

Der falsche Inder (*The Village Indian*) links translation to storytelling and literary resourcefulness and is itself a literary and transformed rendering of some of its author's experiences. Khider, whose five German-language novels have received considerable acclaim, was born in Baghdad in 1972. Through his sisters and his brother-in-law, the literary critic Salhe Zamel, he was exposed to reading and the literary world of Baghdad of the time. An activist opposing Saddam Hussein's regime, he was imprisoned in the early 1990s and left Iraq in 1996. He spent several years travelling through and residing in several countries in the Middle East, Africa and Europe, arriving in Germany in 2000. Having published two poetry collections and a collection of essays in Arabic, he studied literature and philosophy in Munich and began writing novels in German in the mid-2000s and also published a German language grammar book, *Deutsch für alle: Das endgültige Lehrbuch* (German for Everyone: The Ultimate Textbook)[39] in 2019, a book that takes a tongue-in-cheek approach to simplifying German grammar.

In *The Village Indian*, the first version of Rasul Hamid's story centres the theme of mistaken and challenged identities. Rasul narrates how in his childhood and adolescence in Iraq, those around him often doubted his Iraqi identity. Rasul's first narrative, however, does not begin with his own birth, but rather with the AD 762 founding of Baghdad, the 'city of peace' (*madinat al-salam*) that 'has never known peace'.[40] Unlike *Tahta Sama'*, which relates life in Copenhagen to a broader Arabic-language readership that may not be familiar with Denmark, *The Village Indian*'s inclusion of historical landmarks serves both to situate Rasul Hamid's life story in a longer history and to teach readers who may be less familiar with Iraqi and Middle Eastern history about major events that continue to shape the present. After recounting the infamous fire that engulfed the city during the Mongol invasion, he continues,

> I was born in this fire, in this city, perhaps that's why my skin is this coffee colour. I was well-grilled – like mutton – over the fire. For me, the ghosts of the fire have always been present, I've seen this city burn time and again. One war embraced another. One catastrophe followed the next. Each time, Baghdad, or all of Iraq – in the skies and on the ground – burnt: from 1980 to 1988 in the First Gulf War; from 1988 to 1989 in the war that the Ba'ath regime waged against the Iraqi Kurds; in the Second Gulf War in 1991; in the same year again, during the Iraqi uprising; in 2003, in the Third Gulf War; and in between, in hundreds of smaller fires, battles, uprisings and skirmishes. Fire is this country's fate and even the waters of the two great rivers, the Euphrates and the Tigris, are powerless against it.[41]

Rasul describes his dark complexion both as an effect of Iraqi history and the source of doubt and confusion about how he belongs to it. Rasul relates stories from growing up in Baghdad and being mistaken for a foreigner, the Indian actor Amitabh Bachchan, or for a native American and being asked to prove his Iraqi identity. One day his father confesses to him that he had an affair with a beautiful Roma dancer and that this woman, who was named Selwa (just like Rasul's presumed mother), is his biological mother. This story is denied by Rasul's mother and an old woman said to have been present at his birth is called in to authenticate her version of his provenance. Perhaps, Rasul conjectures, his grandmother had a tryst with an Indian soldier brought by the British during the mandate period. 'I am perhaps the product of two British colonies',[42] he muses.

In this first section, the stories of mistaken or counterfeit identities continue as he travels through Africa and Europe. Shortly after his arrival in Greece, Rasul is arrested in a random raid on refugees and he is beaten by a policeman while being held at the station. The beating is soon revealed to result from yet another case of mistaken identity; the policeman's younger brother recently died of an overdose and he mistook Rasul for a Pakistani drug dealer active in the area. Rasul is released, but he is arrested again in Germany, where the police suspect that he is Indian or Pakistani posing as an Iraqi to be eligible for asylum. After 9/11, he discovers that his Iraqi origins arouse fear in strangers.

Rasul suggests in this section that his relationship to writing is in part born of circumstance, in part the result of his forgetfulness. The fact that events quickly disappear from his memory is a boon in his estimation. His writing, which transforms the past as it recreates it, is at the centre of the novel's reflection on the literary.

> I have another ability, another blessing – if something terrible does manage to stick to the edge of my memory, I can embellish it completely and utterly. And in next to no time, the dirt dissolves and only beautiful – *or beatified* – mages remain.[43]

Rasul's shaky memory thus finds resonance in the malleability of events and approaches to telling them. These are metaphors for the literary (indeed an insistence on the literary as a form of resistance to readings of 'refugee literature' as social document) and also an exploration of the potential dangers of writing that gives too much away, both in the context of Iraq during the Saddam years and on the routes and borderlands of irregular migration. Rasul notes that his writing often lacks chronology and details. During his adolescence he even invents an alphabet that no one but he can decipher – until he forgets his own codes. In his telling, writing is both ever-present and abundant, on prison walls, migration routes, on scraps of stolen paper and eminently vulnerable. At many points in the narrative writing is destroyed or lost, such as the time his mother washes his clothes upon his return from prison, destroying the writing carefully sewn into its hems, or the time his father destroys Rasul's library after becoming a Saddamist.

For Rasul Hamid, as well as the narrator of the frame story, storytelling is a survival skill. In the process of telling these different versions of the story, the facts of the story become less important than their malleability and the possibility to retell them in a different way when a story is lost or already told in one way. The ability to turn a string of events – in this case a series of clandestine journeys between Iraq, Libya, Turkey, Greece and Germany – into a series of narratives is a way to ward off amnesia and instead infuse the world with possibility.

The idea that Rasul Hamid is telling the story of the narrator and vice versa points to both the transindividual quality of the writing as well as the defamiliarisation of the migration narrative as a social document. Corina Stan in 'Novels in the Translation Zone: Abbas Khider, *Weltliteratur*, and the Ethics of the Passerby' argues that the true protagonist of the story is neither Rasul Hamid nor the narrator, but rather all of the people along the migratory routes that he so evocatively relates, all the many people who have experienced borderland routes and formed friendships and community along the way. '[T]hese are nesting stories, suggesting lives imbricated with one another.'[44] Commenting on one telling where Rasul Hamid continually sees the faces of people who have died Stan writes,

> The faces suggest that there is no original, no single story, but many, related, albeit each unique; they speak to him, and through him, ex aqua. During the movement of migration, one incurs debts vis-à-vis those lost to watery graves, or on the road; one must continue to carry the memory of others, translate their stories into one's own. A migrant is born translated. As one flees, one must always introduce and explain

oneself while trying to stay out of danger; the person encountered might be a generous soul, or a callous informant. A migrant's life is lived in permanent interpellation.[45]

The novel's subversion of the idea of a true original or a single way of telling a story is a salute to the literary but also a way of emphasising the transindividual quality of the story. The story belongs to Rasul Hamid, the narrator, and also many others. It probes the conditions that so many people in the borderlands outside of citizenship experience while also emphasising the creative capacity and individuality that gives rise to an abundance of tellings. By rendering the stories of so many even as he tells his own, Rasul Hamid is translating and, in the process, translating himself as he encounters the conditions of a shared journey.

Invasion!

The vanishing original in the translation-themed texts discussed here create modes of defamiliarisation that allow for the reinvention of meaning and self in migratory contexts. Jonas Hassen Khemiri's play *Invasion!* masterfully uses mistranslation as a way to deconstruct the idea of the male Arab migrant as a knowable category while also pointing to the creative possibilities of mistranslation.

Khemiri's debut novel *Ett öga rött* (One Eye Red; 2003), which was published three years before the first staging of *Invasion!*, explores a self-styled restorative self-translation in line with that of Huda in Under the Copenhagen Sky. One Eye Red was an instant bestseller and immediately put Khemiri on the literary map in Sweden, though many critics initially mistook the playful use of language in the novel for authentic immigrant slang and the novel as autobiography. In One Eye Red the young protagonist Halim, like Huda in Under the Copenhagen Sky, wishes to translate himself back to a more authentic version of himself as he strives to return to an imagined version of his Tunisian heritage, which he perceives as more authentic. When he and his father move from the suburbs to the socially rarefied and largely white central area of Stockholm, he begins to transform himself into a self-styled 'thought sultan'. He does not rely on a translator, but he meets regularly with an older and mentally unstable woman on a park bench where she shares her theories on politics and some Arabic language lessons with him. Halim believes he has seen through the Swedish integration plan that would erase his identity and begins to pepper his speech with made-up Arabic proverbs, much to the chagrin of his father. Like Huda, Halim's translation project eventually fails and leaves him grappling with the realities of his lived experience. Since One Eye Red, Khemiri has published three more novels as well as numerous plays, short stories and op-eds, many of which centre on themes of language, multi-generational legacies of immigration, and more recently, the intersections of economy and intimate relationships and world views.

The first of Khemiri's six plays, *Invasion!* was first performed at the Stockholm City Theatre in 2006 and was later produced in a number of international theatres, including in France and Germany, and in US cities including Chicago, San Francisco and New York, the latter of which won an Obie Award in 2011. The play begins with two actors placed in the audience who storm the stage (often the audience try to shush them and prevent them from accessing the stage) and loudly interrupt an ongoing and rather uninspiring performance of nineteenth-century Swedish playwright Carl Jonas Love Almqvist's romantic drama *Signora Luna*. Although the two offenders, classmates Arvind and Yousef, are escorted out of the performance and then chided by their teacher, they later recall the name of one of Almqvist's characters, the Orientalised Arab knight Abulkasem, with significant gusto. Within the group of high school friends, the name Abulkasem becomes a flexible slang word, taking on new meanings over time.

> **B/ARVIND**: [...] Then Abulkasem could mean absolutely anything. It could be an adjective ...
> **D/YOUSEF**: (*yawning*) Shit, I'm mad Abulkasem. I was up watching movies all night ...
> **B/ARVIND**: Verb ...
> **D/YOUSEF**: (*irritated*) Come on, Mr. Anderson, Abulkasem someone else, I didn't have time to study ...
> **B/ARVIND**: It could be an insult ...
> **D/YOUSEF**: (*threatening*) Don't play Abulkasem, man, no cuts, it was my turn.

B/ARVIND: It could be a compliment …

D/YOUSEF: Hey! Check out the chica. Look! She's nice yo, she's slim fit, she's flo-jo, she's crazy Abulkasem, admit it!

B/ARVIND: It became the perfect word. But of course sometimes there were misunderstandings …

D/YOUSEF: (*angrily*) What the fuck you mean, Abulkasem? Oh, okay, you mean *Abulkasem*. (*apologetically*) Okay, my bad.[46]

The group of friends graduate from high school and go their separate ways in life. Now, Abulkasem begins to morph into an imagined character or adopted identity. Abulkasem is always other, for better or worse.

As an adopted identity, Abulkasem does offer some temporary cover and reprieve. A few years into his career at a call centre, Arvind tries to impress a young university student at a bar. Nervous, he introduces himself as Abulkasem instead of Arvind. His pseudonym seems to give him enough courage to sweet talk the young woman. Unimpressed with Arvind's babbling, the young woman hands him a made-up phone number to end the conversation and returns to her study group. However, getting annoyed with her fellow students' comments on her supposed oppressed status as a Kurdish Muslim woman, she begins telling them about her favourite director, a radical Muslim woman named Aouatef. However, already agitated, she forgets Aouatef's name and to save face, refers to her as Abulkasem. Arvind begins calling the number she gave him, leaving messages from 'Abulkasem' on a daily basis. The number she made up belongs to an asylum seeker working as an apple picker while waiting for news on his case. As a result of the brief encounter at the bar, the unnamed asylum seeker/apple picker now believes he is being harassed by a man named Abulkasem.

Now, with Abulkasem unleashed into the wider world, a panel of experts appears in several scenes to elaborate on who he might be. The sequence of scenes containing these panels, Scene Two: The Panel of Experts on Abulkasem's Birth,[47] Scene Four: The Expert Panel on Abulkasem's Escape,[48] Scene Six: The Panel of Experts on Abulkasem's Arrival[49] replicate a hostile narrative on migration and on the Muslim Arab male migrant in particular, as well as its adjacent punditry. Mistranslation, or the creative reimagining of a word, may have created a sense of possibility for the characters in the play, but it is also a site of violence.

The commentary of experts in these scenes is very much in line with the play's use of playfulness and irreverence as a means to get to truly weighty issues. The experts provide contradictory and anecdotal evidence on the much-feared Abulkasem. According to the team of experts, he was born in a village in Southern Lebanon, or perhaps in a village in Palestine. He presented very few definable features as a child. 'He was born, grew up, lived a completely average life in a completely average refugee camp.'[50] He is politicised as an adult, but the experts disagree on his positions. According to some experts, he began to vocally support Israeli settlements and applauded American foreign policy in his twenties. According to others, he became a member of the resistance and was labelled a terrorist by the Mossad and an enemy combatant by the CIA.

> **D/EXPERT 3:** Everyone reads him as an opponent.
> **B/EXPERT 1:** And soon everyone agrees that Abulkasem is the greatest threat to our common future.[51]

He travels around the world with the panel of experts close on his heels. When he arrives at his destination (the destination varies depending on where the play is staged) he wreaks havoc on the local political and social systems. Everything from linguistic confusion to a spike in garlic sales and a lack of respect for government is attributed to his arrival.

The absurd punditry points to a question that is at the heart of the play: can the migrant ever be properly represented as a category? Writing on this question of representation, Litvin and Sellman point out,

> The title of the play points to a discourse equating migration, especially from the Arab world, with an invasion of Europe. The play rises to the challenge of staging a highly unstable and slippery figure of the migrant, not as a particular individual, but rather in a way that showcases how individual identities and stories can fade into the distance amidst the chatter of pundits, fears and discourse of 'experts'.[52]

Mistranslation too plays a role in this playful-yet-serious deconstruction of the way the figure of the migrant is constructed. In one scene, the apple picker's Arabic testimony is rendered through a translator who deliberately misconstrues it. While the interpreter begins translating accurately, they soon veer off into the same kinds of stereotypes that the expert panel peddles in.

> **A/APPLE PICKER**: Alraha Alwaheeda Allatii Baqiyat Lii Hiya Fel Musiiqa.
> *[The only comfort I have left is music ...]*
> **C/INTERPRETER:** America is still much better than my homeland.
> **A/APPLE PICKER:** Almusiiqa Kanat Da'iman Mawjuda Wa Lam Tatakhalla 'Anni Abadan.
> *[Music has always been there and never abandoned me.]*
> **C/INTERPRETER:** I come from a relatively terroristic background.
> **A/APPLE PICKER:** Ana Wa Akhii Alasghar Saber Kana 'Indana Firqat pop 'Indama Kunna Sighar.
> *[Saber, my youngest brother, and I had a pop band when we were little.]*
> **C/INTERPRETER:** Saber, my youngest brother, and I used to play suicide bombers when we were little.[53]

While the apple picker is excitedly talking about his passion for music, the interpreter fabricates more and more stories of the apple picker's hatred for Jews, Western women, and his militant activities. It becomes clear to him that something is off when he is belting out Abba songs while the interpreter is talking excitedly about joining the al-Aqsa Martyr's Brigade. The apple picker switches to the language that the play is being performed in and addresses the audience directly instead of relying on the interpreter.

> **A/APPLE PICKER:** (*in English*) No more war. Not good ... Many wars, many violence ... Interpreter not good ... War not good ... Abulkasem not good ... I wait four years ... I stop waiting ... Maybe asylum, maybe torture ... Maybe prison ... No one know ... Not good ... Head feel bad ... Lawyer gone ... Lawyer idiot. Now head sick. Abulkasem everywhere ... Watching ... Threatening ... Maybe Abulkasem is me? Maybe Abulkasem is you?
> (*Silence.* **APPLE PICKER** *looks distrustfully at the audience.*)

Who is Abulkasem? You? Maybe you are. Head very tired. Little sleep. Many many awake.
VOICE MAIL: You have one new message ...[54]

In the play, mistranslation and the continual reinvention of the name Abulkasem point both to the open-ended possibility of re-signifying a term and to the violence of misrepresentation. The play calls attention to the linguistic inventiveness that is often part of translational spaces and the borderlands of migration and points to how translation can be productive of new cultural forms and modes of expression. It is through this creative play with language and mistranslation that *Invasion!* deconstructs the idea of a definable Arab migrant and subverts the us–them binaries that it is based on. Abulkasem, as the apple picker points out, could be anyone as much as it could be him.

Conclusion

In all three literary texts explored in this chapter, translated words, texts and ideas are underscored and originals fade away into the background. The break with the idea of the original is explored through mistranslations, failed translations and translations that cannot be verified against an original. This is true even of *Tahta Sama'*, even as it engages in a lengthy exploration of its protagonist's desire for a more authentic identity, the pre-translated self. This conception of authenticity is predicated on the idea that Huda is living her life as a translation – and here translation is understood as a pale shadow of some previous, more authentic or original version of herself. *The Village Indian* and *Invasion!* also mobilise mistranslation, re-signification and missing originals to target fixed and bounded notions of who the migrant is and can be, especially within European media discourses. Both Khider and Khemiri operate within the languages and discourses of German and Swedish literature respectively, Khider as an immigrant writer and Khemiri as a non-immigrant writer, but with an oeuvre that explores migration and racialisation within European-Arab contexts. The inclusion of these two works points to the overlap between European 'migrant literature' and Arabic migration literature, even as the audiences and discourses that they engage with may differ slightly. Mistranslations and vanishing original in these stories call attention to the literary and imaginative qualities of the story and thus, the role of literature in stretching the limits of how we conceive of migration and the categories that it relies upon.

In the last chapters of *Tahta Sama'*, Huda turns her attention to themes of transformation and imagination. In one of these later chapters, she strolls down the streets of central Copenhagen musing on the cycles of extreme darkness and light that characterise Scandinavian seasons, and how the way that the seasons affect people makes transformation a foundation of being. People in Denmark are also, she suggests, quick to embrace and experiment with different religious identities. In the same way, Huda reads the stories of Hans Christian Anderson through the way that they enact transformation. If he could imagine that people could transform into animals and vice versa, she wonders, how is it that he did not imagine that the Danish citizenry would one day include those who come from places far away and now call Denmark home? She writes,

> But Hans Christian Anderson's childlike and fertile imagination did not help him predict that all of these different nations would one day be transformed into members of his own. It's a pity that such a basic matter eluded him. Did he think that the world of the 19th century, a world whose identities were contained and separate would last?
>
> Why didn't his imagination roam free to consider that the world would become Danish?
>
> Why do we Scandinavians limit our imaginations to talking animals, corpses that return to life, a queen sleeping on a pea, or a nightingale singing for the emperor of China?
>
> How did our image – we, the new Scandinavians – remain hidden from Anderson's imagination? Why does this master of imagination suddenly appear to be so unimaginative when faced with our situation?[55]

Noticing the limits of the imagination in these stories calls attention to the relationship between literature and the habitually thinkable.

The vanishing original in the novel is also the idea of the rooted citizen that the migrant is often juxtaposed to. However, as seen in the novel, the idea of the exile writer is also one that is recognised and anchored, if not in a place, then in an orientation and a discourse. The position that Huda and so many others occupy might be better described as that of the transnational citizen, a transnationalism shaped by forced migration. In contrast to the idea of diaspora, which tends to be more inward-looking and focused on shared histories and identities, the term transnationalism emphasises the outward-facing practices, processes and social spaces that cross national borders.[56] Of course, these outward- and inward-looking processes are often co-present and co-constitutive of migratory subjectivities. Christina Slade suggests in *Watching Arabic Television in Europe: From Diaspora to Hybrid Citizens* (2014) that transnational practices often serve to unsettle myths of cultural and linguistic uniformity and national cohesion within European nations. In response to the rise of nationalist sentiment in Europe, which tends to see such hybridity or practices that link directly to an *elsewhere* as betrayal or conflict, she asks,

> Is the 'dark tribalism' of twenty-first century Europe justified by the clash of civilizations, by an enemy within? Or should twenty-first century Europe hope to be the home of hybrid citizens, drawing on connections across national and ethnic boundaries, a mix of the local, distant friends and allegiances, and underpinned by values of civic engagement?[57]

This, of course, is one of the central questions of *Invasion!* where the idea of an immigrant invasion justifies both discursive and physical violence enacted on the imagined migrant Abulkasem and the asylum-seeking apple picker. While the prescriptive tenor of Slade's questions conjures many pressing issues with respect to defining citizenship and political community in European nations, many citizens and residents are already navigating complex landscapes defined by competing calls for uniformity and loyalty to origins, on the one hand, and the realities of hybridity, flux and the embrace of civic engagement as a basis for citizenship, on the other.

In a 2009 article that discusses the role of translation in contemporary warfare, Mary Louise Pratt argues that in conflicts, the role of the translator shifts from being 'faithful' and an enabler of comprehension to being a possible traitor, suspect to both sides. In addition to embodying this possibility of betrayal of either side, she suggests, the translator has 'the ability to betray both by envisioning, and embodying, something different, a third term'. Although the literary texts explored in this chapter do not focus on war, the way in which languages and the multiple demands of similarity are pitted against one another replicates this idea of difference signalling betrayal and conflict. In Pratt's words,

> multilingualism is translation's mother but thus also, in crucial terms, its definitive other. The multilingual person is not one who translates constantly from one language or cultural system into another, though multilingual subjects are sometimes able to do such work. To be multilingual is above all to live in more than one language, to be one for whom translation is unnecessary. Where there is translation, there are originals and translations but also multiplied identities – subjectivities, interfaces, and agencies born of the entanglement. The image for multilingualism is not translation but *desdoblamiento*, a multiplying or unfolding of the self.[58]

This chapter started by asking 'What would it mean to rely on a translator in order to write your own story?' In different ways, each narrative might be said to ask the questions 'What would it mean to become somebody for whom translation is unnecessary?' or 'What kinds of new stories are born of migration, conceived through translation?' Indeed, translation becomes a terrain of invention and multiplying in these literary imaginaries. There is the multiplying of stories in *The Village Indian*, the sense that these stories are simultaneously shared, individual, and springing from an infinite well of creativity, that of people making new realities and futures. The multiplying meanings of Abulkasem in *Invasion!* creates myriad new identities, some which point toward creative reinvention and some to the construction of the migrant as an outsider and threat.

The narratives explored in this chapter stage this tension between translation, figured through conflict and the potential for violence, on the one hand and multilingualism as a 'multiplying or unfolding of self', on the other. The binary logic that underpins Huda and Rafid's hopes of transformation through translation and the way that it breaks down in the course of the novel suggests a desire to re-theorise the relationship between translation and multilingualism and the questions of citizenship with which it intersects. But the novel also takes seriously a desire for authenticity that echoes the exclusions that can be produced both by nationalist sentiments and by diasporas. Huda's desire to translate herself out of the spiralling constrictions of her exile into an image of an Arab exile author both engages with a literary history of writing exile in Arabic and lays bare anxieties about transnational belongings imagined through this 'multiplying' or 'unfolding' of self in a context shaped by forced migration. The multiplying and unfolding of stories and selves also elicits anxieties in *The Village Indian* and *Invasion!*.

The transnational and perhaps postnational condition that the characters in these works are grappling with are perhaps some of the most central ethical questions of our current age. Feminist philosopher Rossi Braidotti posits that this process of disidentification with national and bounded notions of identity is a necessary yet painful process of confronting a rapidly globalising world and of prioritising interconnections above bounded identities. She writes,

> The qualitative leap through pain, across the mournful landscapes of nostalgic learning, is the gesture of active creation of affirmative ways of belonging. It is a fundamental reconfiguration of our way of being in the world, which acknowledges the pain of loss, but moves further.[59]

This emphasis on recreating ways of belonging is one of the areas where the concerns of Arabic migration literature and European-language migrant literature intersect. *Tahta Sama'* dramatises the trajectory from nostalgia to active creation by beginning with the fantasy of being able to translate oneself to authenticity, then moving to the acknowledgement of the pain of loss which makes moving beyond the framework of many nationalisms and diasporas so difficult, and finally toward a tentative embrace of complex and emergent belongings. We can situate Huda's final declaration of the novel, 'I am Huda', within this mournful landscape, understanding that this Huda is shifting and retranslated just like the changing notions of exile narrated in Arabic migration literature and in European migrant literatures.

Notes

1. Emily Apter, *The Translation Zone: A New Comparative Literature* (Princeton: Princeton University Press, 2006), 6.
2. Moira Inghilleri, *Translation and Migration* (New York: Routledge, 2017), 34.
3. *Tahta Sama' Kubinhaghin* was long-listed for the 2012 International Prize for Arabic Fiction, also known as the 'Arabic Booker Prize'. The nomination received some attention at the time as it was the only book on the list by a female author, and because she was only in her twenties.
4. Hawra al-Nadawi, 'Interview with Hawra al-Nadawi, the only woman on the IPAF longlist', *The Tanjara*, 26 November 2011, http://thetanjara.blogspot.co.uk/2011/11/interview-with-hawra-al-nadawi-only.html.
5. Unlike her protagonist, Huda, the novel's author, Hawra al-Nadawi, left Iraq as a child. Her parents were political prisoners in Iraq, and she spent the first years of her life in a prison with her mother. After an amnesty for political prisoners in 1986, her family received asylum in Denmark. Al-Nadawi grew up in Copenhagen in a multilingual family speaking Danish, Arabic and Kurdish and she embraced Arabic as her language of literary expression.
6. Lori Chamberlain, 'Gender and the Metaphorics of Translation', *Signs* 13, no. 3 (1988): 454–72.
7. Michal Raizen, 'Hebrew-Arabic Translational Communities and the Recuperation of Arab-Jewish Literary Memory', *Dibur* 8 (Spring 2020): 29–42.
8. Al-Nadawi, *Tahta Sama'*, 21.
9. Al-Nadawi, *Tahta Sama'*, 22.
10. Al-Nadawi, *Tahta Sama'*, 22.
11. Al-Nadawi, *Tahta Sama'*, 22.
12. Al-Nadawi, *Tahta Sama'*, 23–5.
13. Al-Nadawi, *Tahta Sama'*, 89.
14. Tobin Siebers, *Disability Theory* (Ann Arbor: University of Michigan Press, 2008), 3.
15. Al-Nadawi, *Tahta Sama'*, 99.
16. Al-Nadawi, *Tahta Sama'*, 128.
17. Al-Nadawi, *Tahta Sama'*, 90–1.
18. Al-Nadawi, *Tahta Sama'*, 134.
19. Al-Nadawi, *Tahta Sama'*, 126.

20. Al-Nadawi, *Tahta Sama'*, 308.
21. Al-Nadawi, *Tahta Sama'*, 309.
22. Lori Chamberlain, 'Gender and the Metaphorics of Translation', *Signs* 13, no. 3 (Spring 1988): 454–72.
23. Chamberlain, 'Gender', 456.
24. Chamberlain, 'Gender', 461.
25. Al-Nadawi, *Tahta Sama'*, 323.
26. Al-Nadawi, *Tahta Sama'*, 368.
27. Al-Nadawi, *Tahta Sama'*, 9–10.
28. Al-Nadawi, *Tahta Sama'*, 10.
29. Al-Nadawi, *Tahta Sama'*, 117.
30. Al-Nadawi, *Tahta Sama'*, 14.
31. Al-Nadawi, *Tahta Sama'*, 325.
32. Al-Nadawi, *Tahta Sama'*, 326.
33. Al-Nadawi, *Tahta Sama'*, 375.
34. Al-Nadawi, *Tahta Sama'*, 376.
35. Al-Nadawi, *Tahta Sama'*, 329.
36. Al-Nadawi, *Tahta Sama'*, 330.
37. Hanan al-Shaykh, *Only in London*, trans. Catherine Cobham (New York: Anchor Books, 2002).
38. Al-Samman, *Anxiety of Erasure*, 197.
39. Abbas Khider, *Deutsch für alle: Das endgültige Lehrbuch* (Munich: Carl Hanser Verlag, 2019).
40. Khider, *The Village Indian*, 7.
41. Khider, *The Village Indian*, 7–8.
42. Khider, *The Village Indian*, 17.
43. Khider, *The Village Indian*, 20.
44. Corina Stan, 'Novels in the Translation Zone: Abbas Khider, *Weltliteratur*, and the Ethics of the Passerby', *Comparative Literature Studies* 55, no. 2 (2018): 292.
45. Stan, 'Novels in the Translation Zone', 294.
46. Jonas Hassen Khemiri, *Invasion!*, trans. Rachel Willson-Broyles (New York: Samuel French, 2013), 16.
47. Khemiri, *Invasion!*, 21.
48. Khemiri, *Invasion!*, 32.
49. Khemiri, *Invasion!*, 45.
50. Khemiri, *Invasion!*, 22.

51. Khemiri, *Invasion!*, 23.
52. Litvin and Sellman, 'An Icy Heaven', 49.
53. Khemiri, *Invasion!*, 39–40.
54. Khemiri, *Invasion!*, 43–4.
55. Al-Nadawi, *Tahta Sama'*, 202.
56. Thomas Faist, 'Diaspora and Transnationalism: What Kind of Dance Partners', in Rainer Baubröck and Thomas Faist (eds), *Diaspora and Transnationalism: Concepts, Theories and Methods* (Amsterdam: Amsterdam University Press, 2010), 9.
57. Christina Slade, *Watching Arabic Television in Europe: From Diaspora to Hybrid Citizens* (Basingstoke: Palgrave Macmillan, 2014), 22.
58. Mary Louise Pratt, 'Harm's Way: Language and the Contemporary Arts of War', *PMLA: Publications of the Modern Language Association of America* 124, no. 5 (2009): 1527.
59. Braidotti, *Transpositions*, 84.

5

Writing against 'Crisis': Defamiliarising the Refugee Narrative in Arabic Literature and Theatre in Berlin

After the arrival of more than one million Syrians in Germany in 2015–16,[1] Berlin has become host to a thriving Arab arts, literature and theatre scene. Some artists and culture critics have even posited Berlin as a new capital of Arab culture. As the arts scene in Berlin has been both invigorated and transformed by the visibility of Syrian and Arab writers and artists, there has also been increased interest in curating, performing and attending both arts-based and academic events that touch on contemporary migration, especially the forced migration of the post-Arab Spring moment. Arabic theatre and literature in Berlin are negotiating these emergent social and artistic spaces, where creative and often collaborative and multilingual approaches coexist with, negotiate, and sometimes resist, dominant representations of the exile, refugee and forced migrant. In the process, writers and other cultural actors are creating experimental and speculative modes of writing and performance that upend expectations placed on migration literature and the figure of the refugee while imagining mobility and diaspora alongside the complex questions raised by forced migration.

In this chapter, I discuss the emergent Arabic literary, theatre and arts scene in Berlin and analyse several literary and theatre texts and performances that are defamiliarising migration in ways that create openings for transformative reflection. This discussion anchors Berlin's collaborative, translational and internationalising ethos within a range of different institutions, cultural actors and efforts to define it. This new exile, what political sociologist Amro Ali calls 'the new Arab exile body',[2] whose history, conditions and cultural institutions diverge significantly from the postcolonial centres of London and Paris, is being theorised in multiple spaces, including literature, theatre, the arts and in forums for critical inquiry, but also in the everyday lives and practices of those who are living and shaping it. In the chapter, I discuss the short stories from two collections by Rasha Abbas, a journalist and author from Syria who has been active in Berlin over the past few years. Her *Kayfa Tamma Ikhtira' al-Lugha al-Almaniyya* (How the German Language was Invented), which was first published in German translation in 2016 as *Die Erfindung der deutschen Grammatik*[3] (The Invention of German Grammar) is a collection of short stories, or vignettes, depicting life in Berlin from the perspective of a newly arrived refugee. Her main character braves a sometimes absurd housing market, the effects of sun deprivation, and Berlin hipster culture, and imagines the sadistic tendencies of those who invented German grammar. Her 2018 short story collection, *Mulakhkhas Ma Jara* (A summary of what happened, or 'The Gist of It'),[4] has been described as 'psychedelic'; the short stories, many of which take place in the midst of the Syrian war and in migratory contexts, delve into speculative modes of writing and altered states of consciousness. Both collections reframe mobility and migration in ways that defamiliarise the tropes and vocabulary of contemporary forced migration, placing them in speculative contexts or novel situations. Finally, the chapter discusses Ziad Adwan's play *Please, Repeat After Me*,[5] a work of performance art that seeks to refigure audience expectations of migration theatre and testimony through the deliberate performance of mistakes. Written in English and performed in Munich (2018) and Berlin (2019), the play explores the impact of mistakes and the performance of the absurd on the power dynamic between audience and performers, especially when the actors are presumed to be Syrian refugees or representatives of authentic culture or testimony. Both Abbas's short stories and Adwan's play draw on speculative and performatively subversive strategies to inquire into what is possible as they theorise exile from the vantage point of communities emerging post displacement. In a context where migration and displacement are hypervisible in the media, eliciting both responses of solidarity and calls to harden borders, Abbas and Adwan intentionally move away from direct representation of migration and insist on art doing something different. In their work, we find a deep probing of subjectivity and choice that invites the fashioning of new, perhaps yet unformulated, responses and imaginings of the meanings of mobility.

Berlin as a Capital of Arab Culture

The so-called migration crisis made the Syrian refugee the face of global migration and displacement. Mass media and social media images of large groups of people crossing borders on foot or by boat (perhaps the most painful image of the toll of these journeys is that of Alan Kurdi, the Kurdish Syrian toddler who drowned off the Turkish coast) played a large role in creating both spaces of solidarity with migrants and calls to tighten borders. Syrian migration to Europe and to Germany in these years has been hypervisible. Although many Syrians in Germany have taken the so-called sea routes or precarious migratory routes across land, unlike the *harraga* literature discussed in Chapter 2 or the post-human refugee literature discussed in Chapter 3 of this book, the Arabic literature and theatre of migration in Berlin largely eschews artistic representations of these journeys, likely in response to the oversaturation of these images in the media and the expectation that Arab writers (and Syrian writers in particular) will be focusing on topics like migration and revolution in their work. Against this oversaturation of images and expectations, many writers are turning instead toward different modes of defamiliarising the images, ideas and texts that are already circulating and to writing that seeks new ways of imagining mobility.

A commonly cited sentiment by Syrian artists in Berlin is that efforts to make them more visible, while often well intentioned, circumscribe the work of Syrian artists to themes of war, revolution or the refugee. When people hear 'Syrian', '[they] immediately think "refugee"', states artist and curator Khaled Barakeh.[6] 'There is no such thing as refugee literature',[7] states writer Rasha Abbas, at least not the way it is sometimes framed in public events featuring Syrian artists in Berlin. Barakeh's and Abbas's points are apt – there is a tendency for the political and social to overtake the artistic contributions of artists when events and literature are framed around the topics of exile and migration. The abject often permeates efforts to represent refugee experiences. This flattening can have the impact of turning artists into informants or spokespeople for otherwise pressing political issues. It is by taking their works seriously as works of art and literature that we can see the multiple ways in which they are transforming Arabic literature of forced migration.

The arts scene in Berlin is open, translational and collaborative. Individuals and institutions are creating spaces for art with and against the pain of the war and the massive displacement and migration it has caused. My intention here is not to idealise the city of Berlin or in any way minimise the real pain of living – and creating – synchronously with the ongoing war in Syria. Rather, I aim to describe some of the conditions of the arts scene that Syrian artists are creating in Berlin, often in productive collaboration and conversation with local institutions and actors. For one, the experimental and avant-garde ethos that has long been part of Berlin's arts scene has translated into a relative openness to collaboration with newcomers. In addition to the talent, training and ideas that Syrian and other artists are bringing to Berlin, there are the institutions and local actors that help make their work visible. Whether or not the writers or artists arrived as refugees during the war, such collaboration is to some extent supported by Berlin's predominantly left-wing politics and by a cultural climate that is relatively open to new influences. In fact, some Syrian writers and artists describe this hospitality as a double-edged sword ('hostipitality', in Derrida's words), whereby their art gains a certain visibility, but sometimes at the risk of their identities being reduced to their nationality or equated with topical issues.

The fact that Berlin is sometimes touted as the capital of Syrian and even Arab culture is an interesting turn of events in itself, but it points to the way that the relationship between diaspora and the nation(s) is being reimagined. Indeed, the locating and theorising of centres and capitals perhaps hinges on finding new geographies following large-scale dispersal. In May 2018, for instance, a programme titled 'Is Berlin Today a Capital of Arab Culture by Virtue of the Number of Arab Artists and Intellectuals who Live There?'[8] aired on BBC Arabic. The featured panel of Arab writers and cultural brokers living in Berlin offered varied perspectives on the question. One of the participants, Widad Nabi,[9] noted that the Arab and Arabic-language culture scene in Berlin has a lot of visibility but lacks the Arabic-language publishers and cultural institutions of some European cities, such as London and Paris.

Nabi's point is significant in that it touches on the questions of what institutions and practices are necessary for a city to be considered a cultural centre, both in a general sense and in the context of Arab diasporas. However, the fact that Berlin is operating *differently* from more established centres of Arab diasporic culture in Europe is precisely the reason that these conversations are unfolding. Berlin is being experienced and thought of as a site of possibility in the period following the Arab uprisings but also in the post-2015 period. It is true that there are no well-known Arabic bookstores, presses or literary institutions in Berlin; yet events, performances and public discussions are part of many of the mainstream and emergent cultural institutions, festivals and publishers. Some artists cite the absence of established Arabic-language institutions and long-time cultural elites in the city as one of the reasons that newcomers have been able to quickly create new spaces and practices.

Two of the participants in the BBC discussion were Mohannad Qaiconie and Dana Haddad, founders of Berlin's Arabic library, Baynatna (Between us). Baynatna, itself an institution that reimagines what a library can be, lines up well with the open-ended and emergent ethos of this culture scene. The library was initially located in an emergency refugee centre, the Arabic collection generated by donations. The founders eventually won a grant that allowed them to relocate the library to a space in central Berlin. An architecture class at Berlin's Technical University donated moveable furniture and shelves, thus creating a flexible library that can be reconfigured for different types of events. Since then, in addition to operating as a traditional lending library, Baynatna has hosted discussions, literary events, performances, musical jams, and more. As the founders explain on the library's website,

> 'Baynatna' means 'between us' in Arabic: this very popular phrase creates a special kind of intimacy between people who agree to share insights, thoughts or stories even if only just for seconds. In the process of establishing Baynatna, our international team relied on humour, trust,

and sensibility to facilitate a space for dialogs [sic] no one knows where exactly they may lead us.¹⁰

As is the trend in many libraries, the founders express an intention that Baynatna be a space where ideas and resources are not only stored and shared, but also curated and created in Arabic, German and English.

In addition to creating spaces whose use goes beyond their earlier functions, established, mainstream institutions are also featuring some Arabic literature, theatre and visual arts. These processes are not without friction. Antimigrant nationalist currents that have been spreading in Germany are not completely absent in Berlin. Yet the scene is dynamic and generative. Readings, screenings, exhibits and talks, often advertised on Facebook, draw people together. A few examples: The Literaturhaus, traditionally a stronghold of German literature, held a landmark, all-Arabic conversation between prominent Arabic-language exile authors in June 2019, in which conversations quickly moved between the literary and the question of politics in the post-Arab Spring moment. The Berlin Arab film festival brings in prominent films and filmmakers. A robust number of educational institutions and foundations shape academic and public debate.[11] Events are by no means limited to audiences who speak and read Arabic. Plays are staged in translation, with subtitles, or written in English. Literary texts are translated and literary events often have simultaneous interpreters present. The current arts and literature scene is often collaborative, creating a wide and engaged audience and possibilities through encounters and shared questions. In some instances, collaborations between German and Syrian artists and writers have created reflections on Germany's history of war and the devastating impact of displacement and borders.[12]

Importantly, the Ballhaus Nynaunstrasse theatre, strongly associated with the concept of 'post-migrant' theatre (*postmigrantisches Theater*)[13] and Shermin Langhoff's long-time leadership, created a forum for theatre and multimedia art that grapples with issues associated with second- and third-generation immigrants. Though post-migrant theatre creates a forum to see and reimagine the issues facing second- and third-generation immigrants to Germany, it has paved the way for more experimental and intersectional approaches to staging theatre that deal with migration and social identities. A prominent example of the transfer of knowledge and approaches to theatre is artistic director Shermin Langhoff's move to becoming the artistic director of the Maxim Gorki Theatre in 2013. From founding the current iteration of Ballhaus Nynaunstrasse and defining the meaning of post-migrant theatre, she went on to transform a prominent theatre in Berlin to a space that now prides itself on its work on borders and belonging. The Gorki Theatre's website states that 'Under Langhoff's direction, the Maxim Gorki Theatre understands itself as a place in which constructions of nation, identity and belonging are questioned by dealing with history and presenting trans-local references.'[14] Specifically, the theatre's Exil Ensemble,[15] composed of artists from Syria, Palestine and Afghanistan who, as the theatre states, 'have been forced to live in exile', has become one of the institutions through which Arab playwrights, directors and actors have produced and performed their work.

In line with these transformations of established cultural and educational institutions and the emergence of new institutions and spaces, some have noted a need to theorise this new exilic situation in Berlin in ways that depart from reductionist approaches to the forced migrant; rather, they approach the condition of the exile, situating them as producers of vision and an emergent cultural politics. A visionary example of this kind of conceptualisation is political sociologist Amro Ali's intervention, which began with a January 2019 essay titled 'On the Need to Shape the Arab Exile Body in Berlin', published on the *AlSharq* blog (now *dis:orient*) and developed in a series of public speaking engagements, debates and a documentary produced for German television. Ali's essay represents a call to both theorise and more fully realise the cultural and political potential of the burgeoning Arab community in Berlin. In this essay, Ali argues that the Arab community in Berlin today is uniquely positioned to constitute a body politic, that is, an organically fashioned and self-aware community that might continue to build on the yet largely unrealised aspirations of the Arab uprisings through a deep connection to Berlin on the one hand, and to the Arab world, on the other. Berlin today, he suggests, has the potential to become what New York was for Jewish exiles who fled European persecution in the 1930s, and Paris was for Latin American exiles fleeting dictatorships in the 1970s and 1980s.

Ali lists a number of material and social conditions that have made the Arab diaspora in Berlin such a fertile ground for shared reflection and creativity. For example, he notes that Berlin, in contrast to many large European capitals, is still relatively affordable and its Arab diaspora is not associated with any one political movement or party. In contrast to Paris, it is not bound to the francophone world. It is a major European city, yet perceptions of the city are not overly defined by its colonial past and lingering postcolonial ties. The long grappling with the country's own fascist past (even as far-right nationalism is on the rise) has led to a relative political openness. In contrast to many of the hyperpolished European capitals, many parts of Berlin remain gritty, the city still has space to grow, and it 'offers a sense of incompleteness' which invites newcomers to participate in an emergent culture.

Yet Ali's call goes beyond the city's material conditions and asks readers to consider a manifestation of politics deeper than the political institutions of the state, into 'the existential level that shores up the transnational Arab sphere. This is the very area where the stream of human life animates a language of awareness and the recurring initiative helps to expand the spaces of dignity for fellow beings.' Along with this romantic vision of diasporic becoming, a call to revisit *Nahda*-thinker Butrus al-Bustani's 'Ruh al-Asr', this is also a call for an intellectual movement:

> In effect, there is a dire necessity for this community to acquire a name, shape, form and a mandate of sorts. With a vigorous eye to a possible long-term outcome, this may include a school of thought, a political philosophy or even an ideational movement – all cross-fertilized through a deeper engagement with the Arab world.[16]

To theorise this body politic is necessarily to revisit the meaning of exile, where the refugee might be its central figure. Ali notes that previous instances of large-scale forced migration of Arabic-speaking populations have mostly been national (Palestinian displacement, the Lebanese Civil War, Libyans leaving Gaddafi's regime, etc.), but the Arab uprisings of 2011 and the conflicts that ensued have created the first pan-Arab and transnational exodus. Although the most recent immigration to Berlin is largely comprised of Syrian arrivals, the thriving Arab cultural scene is decidedly transnational.

Importantly, Ali theorises exile as a collective practice, quite distinct from its modernist imaginings. He recognises that the categories ascribed to people in movement (refugee, intellectual, emigré, immigrant, etc.) overlap and shift and that no group has a monopoly on creating exilic culture. As such, the binary of the voiceless refugee and the exilic intellectual is not useful for theorising exile. He uses the example of the Arab barber, who through daily sociability forges transnational ties and, like the intellectual, is playing a role in creating exilic culture. On this subject, Ali writes,

> The Arab author is simply one manifestation of the same political spectrum that produced that barber. The author just happens to be one of the most visible, most political, most clearly articulated expression of Arab grievances. Yet the author should not forget that he or she developed, consciously or not, from the same background and reservoir as the rest of society and the upheavals of the Arab Spring. This is where they draw their strength and legitimacy from; and this society has a very large reservoir of pain, unhappiness, confusion, and uncertainty. But when the intellectuals and activists not only recognize the futility of separation from that background, but also return to and engage with it, not as shewerma-buying customers but as citizens-in-exile in an ever-expanding conversation with moral obligations, the securing of a steadfast future is aided.[17]

Ali's rendering of Berlin does include a discussion of some important contradictions that result in Germany being seen as a sight of possibility less burdened by colonial histories, despite its historical and present powerful role in the world. For example, he notes that Germany is not acutely linked to colonialism even though its global companies have been associated with exacerbating economic underdevelopment in their countries of operation. Furthermore,

> The paradox of its power is that the savagery Germany committed in the first half of the twentieth century skirts around the Arab world. While

> German orientalism is not alien to Arab scholarship, this is not what is usually or immediately deplored in Arab scholarly circles and the Arab imaginary regarding Germany – to that country's stroke of luck. Even strong German support for Israel does not elicit the same degree of Arab anger towards it as with the US and UK, partly because of the sound popular view that Germany is coerced by historical guilt. So, in a sense, Germany is conditionally, if not grudgingly, let off the hook.[18]

Adding to Ali's examples, I'll note a number of further contradictions: Berlin may be affordable relative to some major European cities, but it is also a site of rapid gentrification. Berlin is often perceived as less burdened by colonial ties than other major European cities, but it was also host of the 1885–6 Berlin Conference that set the stage for European colonisation of Africa. Its culture is deeply shaped by antifascism even as far-right nationalist currents are gaining strength in Germany. However, the focus of Ali's essay is on the spaces of possibility that migrants and exiles are co-creating in the city and as such, these contradictions remain largely implicit.

The very idea of Berlin as a capital of Arab culture requires seeing belonging as a practice and creation rather than anchored to a fixed geography. Another example of how the Syrian nation in particular is being imagined through a displacement from its own geography can be found in Syrian artist Khaled Barakeh's participation in the Ford Foundation-sponsored project CoCulture,[19] an online platform that includes 'Syria Cultural Index', which maps Syrian artists as a web of connections spread across the globe. The planned 'Syrian Biennale: Roots En Route' aims to create a mobile biennale along migratory routes and in the cities and towns that have become the new homes of displaced artists from Syria. The 'Roots En Route' aims to strengthen Syrian identity precisely by anchoring the nation not in a fixed geography but through connections, open-ended cultural production, and the geographies of dispersal:

> Hoping to counteract the defragmentation and displacement of the Syrian identity, the Syrian Biennale serves as a contribution to a much-needed conversation around Syria's media-generated image; through supporting, empowering and connecting Syrian cultural producers around

the world it represents and preserves Syria's cultural heritage beyond national borders.[20]

Here, diaspora becomes the nation rather than being secondary to it.

Literature and theatre are important sites for this aesthetic and political reimagining of exile, which places the forced migrant and dispersal at its centre. The following sections discuss Rasha Abbas's short stories in *Mulakhkhas Ma Jara* ('The Gist of It') and *Kayfa Tamma Ikhtira' al-Lugha al-Almaniyya* (How the German Language was Invented) and Ziad Adwan's play *Please, Repeat after Me*. Both use narrative and performative strategies to defamiliarise migration and mobility and thus subvert dominant perceptions of the refugee and the power dynamics that underpin them. Each in their own way, these pieces are invested both in the dynamics and possibilities of both the local scene and the transnational Arabic-language literary sphere.

Rasha Abbas's Short Stories and the Project to Reinvent Exile Literature

Rasha Abbas is a Syrian writer residing in Berlin. While she insists that 'there is no such thing as refugee literature', she is among a number of writers and cultural actors in Berlin's Arab cultural scene who are rethinking how this moment of forced migration can be written and imagined outside of dominant discursive parameters. While many of her short stories are set against the backdrop of the Syrian civil war or in migratory or post-migratory contexts, they actively resist the way the term 'refugee literature' is often made to signify.

Rasha Abbas was born in Latakia, Syria, and grew up in Damascus. She studied journalism at the University of Damascus and, after graduating, worked as an editor for Syrian television. In 2008, she published her first short story collection, *Adam Yakrah al- Talifiziyun* (Adam Hates Television),[21] for which she won an Arab Capital of Culture young writer's award. As a public figure who had become involved in the popular uprising against the Syrian regime, she was forced to relocate, and so moved to Beirut, Lebanon, in 2012. Then, after receiving a Jean-Jacques Rousseau fellowship at Akademie Schloss Solitude in Stuttgart, she moved to

Germany. Unable to return to Syria, she applied for asylum in Germany and has lived thereafter in Berlin. In 2016, Abbas published *Kayfa Tamma Ikhtira' al-Lugha al-Almaniyya* (How the German Language was Invented), a collection of humorous stories on navigating life in hipster Berlin. It first came out in German translation and was later reworked and published in Arabic. In 2018, she published *Mulakhkhas Ma Jara* ('The Gist of It'), a collection of very short stories. And she is currently working on a novel titled *al-Ku'us al-Sab'* (Seven of Cups), a work that uses tarot cards as a starting point to narrate the brief union between Syria and Egypt (1958–61), an interesting experiment in using the future-oriented modes of tarot to examine a moment in the past that seems to exemplify the contingency of national borders.

Abbas's experimental, 'psychedelic' and often humorous voice is in part a conscious response to the socialist realist style that was long an important presence in modern Syrian literature. Since the 1950s, an ideal of literature participating in a progressive – even revolutionary – reimagining and improvement of society coalesced around dominant socialist realist style oriented around 'nationalism, class consciousness and dialectical materialism'.[22] Socialist realism's association with anti-imperialism and the Soviet Union meant it remained dominant even as Sartrean political commitment (*iltizām*) rose to prominence in the 1960s in many Arab literary contexts.[23] The Writer's Union in Syria has long set the tone of literary discourse and the facts that many writers were employed by the state and that the Ministry of Information and the Ministry of Culture were long Syria's largest publishers strengthened this literary approach.[24] 'The writers' duty was the service of the nation',[25] writes Mohja Kahf, just as literature, in the socialist realist school of thought, was to serve the vision of a just socialist society. Though the socialist realist style and ideals did create and shape innovative literary styles and ideals of greater social justice, it tended to centre masculine narratives, as evidenced by the common trope of the noble (male) hero struggling for a just cause against oppressive social classes. These tropes extended to exile literature, such as Hanna Minah's exile novel *Al-Rabi' wa-l-Kharif* (Spring and Summer),[26] which presents an upright and politically committed hero in exile in Hungary who, despite enjoying the fruits of socialism in exile, returns to his country to struggle for justice. Women, in this novel, appear mostly as the hero's lovers and metaphors for the nation or political causes.

At the same time, in modern Syrian literature there is also a long history of resistance to dominant styles and evasion of censorship. As noted by Kahf, state censorship has the tendency to give rise to both conformist writing and new forms of artistic expression, especially ones that makes use of silence or ask the audience to read between the lines:

> Contemporary Syrian literature is created in the crucible of a tenacious authoritarianism. Manifold silence, evasion, indirect figurative speech, gaps and lacunae are striking features of Syrian writing, habits of thought and wary writerly techniques that have developed during an era dominated, in Syria more overwhelmingly than in other Arab countries excepting Iraq and perhaps Libya, by authoritarian governments with heavy-handed censorship policies and stringent punitive measures.[27]

Rasha Abbas's own fiction simultaneously counters both a socialist realist heritage and the expectations of a local audience in Europe, and in Berlin specifically, of how literature on war and displacement should be written.

Abbas has addressed the question of how to address war and migration in her own pieces of literary criticism, such as in the essay, 'How Political Should We Get While Writing?'[28] which she published while an international artist in residence at the Akademie Schloss Solitude. In this text, she asks: 'So, how far should we go in trying to be faithful to the political necessities of our times in what we write? Maybe, the answer is in not getting far at all.' In the essay, she refers to Leon Trotsky's work of literary criticism *Literature and Revolution,* in which he compares the approaches taken by novelist and playwright Alexey Tolstoy (a distant relative of Leo Tolstoy) and the poet Tikhonov. While Alexey Tolstoy wrote overtly communist fiction featuring, for instance, communist revolution on Mars, Tikhonov's poetry focuses on everyday settings and makes little or no overt reference to either revolution or communism. In *Literature and Revolution* Trotsky argues that one of Tikhonov's poems, set in a grocery store, captures the spirit of revolution in ways that more overtly political works cannot. Using this example to capture the role that she ascribes to political messaging in her own work, Abbas writes,

Here the Lacanian maxim 'the letter always reaches its destination', comes in handy, because it's not up to you to decide where the letter arrives; if it ends up burned in the post office during a civil war or safely reaches the recipient. Your message's destination is wherever it arrives.[29]

In another online post, titled 'We Can't Compete in Writing',[30] she addresses her own reluctance to write in a direct manner about the war in Syria, noting that direct messaging easily undermines the literary qualities of a text and that the context shapes the text in less overt ways. Furthermore, she points to a sense that fictional writing cannot 'compete' with the brutal realities of the war. Like the fictional narratives examined in earlier chapters of this book, she asserts that literary narratives need to 'do' something different from other discursive practices.

Rasha Abbas's *Kayfa Tamma Ikhtira' al-Lugha al-Almaniyya* was first published in German translation from the Arabic as *Die Erfindung der deutschen Grammatik* (2016) by the Berlin-based publishing house Microtext and later published electronically in Arabic through the Beirut branch of the Heinrich Boll Stiftung. The short book consists of humorous and episodic short stories, or vignettes, detailing the travails of a Syrian refugee navigating the vagaries of German grammar, Berlin hipster culture, the challenge of finding good housing, surviving sun deprivation during the long grey winters of the German capital, and the bureaucracy of visas, residence permits and asylum applications that also are part of being a newcomer. *Kayfa Tamma*'s humour is situational – often deadpan and farcical. The book's narrator is sincere in her comical attempts to learn German. However, faced with the discovery of ever more complicated grammatical rules as well as the contradictions and absurdities created by gentrification, hipster cultures (the anarchist who calls the police on her, for example) and the Berlin arts scene, she takes shortcuts, daydreams, and bargains to much comical effect. The book places the reader in a position to both laugh at the narrator and identify with her situation, just as they might laugh at the hyperbolic rendering of Berlin, rendered here through a banter that is at once loving and critical.

As suggested by the book's title, language is central to its social critique and humour. The confident and formal tone of the first part of the title, *Kayfa Tamma*,³¹ contrasts with the choice of words that posits the German language as something that was 'invented'. In the book, two civilisational languages meet. The narrator, whose efforts to learn German and make sense of the grammar through another language that is infamous for its difficult grammar – Arabic – inhabits the crevices between the two, where she can draw attention to absurdities and also humanise the struggle to learn a new language as an adult, a struggle that many can relate to. (Interestingly, Iraqi German author Abbas Khider published a book in 2019 titled *Deutsch für alle: Das endgültige Lehrbuch* (German for Everybody: The Ultimate Textbook), a humorous but also a linguistically based discussion of the possibilities for simplifying German and making it more hospitable to learners.)

The opening vignette in Abbas's book is an imagined conversation between two dukes (the humorous effect comes in part from the self-aware historical inaccuracies of the two men) conspiring to create a language that will be exceptionally difficult for foreigners to learn. The two engage in a giddy conversation where Duke Ludwig's position that they should create as complicated of a grammar as possible prevails. 'Let's make up scores of verbs with no regular conjugation', Duke Ludwig suggests, 'verbs that are written differently in the middle of the sentence and at the end of the sentence'. He chides his fellow duke, who is more moderate in his ambitions,

> But Duke Karl, aren't you being a bit sensitive? To be honest, I have a few immediate objections to your suggestions. We're about to embark on deciding the role of gender so you shouldn't even be aware of these issues yet (unless through heresy or knowledge of the unseen). I'm afraid your behaviour is turning this session into a bad drama. I don't think our aims should be constrained by making things easier for language students. What do I look like to you? A tourist welcome centre? Look at me now Mr. Duke and tell me: Do I look like a tourist welcome centre to you? Is it the wig that I am wearing? Alright, I'm actually going to suggest that we do the opposite and propose that the tenses be deliberately misleading. Let 'apple' be masculine.³²

The dukes are supposed to be speaking weak English (since German has not been invented yet) and at the same time, the Arabic text makes reference to concepts and logics that are anchored in the Arabic language. The word for divination used is *'ulūm al-ghayb*, knowledge of the unseen, a concept that in different Islamic schools of thought is usually only attributed to the divine and select individuals who are granted access to such knowledge. The blundering dukes would be unlikely candidates. The word 'apple' is obviously feminine in Arabic since it ends with the feminine marker, and the statement about German will make sense if the Arabic is brought in alongside it. The presence of Arabic in the discussion adds to the effect. 'Are you thinking what I am thinking?' asks one of the dukes. 'If we do this no crazy foreigner will dream of learning this language.'[33]

After an episode in which our hero searches for affordable housing (she finds a keyless room that is only a two-hour train and swimming commute from central Berlin that she can share with a bitter Kemalist, a washed-up Italian artist sniffing paint varnish, and unknown others), there is a section titled 'How I Became an Artist'. Here, the narrator, who has been struggling to learn the gender of German nouns, decides to start drawing the gendered words on her wall. She paints an orange with breasts, a soup on birth control, and fills her walls with images aimed to aid her memorisation. To her own surprise, her walls become a destination for art connoisseurs and her work is featured in some of the important galleries in the city. She decides to join the ranks of artists who refuse to offer interpretations of their works – she draws the conclusion that they might be learning German, too. Later in the book, frustrated with the grammar lessons offered in class, she embarks on a project to learn German from 'the school of life', an effort that offers its own surprising pitfalls.

In the vignette titled 'Visa?' the narrator makes the decision to begin the process of applying for refugee status in Germany. As in some other sections, the situational humour derives partially from the narrator walking into situations naively, discovering how they are complicated, and then resorting to tricks and comical manoeuvres to get herself out. She declares her lack of knowledge about the asylum process upfront: 'I had no idea how to do this, and I was wary of the process itself. Maybe this is because I had just made the mistake of reading *Maus*, the graphic novel about a survivor of the Nazi holocaust.'[34]

While the asylum interview and the stories it solicits are an important contemporary narrative genre and an important feature of migration literature, 'Visa?' focuses not on the asylum interview but rather on the questions that she receives from the other Syrians who are standing in line with her. When she arrives, she is excited to be among Syrians again and finding herself in a friendly disposition, she begins her interactions with them by earnestly answering questions. However, the questions and answers – though straightforward – prove surprisingly challenging. Noting that she is one of the few lucky ones who travelled to Germany on a visa and thus avoided the dangerous sea and land routes that most Syrians arriving in Germany were forced to take, she immediately elicits surprise when a woman asks her when she arrived and she says that it was about three months ago.

> She responded: 'And why didn't you declare yourself during this period?'
> I answered stupidly: 'Because my visa was valid for three months.' Cue the suspicious silence and then the nice lady's slow repetition of my own word: 'Visa??'[35]

The narrator, feeling slightly guilty about her privilege at this point, begins to imagine that the lady's tone is hostile. She compares it to the tone her mother used to use when she caught her smoking as a teenager. '"*Ci*garettes?" The question sounded scornful to the degree that it revealed what she really wanted to say: "Who are you to have a visa?"'[36]

The questions of those standing in line continue, each more difficult to answer than the last. Who is with you? (It's a friend, but many in line assume he is her fiancé or spouse). Where are you from? (This one is complicated because she is from a town known to be a stronghold of the feared Syrian intelligence agency, the very reason that many have become refugees.) She has spent her life in Damascus, but knows that she cannot claim to be of Damascus, since her family's roots in Damascus do not stretch back far enough. Eventually, finding these questions and social circumstances too difficult, she begins to spin stories, or scenarios, of boat crossings, smuggling, and dangerous land crossings. Sneaking away from her friend, she registers quickly with the administrators of a refugee camp and later, pretends to her roommates that she does not speak Arabic.

In the story, the very questions that pertain to personal status, arrival, origin, et cetera are also those of bureaucracy and the asylum interview specifically. However, those doing the questioning and judging here are well-meaning (though stress-inducing) fellow Syrians who are also standing in line to face similar questions. The story calls attention to the stakes of presenting oneself as a refugee and the dissonance that might exist between personal histories and both the versions that are recounted and the commonly circulated narratives about who a Syrian refugee in Germany might be. The narrator's narrow escape into anonymity in the refugee camp might be sheepish, but as in many of the stories in the book, she makes do in situations that elicit both social critique and humour.

The stories in *Mulakhkhas Ma Jara* inhabit the world of the post-2011 Syrian revolution and conflict and all that it has entailed, including violence, displacement, and the discordant dissemination of information during the war. Alice Guthrie, who has been working on an English translation of these stories, aptly describes them as 'eclectic, intense, often psychedelic' and as 'dreamscapes which creep up on the reader with sudden plunges into haunting hyper-realism, operating within a punk aesthetic'.[37] Different nonrealist modes of writing weave in and out of the stories (from science fiction and fantasy to stories where magic has a real role to play), but The Gist of It cannot really be defined by one genre of speculative writing. There is perhaps a touch of what Finland-based Iraqi writer Hassan Blasim calls 'nightmare realism'[38] or what Haytham Bahoora calls the 'the aesthetics of horror'[39] in Iraqi war fiction. There is also a sly and situational humour.

In particular, Abbas's characters seem to parody the noble (male) hero of socialist realist writing long present in Syrian literature, who ceaselessly struggle against oppressive social classes and espouse a clear and correct political vision. Instead, her characters are caught up in their worlds, trying to make do and discover what there is to discover. They often inhabit alternate realities or altered states of consciousness that are either drug-induced, sleep-induced, or trauma-induced, or simply part of a setting that does not correspond to laws of nature. Many times, surprising and even fantastical forces shape their journeys. When the characters are mobile, they get lost, become victims of magic that misfires, or accidentally 'end up' in strange places. In the following section, I will discuss two stories from *Mulakhkhas Ma Jara*, 'The Day I Returned to the Ruins' and 'Seven O'Clock Yesterday', considering how they reframe the travelling hero around subjectivity, the speculative and the language of forced migration.

Mobility in 'The Day I Returned to the Ruins' and 'Seven O'Clock Yesterday'

In the short story 'Yawm 'Idtu ila al-Kharab' ('The Day I Returned to the Ruins') it first appears as if an unnamed narrator – an exhausted journalist – is being sent off on a vacation by her colleagues at the newspaper where she works. But as she journeys, so does the logic of the story. First, it reveals the trauma that precedes the story, then the disjuncture between the narrator's perception of reality and the setting. Finally, the story begins to unfold like a dream, then an absurd nightmare, until we arrive at an ending that completely reframes our understanding of the narrator's trip.

In the beginning of the story the narrator reveals a recent trauma while chatting with a very uninterested taxi driver about her chakra stone necklaces. The narrator also reveals her fascination with causation, which she projects onto her necklaces. She explains:

> There were other stones too, but they're still hanging around my sister's neck. Now, they're under the rubble of a building. She got the necklaces with the earth stones and I got the ones with the air stones. That's why she stayed in the house. She remained there after two consecutive pregnancies and births and now she's buried there. After the house collapsed. Meanwhile, I flew here and was saved.[40]

The story's geography is that of a vague 'here' – the hotel where the taxi eventually drops her off – and a 'there' that signifies the home and ruins that she left behind. The initial description of mobility is transactional. She has traded safety 'here' but not yet lost 'what she has'. What she has seems to refer to her magical, likely delusional, ink and water divination practice through which she solicits signs from her stone chakra necklaces. The taxi drops her off at what she refers to as the hotel. She concedes that it bears a certain resemblance to an in-patient facility but insists to herself it's just the modernist aesthetic. Once she has reassured herself that none of the friendly yet insistent white-clad hotel employees are present, she immediately starts her ink and water divination practices. It is when the expected messages fail to appear that she begins to regret her travels, noting that she has exchanged safety for 'what she has'. And 'what she owned' remains 'there', in the ruins.

After a man she refers to as a hotel employee administers her medication and assures her that she can leave whenever she wants, the story departs even further from an expected sense of the real and from the transactional metaphors of movement.

> I was worried that the man might be lying, but it turned out he wasn't. I rose from the bed cautiously and walked up to the castle. I walked a little further until I reached the shore. I gripped my necklace tightly and proceeded to cross the ocean. I didn't feel afraid because when the necklaces were first cast, they were engraved with a promise that those who wear the stone of speech will be permitted to cross the ocean unharmed.[41]

This journey of return, toward her home, the ruins, first appears as a dream sequence in which oceans can be crossed instantly. But it quickly turns into a nightmarish hallucination. Everyone she encounters is clad in white, from the kids who look like karate students and help her on the way and the young man who looks like a karate instructor but is suddenly dressed as a soldier, to the relative she finds in her house who instructs her to announce her family's death to the neighbourhood. Back in her house, she is overwhelmed by the shadows of rats. She and her colleagues discuss plans to film a report on the rats that have invaded the city, which is under siege. Grotesque examples of violence are on display. The story becomes structured through a countdown of various strange and seemingly nonsensical numerical combinations of seconds (marking time in a way that feels incomprehensible to the reader). Finally, the white-clad men return to bring her back to the hotel. But as the city burns, she refuses to move. As she is about to meet her death, she looks at the fresh footsteps in the grass, considering the woman who must just have walked there. In the final moment, the narrator, who seems to have been tossed on the waves of various states of altered consciousness, is the one who sees and knows. She notes,

But I knew more than anyone else. She hadn't just been walking on this grass. Rather, it was a long time ago, after she threw herself off the balcony of the hotel facing the ruins of the castle. This piece of knowledge won't be of use to anyone now, in any case.[42]

The main character is a journalist who engages in murky divination practices and has descended into a long hallucination. As she narrates the story, her reporting seems to defy all of the tenets of her profession. Yet as an account of her traumas, it is painfully convincing. While not anchored in a reality that is shared with others, she is the one who sees the footsteps in the grass for what they are. Brushing away a sense of instructive or objective truth, she wonders whether her knowing of the truth matters. When she first describes crossing the ocean, it seems as if she is describing a dream, but by the story's end, we understand that this journey was the death that the chakra necklace could not avert. This is a narrator who sees and knows, yet makes no pretence of objectivity or heroism.

In the story 'Al-Saʿa al-Sabiʿa fi Yawm Ams' ('Seven O'Clock Yesterday') the uncanny takes centre stage when a man becomes lost while travelling to visit his relatives and accidentally ends up in a small town where time does not exist. This short story reframes key types of mobility, merging the terms of escapist tourism and forced migration. For example, the terms 'fleeing' and 'taking refuge' are often repeated and here, transferred onto a desire to escape the limits and impediments that time imposes.

The story opens on a wistful note sometime in the future. The narrator states: 'If I could one day find the way again, everything would be better. I went there once, but I lost my way and never found it again.'[43] There is humour in the statement as it renders his inability to navigate back to the town the crux of the matter rather than the curious fact that time is absent there. The repetition of *yawman*, 'one day' or 'once', places the narrator's past travels vaguely in time and space. The vague, almost storybook feeling of the opening is soon replaced by his very specific rendering of how bothersome and difficult the journey there was. Retracing his steps, he recounts first taking a train, then trekking far on foot while dragging a heavy suitcase. Exhausted, he finally stumbles upon a taxi parked in a landscape that has no distinguishing features. After some negotiation, he is eventually transported to a little town and checks into Ricardo's Inn, a mediocre hotel where guests must make their own drinks at the bar. Once there, he notices a number of things that seem strange. His phone will not connect to a network and no longer displays time. There is no television in his room, and there are rarely any employees in the hotel. After some enigmatic conversations, he discovers that the town has somehow been liberated from the constraints of time.

The taxi driver did say something about this, he recalls, but he notes: 'I thought it was more like a figurative description, like saying "This beach transports you to paradise without the need to purchase a ticket." Or "Take a break in the mountains that will take you far from your everyday worries."'[44] The town is, indeed, a destination for a kind of escapist tourism. And the language reinforces this link between the ways we talk and write about different kinds of mobility. The inhabitants and visitors are repeatedly referred to as people who are *fleeing* and people who are *taking refuge* from time.

A young man guides the narrator around the town and tells him about its original inhabitants and those who have fled there. The way the stories of these 'time refugees' are told mimics the narrative devices that often structure the understanding of the exile versus the refugee: the modernist exile is a privileged interpreter of the modern condition whereas the refugee is subject to the forces of history. Some of the people in the town have individual stories and others are described as fleeing the general limitations of time. There is a well-known film star who was famed for her beauty and is now escaping the detrimental effects that aging has had on her career. There is an inventor who is competing against his own mortality as he makes all-too-slow progress toward inventing an artificial bladder that will solve humanity's urination problems. Other visitors and inhabitants are described as people who, in general, are always in a hurry and feel that they lack time. Paradoxically, no time is experienced as an abundance of time and after a while, old habits fall away.

The guide explains that there is a magnetic field under the ground that is causing the standstill in time and that its pull is at its strongest within a portal located in an abandoned building. The people, the narrator learns, are generally not interested in entering it, even though it transports one to the previous day. Unlike the other inhabitants and visitors, the narrator decides to venture through the portal and returns to find the sunset of the previous evening at 7 pm. Presumably, it is this that makes him lose his way once again.

The characters' ways of knowing in these stories are shaped by hallucinations, warped time and altered states of consciousness; they are very distant from the heroes of the social and socialist realist exile narratives and even modernist narratives, which made the exile a privileged interpreter of their time. This parody of the old guard and of the hero narrative is in and of itself nothing new; however, Abbas is mobilising it in interesting ways in her current moment. Her antiheroes, in their very distinct states of consciousness, see but do not purport to instruct through their particular vision. Instead, they invite readers to consider how they are seeing.

Returning to the question of refugee literature and whether it exists as a genre, we see that these stories both defamiliarise the language and tropes that are ubiquitous in the framing and language of forced migration and deliberately use them out of context, thus both displacing and generalising them. From the transactional idea of trading home for safety but linking them to divination practices in 'The Day I Returned to the Ruins' to the people who 'flee' and 'take refuge' from the effects of time in 'Seven O'Clock Yesterday', we see that Abbas is exploring *how* these terms can signify.

The humorous and the flippant are juxtaposed with the deeply sorrowful, sometimes to rather shocking effect. As Michal Raizen notes,[45] there is an 'accordion' effect. We are stretched far from the immediate context of war and migration (while staying with some of its language), through the humour, through the speculative elements, through the narrators – and then we are snapped back with an image or word that conjures the war and its ruins. And the effect is amplified. In all that is being created here, these are just some of the ways that fictional writing is undoing paradigms long associated with exile literature and the idea of refugee literature.

Performing Mistakes in *Please, Repeat After Me*

Written in English, Ziad Adwan's play *Please, Repeat After Me* premiered in 2018 at the HochX Theatre und Live Art in Munich and was later performed at the English Theatre in Berlin in May 2019 and then again in November 2019. The promotional materials bill it as a play about stereotypes and choice:

> *Please, Repeat After Me* is a play about decision-making and labels.
> (We)* are left abandoned in the theatre with a real mermaid: a fish incapable of being eaten and a woman incapable of seduction.
> But the mermaid is real!
> When does a stereotype stop being a stereotype?
> When does a refugee stop being a refugee?
> When does an actor stop being an actor?[46]

The formulation (We)* is self-referential; the asterisk leads nowhere, thus simultaneously calling attention to and calling into question the collective experience of theatre. While the audience is never literally abandoned with a mermaid (one of the characters, the Hakawati storyteller, references the figure of the mermaid in a speech), the figure of the mermaid metaphorically invokes the playful yet serious treatment of the refugee actors who also defy the utility and expectations ascribed to them.

Please, Repeat After Me draws on Brechtian and other practices of defamiliarisation[47] to create a theatrical space in which audiences are invited to confront their own preconceived notions of what migration theatre is and does. It is a play about stereotypes, but not necessarily the stereotypes that we might expect. In fact, when Ziad Adwan, the play's writer and director (and also one of its actors), steps up to introduce the play, he assures the audience that the play will feature authentic testimonies that are based on years of research and are thus far from the stereotypes that plague representations of Arabs. In the 1990s, Ziad declares in this speech, Arabs were wealthy tourists. Then, in the 2000s, they became terrorists. Now they are refugees. What will they be in future years, in the coming minutes? This laid-back introduction to the play (in which a casually dressed Adwan holds a cup of mate tea and invites audience members to keep their mobile phones on and even film the show if they want) establishes a joking yet intimate rapport with the audience and extends a promise that something authentic will be delivered. In addition to the testimonies of refugee actors, he explains, he has invited a Syrian storyteller, an English-speaking Hakawati, who will videoconference in to deliver an epic in English. As the play continues, however, things appear to go wrong. Lights flicker, technology fails, the four 'refugee' actors'[48] personal problems disrupt their performance of testimony. The Hakawati gets into a squabble with one of the actors. The interventions of Ziad, the director, and Ineaki, the European manager, only complicate matters. The play's descent into chaos and absurdity is intentional. The audience is suspended in a space of uncertainty about the performance, a space where they must confront their own expectations of migration theatre and consider how to act and respond within the framework determined by the play.

The theoretical questions underpinning *Please, Repeat After Me* were developed during Ziad Adwan's already rich career as a theatre maker and academic. The son of famous playwright Mahmoud Adwan, Ziad Adwan has inhabited a range of roles and spaces within the world of theatre. As an actor, he has performed in many plays and also in films such as Steven Spielberg's *Munich* and *The Hamburg Cell*. He has directed plays and street theatre. Adwan earned an MA in Text and Performance Studies at the Royal Academy of Dramatic Art at King's College in London and then a PhD in Theatre Studies at Royal Holloway, during which he wrote about mistakes and authenticity in folkdance performance. When he returned to Syria, he taught theatre and performance theory at the Higher Institute of Dramatic Arts in Damascus and served as artistic director of *Invisible Stories*, a series of performance events that took place in different neighbourhoods in Damascus. An active academic and researcher, he is currently affiliated with the Global Theatre Histories Research Project at LMU in Munich (where he has published articles on theatre culture in Syria and the Gulf) and a partner at Tanween Theatre and Dance Company, founded by Adwan's wife, choreographer and activist Mey Seifan. In 2016, he published a magazine on Syrian exilic culture in Berlin titled, *A Syrious Look*, with several German and Syrian artist colleagues in Berlin. About the culture of Berlin, Ziad noted in a 2017 interview that 'Berlin ... is a city mixing history with authenticity. Due to the war, it appears open to everything new, after having lost a lot. It is a city aspiring to the future, despite the war.'[49]

Please, Repeat After Me extends the questions of Adwan's PhD thesis into the world of migration theatre. In his dissertation, Adwan analysed the folk dancer as a figure of cultural authenticity. In it, he argues that in contrast to the professional actor, who would fall out of character as soon as they make a mistake, the folk dancer remains a folk dancer in the eyes of the audience even when they make mistakes. This is because they are perceived to be performing an aspect of their identity that is authentic, independent of their performance in front of an audience. In *Please, Repeat After Me*, Adwan experiments with the relationship between the figure of the refugee and conceptions of authenticity that are implicit to many articulations of migration theatre. He posits that the refugee actor (or rather the actor who is perceived as a refugee) occupies a position similar to the folk dancer; they are not perceived to fall out of character even when something goes wrong. Cynically, one could say that if they step out of character they paradoxically remain even more *in* character, especially if there is an assumed dichotomy between professional theatre and migration theatre. In *Please, Repeat After Me*, the character Sabah, who holds a fluid identity with regard to gender, personality and origin, voices this position directly to the audience:

> My dear audience! Who said that a simple technical difficulty can stop us from saying who we are and what really happened to us? We are presenting our stories and our background. We either survive or we are forgotten. Our experiences do not depend on electricity and recorded music. Telling you the truth does not need technology. It is blood and soul. (*Pause*). Listen my dears! This play is not a normal play! In a normal play, actors return back to who they are when such a mistake happens. If a mistake takes place when I am playing Hamlet, I will stop being Hamlet, and I become myself. But, we as refugees, we are still refugees despite everything. Whatever happens we remain the same, we remain our authentic self. And this is the unique thing about us. We are refugees in theatre and in real life. We either survive or we are forgotten.[50]

The play pushes this thesis to its breaking point as repeated failure to perform a seamless authenticity turns into humour and farce.

This theatrical experiment must be situated in relation to the upsurge in migration theatre in Europe (and Berlin especially) following 2015 and, specifically, to the range of ways that authenticity is made to signify, at times through the crowdsourcing stories, staging nonprofessional refugee actors, or the staging of plays that emphasise content and social solidarity. While these experiments may create interesting aesthetic and social effects, *Please, Repeat After Me* pursues a different line of inquiry. Instead, the play takes on the underlying assumptions and power dynamics of migration theatre in Europe, where Middle Eastern others provide authentic materials and the audience is placed in a position of power. It redirects attention toward how theatre may, within the short time that actors and audience interact, create conditions for exposing, grappling with, and potentially transforming the power dynamics that are often part of migration theatre.

The performance of testimony is part of the ecosystem of migration theatre. As Margaret Litvin and I have noted in a previously published article, there are a number of 'traps' related to perceived authenticity that often structure Arab theatre of migration in Europe. These include the expectation that meaning is anchored in autobiography, national allegory and Orientalist tropes. Arab theatre in Europe often both trades in and subverts these expectations, or 'traps', in an effort to both capture the audience's attention and navigate toward an understanding that their art form transcends one particular social context.

> well-intentioned projects to elicit and stage refugees' stories, including both verbatim theatre and adaptations of Greek tragedies, can cause an unintended reproduction of racism and (colonial) stereotypes, leaving the migrant participants neither really seen nor really heard. Perhaps inadvertently, these projects treat migrants as raw materials, not creators, for the theatre process. That they often present amateurs also works to obscure the fact that trained professional Arab artists exist in Europe.[51]

In a later piece on the Arab migration theatre scene in Berlin, Litvin reflects on how some of these dynamics have shifted in the contemporary theatre scene in Berlin:

Unlike some more typical cases of post- 9/11 'Arab/ic theatre for Western audiences', Berlin audiences are diverse, comprising viewers with different language skills and expectations, including some who are Arab immigrants themselves or know Syria or other Arabic-speaking societies intimately, along with others who do not but want their play-going to be timely. Yet, the Syrian-German arts community is relatively new, compared for instance to the generations-old Turkish-German arts community and the 'post-migrant' theatre it has created. The Berlin-based Syrian artists do not fit neatly into the 'Sindbad vs. Houdini' typology that Johanna Sellman and I recently proposed within another European context; they are neither exotic visitors on tour nor Arab Germans.[52]

Even with this changed reality (and truly, the audience of *Please, Repeat After Me* was multilingual and of diverse origins), the play targets the power dynamics that remain part of the theatre scene. Specifically, it calls attention to the desire for authenticity, which coexists with a downgrading of the kind of art that corresponds to its parameters. In an interview, Adwan states that one reaction that the play both elicits and invites the audience to face can be summed up as a curiosity about the authentic other than can easily turn to annoyance: 'We respect theatre. We are here, so you can't make mistakes.' Witnessing this reaction in others (or perhaps observing it in oneself) puts the power relationship between audience and performers on display. As an experiment, the play seems to ask: can the embarrassment, exposure and alienation triggered by mistakes in a performance create shifts in perception?

Disrupting Authenticity

In what initially seems like an impromptu opening speech, Ziad Adwan, playing the role of Ziad, calls out to Ineaki, the European manager of the show, to come up to the stage and greet the audience. Ineaki, Ziad explains, is among the Europeans who truly understand 'us'. Ineaki, however, fails to appear. Thus begins the series of mishaps and mistakes that shape the performance. The representation of the subject matter at hand – the Syrian war, migration, stereotypes – becomes increasingly chaotic and even flirts with the absurd. The audience is invited to pass through a landscape of uncertainty before arriving at any conclusions about the play, facing questions such as: is the intent of the play representation or the breaking down of representation? Who are we coming to see, the Syrian refugee or our own presumptions projected back at us?

Before we see actors playing refugees in person, their faces are projected onto a grey plastic screen. Since the screen is somewhat wrinkled and the projector does not seem to give off enough light, the images are somewhat difficult to discern. The faces on the screen read the following lines:

> **SABAH** (*On the screen*) Yes Sir! This is me in the passport.
> **HALA** (*On the screen*) I don't know where I am going next.
> **REEM** (*On the screen*) What do you want me to do sir?
> **ARMAJ** (*On the screen*) I'm not lying sir! I really don't know![53]

The lines, which seem to be responses to questions in an asylum interview, or perhaps the questioning of a border agent, are repeated monotonously until they overlap and come to a crescendo. The actors move from behind staggered and wrinkled light-grey plastic panels hanging on both sides of the screen, entering the stage, making stumbling motions. Suddenly, the lights begin to flicker and the projector turns off. As the actors look around in confusion, Ziad comes out on the stage again to apologise for the technical difficulties and asks the audience to turn off their phones since one actor is upset about not receiving any calls for her birthday. The play soon resumes, and the actors continue to repeat the lines.

The character Hala, played by the Turkish actress Selin Kavak, dressed in a formal gown, performs a remake of a song by Youmni Abou Al Zahab's heavy metal band Ascendant. Then, a traditional storyteller, the Hakawati Abu El-Fasel, appears on the screen wearing a tarboosh, flowing robes, and clasping a stick in one hand and an old book in the other. His demeanour straddles the loudly sincere and the comically serious. On screen, he begins to tell the story of the Syrian revolution in language that gently parodies Orientalist tropes of the mysterious other:

> We are no different from the old times when our ancestors wrote their magnificent epics about our legends. And I wrote this story, when I saw

my people making miracles no different from the pyramids, Babel and the alphabet. We invented language, but we did not tell people how to use it.

We come from a land, best described as All-Secrets Land. It should be called All-Secrets Land. All through history and throughout the written stories, invaders from distant lands wanted to control these secrets. And my story tells you, my dear ears and my dear eyes, that the problem is; these invaders do not know how to deal with the secrets of our lands.[54]

In this first speech he introduces the 'young dreamers' or 'Gray Ghosts', who, he notes, are as numerous as the stars in the sky or the grains of sand in the desert. The ruler has ordered their arrest, but the secrets continue to spread, now into foreign lands. In this mythologised version of the war, the actors on the stage are positioned as grey ghosts, the young revolutionaries who are now scattered in foreign lands. The insinuation is that they are about to share their secrets with the audience. For a moment, there is harmony between these two sources of authenticity: the stories of the traditional Hakawati and the testimonies of the refugees. However, as the play continues the Hakawati's performance becomes repetitive, ornery, even ridiculous – and increasingly at odds with that of the other actors. The testimonies that each of the four refugee characters deliver are also far from what might be expected. Internal and external conflicts bubble up and mistakes continue to interrupt and subvert the performance of authenticity.

Interspersed between the testimonies are songs, a slideshow about war, dancing, recurring lines repeated by the actors, and the Hakawati's monologues on the screen. In the first testimony, Armaj is alone on the stage. He leans into a backwards-facing chair, looking intently at the audience and smiling, as if ready for an intimate conversation between friends. There are numerous elements of testimony present. For instance, his speech begins by documenting a specific moment in place and time: Wednesday, 24 October 2012, Damascus, 4 pm; and he signs off with his name, Armaj. The specificity of the information, however, is destabilised by the content of his testimony, which reflects on how 'war is paradise' because it is one extended experience of living in the now.

Sabah opens their testimony with Foucault's theory that the sovereign is that which holds power over life and death. Then, pacing the stage clad in a dress and high heels, they deliver a speech in a floaty voice about the arrest and torture that protesters faced in the Syrian revolution. In their testimony, their nonbinary gender identity intersects with the play's theme of the fictitious nature of playing/performing an authentic self:

> My name is Sabah. This is a unisex name. My parents thought that I could fit anywhere with this name. And the secret police once fitted me in a car trunk, while I was walking the street just like any other person. I was held for twelve days in solitary confinement. I was tortured; raped, electricity shocks, put on the German chair, and they hanged me by my wrists whenever the jailors were bored. When they interrogated me for the first time, it was on the twelfth day. And there was the surprise; the officers realised that they were looking for someone who has my same name, same name of my parent, and same date of birth, but the different sex. The officers were shocked. As a matter of fact, they had sent their jailors to rape me for the past eleven days without knowing if the jailors were raping a man or a woman.[55]

Next, Hala delivers a testimony with gusto, head held high. Hers is a story that takes place somewhere between dreams and waking life. She recounts awaking to find a recording device under her pillow. In the dream the floor is wet and there is a large hole in her house that creates a view of the whole city. She is afraid to fall through it. The stumbling motion that she makes as she recounts this fear of falling is recognisable as the stumbling motion that the actors in the play made when entering the stage. As she delivers her testimony, the other actors, following her cue, begin to repeat this motion again.

Soon, a new cascade of disruptions forces Hala to jump in to play the roles of the other characters. When the screen breaks yet again, she says the Hakawati's lines. When Reem is unable to give her testimony (the trauma she is recounting appears to be rendering her speechless), Hala steps in to say her lines until Reem remembers them. Reem, played by Turkish actress Gizem Akman, is dressed in a glittery skirt and a loosely fitting hijab. Throughout the play, she often smiles intently yet absently, and frequently forgets her lines. When she delivers her testimony, however, she wears a look of horror:

> Yes! Now I remember ... Our senses were the real threat against us. My sister was weak, and she couldn't handle her senses. We had to run away ... We ran away from hearing the sound of bullets and the screams of the innocents. We ran away from seeing a sniper staring at us. We avoided touching the burning walls. We ran away from the smell of ...! (*Pause*.) We ran away from the smell ... No![56]

As Reem struggles to continue her story, more things go wrong. The screen breaks yet again and Reem has to be escorted off the stage. Only Armaj is left. Visibly pleased to have the audience's undivided attention, he addresses them earnestly:

> You've probably noticed that we've had some difficulties tonight. The actors withdrew. One sister is nervous today, the other sister has lost control. Al-Hakawati didn't appear on the screen. It's quite unbelievable, isn't it? I don't know if you believe me or not, but it doesn't really matter. I will continue the play. Stay and watch. You won't regret it. I can play all the parts if you want. Do you believe me? I've memorised the entire play, apart from the songs. I'm not allowed to learn the songs, because they think I'm not Syrian.[57]

Here, Armaj directly addresses the question of believability. Does the audience at this point believe that the mistakes are part of the play? A sign of unprofessional theatre? Fluke incidents in an otherwise well-intended effort to present authentic Syrian culture and experiences? Reactions to these mishaps and playful parodying of authenticity were varied but pronounced during the two performances I attended. They included smiles and laughter, visible confusion, irritation, and even anger and frustration. At each one, a couple of people left the theatre in the middle of the performance.

It is also at this point that the question of mistakes is discussed openly on stage and the play takes an even more chaotic turn. Sabah takes the stage and in a confessional tone delivers a monologue that includes the previously quoted reflection about how they, as refugees, remain refugees despite anything that happens in the performance. The Hakawati appears on stage and a struggle ensues between him and Armaj about who should be speaking. Reem begins to meander, crawl, climb through the audience, asking: 'What do you want, sir?' We learn that that Armaj's Syrian identity is in question. He says he is from a border town that only sometimes is Syrian. Since it was forbidden to speak Arabic in the town, Armaj never learned Arabic and is thus unable to sing the authentic Syrian songs they had planned for the play. Sabah insists that they need to be performed:

> WHAT! To continue without the songs! This is culture. This is us. There is no culture without songs and music. You don't care about the songs because you are still unsure whether you are Syrian or not. But songs are culture. Nothing is more real than a song.[58]

However, since Sabah is unwilling to perform personal identity anymore and with none of the actors up to the task, Sabah suggests that Syrian audience members be solicited for the task.

The Political

The title *Please, Repeat After Me* invokes the idea of soliciting a mimetic response, a straightforward repetition of what has been said or meant. The irony is that the audience is left not knowing how to respond; the play places us in the uncomfortable yet productive position of not knowing where the testimony or topical matters of the play end and where the ruse begins. Even with the parody, mistakes and dark humour that are being performed, the representation of the topical content is also often haunting and powerful. We are left in an ambiguous space where both representation of the war and the critique of representation coexist in a generative tension. The play, however, does shift attention from newsworthy subject matter, such as the war in Syria and the displacement of Syrians, toward more ontological questions of being and what it means to be a witness to such a performance, mistakes and all.

As the chaos crescendos, authenticity is transformed from something that validates the performances to a marker of absurdity and play. The actors continue to verbalise the importance of authenticity even as they disqualify themselves from aligning with its framework. Armaj states that he is wealthy and made the undocumented journey to Europe so that he could try to travel to the moon. He is not sure if he is Syrian but he knows what he wants. Sabah enthusiastically supports the very authenticity ('It is blood and soul') that the play toys with but refuses to perform the authentic Syrian songs that the actors had planned to perform. With Hala upset (she has delivered a monologue about a relationship with Ziad that just ended and pleads with the audience for a place to stay) and Reem deeply affected by traumatic memories and unable to remember her lines, the actors decide to solicit authentic Syrians from the audience to perform the songs. Armaj begins to walk through the audience looking for 'Syrians'.

> You see! This is quite normal. Don't be shy please! We need an authentic Syrian volunteer please. Any Syrian please! (*Pause*) Who is Syrian here? Our dear audience! We want to know if we have Syrians among you to play the song.[59]

Armaj, whose own membership in the category 'Syrian' is in question (the other actors frequently mispronounce his name, 'Ajrash', 'Sharjam'), walks through the audience, approaching people and asking them if they are Syrian. The mirror is now reversed. Even if the audience understand that this is a game, there is a discomfort in being approached in this manner, in being asked to do something that you are not prepared to do or be something you are not prepared to be. In the stage directions, it states that the audience members approached need not be Syrian. In both performances that I attended, Armaj approached audience members who were not likely Syrian, of course, and the play brings this point home: there is no way of really knowing. Armaj engages in quiet conversation with audience members, asking if they are Syrian and when they respond that they are not, he responds that he *thought* they were. Are they sure they are not Syrian? Regardless, maybe they can come up on stage to perform the song? The audience thus becomes a part of the stage and a variety of reactions are put on display. Some smilingly play along and agree to go up on the stage; others are visibly embarrassed and insist they are not Syrian and decide to stay in their seats. There is clearly no 'right' answer: to play along is to submit to a gentle humiliation; to refuse to play along is to make visible the 'us versus them' binary that the performances of testimonies to largely European audiences depend on. Either option produces discomfort.

This act of turning the mirror of authenticity onto the audience is amplified when the character Ineaki appears on stage toward the end. He is the European manager of the company, the one who failed to appear when Ziad called out to him in his introductory speech. He assures the audience of his goodwill toward his Syrian friends and reveals his propensity for projecting his own dreams of being a political being onto them.

> I have always wanted to do something for their sake! I have been watching them in the rehearsals and the shows when I took them touring. They are really nice people! I have always been very close to their cause! It is something in my family! My parents were very revolutionary. My father met my mother in France during the 1968 revolution. They fell in love and got married. They get divorced afterwards but they had me. The revolution in France is the very reason of me. It makes me proud to call myself the son of the revolution. And now my Syrian friends are my revolution. And, thank god they came here! I discuss their problems more than I discuss my debts. I was dead before they arrived. They provide me with the political life I always dreamt of living. My political awareness was triggered when they arrived here. And now I will leave you to our play and hope you enjoy the …[60]

Although his arrival is initially greeted with enthusiasm by the other actors, his propensity to interrupt them to explain Syrian culture to the audience (even to his 'Syrian' friends, the other characters) contributes to the building chaos and showcases the paternalism that sometimes lurks beneath the surface of solidarity. Ineaki, for example, waxes on about the democratic elements of *dabkeh* line dance and how he has participated in many a *dabkeh* dance in the context of political demonstrations. He interrupts Sabah to teach the audience about falafel and boasts of how the globalisation of food culture was resisted in Syria.

Ineaki's character is at the heart of the critique that the play is performing: audience expectations of authenticity are linked to the way that Arabs and especially Arab migrants are politicised. Here, the play is not taking aim at the far right or anti-immigration rhetoric or even the rhetoric of the War on Terror that positions Middle Easterners as potential terrorist threats. Rather, it delves into the rhetoric that the audience has more likely at least partially bought into; that is, the way that the idea of the Syrian and Syrian migrant become canvases for a desired politics. In a conversation I had with Adwan in the summer of 2019, he reflected on his experience of being a cultural actor in the world of theatre in London, Munich and Berlin, encountering a European propensity to project the political onto an 'other', in this case Arabs:

> As if there are no political problems here! We want to be political so we speak about Palestine, we speak about the war in Iraq, we speak about Osama Bin Laden! ... They believe that they have reached the end of history. They have reached stability, the end of man, or the utopia, as if there are no problems. And if you want to speak about politics so you speak about the *other*. As if all of Europe became Tintin. Yeah look at Tintin! When he goes abroad there are major problems. When he's in Europe it's Casa Fiori. It's a little bird who stole jewellery. And my standpoint back in the time, during the terrorist time, was, it's not that they are stereotyping us as terrorists or not. No no, we are stereotyped as political creatures. So whenever you speak about Arabs you speak about politics.[61]

With the authenticity trap projected back on us, the play places the audience in a position where we need to make choices in how to witness, how to respond, and how to flow with changing realities and expectations. Each choice we make is necessarily a compromise within a framework that is determined by the play, not us; we experience ourselves as political beings and the political as something shared. However, since we are being played, there is no way around it – the power is in the hands of the theatre makers, thus reversing the power dynamics that are often part of migration theatre. As Adwan states,

> But there is something cultural that is forgotten when refugees want to represent themselves on a European stage. That the audience is stronger. And the actors are the inferior. And this is not how theatre is. In theatre the actor is stronger and the audience is ... so I started with this cultural experience and said, 'ok let's accept it'. The audience as being stronger

and my intro as Ziad ... it has it all, like we are here for you, we are touring just to exist. And then with the mistakes it shifts it all political event not cultural and the actors are gaining power back again because of their responsibility. And the audience feels intimidated.[62]

The play is not necessarily situating itself against either solidarity or engaging with migration topically, but rather inviting a subversion of the us/them boundaries that often structure both.

In the visceral experience of choice and needing to align oneself within a constantly shifting reality, we are forced to confront what we wanted out of the play to begin with. It is not only individual desires and projections at stake. These are clearly varied, especially in an audience such as the one that gathered at the English Theatre. Armaj has declared that he made the undocumented journey to Europe because he really wants to travel to the moon (yet nobody believes him). His statement does not align with realistic expectations for mobility for most, but certainly not with discourses on mobility for Syrians. Reem makes acrobatic ventures through the audience where she hangs on pipes in the ceiling, crawls between audience members, and climbs on handrailing. In her movement through the audience, Reem, in a floaty voice and manner alternates between asking individuals in the audience, 'What would you like me to do, Sir?' and statements like, 'Some want to play cards and some want to follow the rabbits' and 'Some want to lie and some want belly dancers'. These events call attention to our own desires from the play but put them in relationship to the comically absurd. The subversion of wanting along with the constantly shifting relationship between performers and audience allows for an alienation or defamiliarisation that creates a critical distance from which we might contemplate what it is we expected from the play and why.

An argument breaks out about who is going to finish the play and who is going to leave. We wonder, has the 'play' that we anticipated even started?

Conclusion

To understand Berlin as a capital of Arab culture is to both reimagine geographies of belonging through routes of displacement and to take seriously efforts to theorise exile and diaspora through forced migration. Perhaps understanding Berlin as a capital of Arab culture requires a different conception of the nation, now imagined through displacement and especially this current moment in Syrian history, at a moment when displacement and mobility are both ubiquitous and understood through 'crisis'. As discussed, earlier, the emergent Arabic literary and theatre culture in Berlin is distinct from that of other major European capitals in many ways. In particular, its institutions and practices differ from the postcolonial centres of London and Paris, which are host to more established Arabic-language cultural and literary institutions. Arabic literature and theatre in Berlin have been characterised by collaborative and translational practices and by an effort to reimagine the images and discourses on the refugee that have been hypervisible and mediated in the past years. Furthermore, a major world city, Berlin is host to a much larger and more visible arts scene than many of the newer diasporas that have been discussed in this book. In Berlin, as Amro Ali has argued, exile – a category that has been important to Arab intellectual history – is being reimagined transnationally with forced migration and the varied experiences of refugees at its centre.

In comparison to the literature of forced migration discussed in previous chapters – also from more recent Arab diasporas – the literary texts discussed in this chapter are less invested in imagining routes and migratory journeys, in part because of the oversaturation of images, discourses, and reporting on migration to Europe and Germany in 2015 and after. There is a decided move against both realist representations of migration and art that is prescriptive. While the speculative elements discussed in previous chapters were amplified in writings of journeys, routes and border crossings, the defamiliarisation that we see in Rasha Abbas's short stories and in Ziad Adwan's play is focused on displacing expectations of migration literature and theatre and creating spaces to imagine them differently. These represent conscious efforts to defamiliarise dominant images of migration as a 'crisis' and, instead, put meanings, genres and expectations in crisis.

In Rasha Abbas's stories, the speculative elements and emphasis on highly subjective perception and altered states of consciousness are an enduring theme. The vocabulary and contexts of forced migration are very present in her stories. But by deploying the terminology of migration in novel situations, she displaces words and meanings from the current overdetermined context and insists on the mutability of both discourse and our experiences of it. The proverbial letter does reach its destination, but in a way that calls attention to the subjective rather than the realist or prescriptive.

Please, Repeat After Me probes the capacities of theatre as a laboratory for dialogue and potential shifts in perception. It invites the audience to not only see, but also *feel* their expectations, thus pushing them to reflect on what to do within the parameters determined by the play. In this sense, it is an example of Saadallah Wannous's understanding of theatre as a space of multi-layered dialogue between audience members, between performers and the audience, and with the city outside of the theatre.[63]

The experiment happening within the theatre and between the audience members and the performers is also one for the 'city outside' – that is, Berlin. To what extent do we, as Wannous suggested, shed a measure of our lonely depression and acquire a new sense of societal affiliation? The play asks us to think about the foundations of our belonging and address the assumptions that underpin a binary logic that keeps a perceived other pinned within a narrow conceptual framework. Taking on the assumption that the *other* (the Syrian migrant, in this case) has an intensified political existence, the play enacts a role reversal.

The collaborative ethos that is so much a part of the Arabic-language literary scene in Berlin is also a part of the short stories and play discussed in this chapter. If the notion of refugee literature or theatre often presumes that art concerning forced migration functions only to tell a truth about itself – to offer a testimony to a reality, in these works, the political is instead projected onto the reader and audience and the art resumes its place as art. As Adwan notes, this is a matter of exploring and potentially shifting entrenched power dynamics, and allowing us to mine within ourselves a different starting point from which to engage the topic. The invitation is to co-create meaning within a space of Arabic literature and theatre in a city where exile is being reimagined through forced migration.

Notes

1. In the middle of 2019, there were 1.1 million registered Syrian refugees in Germany. The arrival of a large number of Syrian people in 2015–16 followed German Chancellor Angela Merkel and Austrian Chancellor Werner Faymann's decision on 4 September 2015 to open the border from Hungary to Austria and from Austria into Germany. Angela Merkel's statement '*Wir schaffen das*' ('We can do this'), that is, we can manage to welcome and host the new migrants, epitomised a moment that deeply affected German politics. As a point of reference, at the same date there were around 3.2 million registered Syrian refugees in Turkey and many million internally displaced in Syria and living as refugees in Lebanon, Jordan, Iraq, and elsewhere in the region.
2. Amro Ali, 'On the Need to Shape the Arab Exile Body in Berlin', *Alsharq Blog* (now *dis:orient*), 25 January 2019, https://www.disorient.de/blog/need-shape-arab-exile-body-berlin.
3. Rasha Abbas, *Die Erfindung der deutschen Grammatik*, trans. Sandra Hezl (Berlin: Mikrotext, 2016); Rasha Abbas, *Kayfa Tamma Ikhtira' al-Lugha al-Almaniyya* (Beirut: Heinrich Boll Stiftung, 2016), https://lb.boell.org/sites/default/files/german_grammar_arabic_e_book_2016_08_23.pdf.
4. Rasha Abbas, *Mulakhkhas Ma Jara* (Milan: Manshurat al-Mutawassit, 2018).
5. Quotations from the play are from Ziad Adwan, *Please, Repeat After Me*, unpublished script.
6. Khaled Barakeh, 'The Role of Cultural Organizations', talk at the *'Beyond Trauma' Conference*, Berlin, Germany, 13 June 2019.
7. Rasha Abbas, interview with Johanna Sellman, Berlin, Germany, 13 August 2018.
8. 'Capital of Culture', *BBC News Arabic*, Berlin, *YouTube* video, 52:25, 21 May 2018, https://www.youtube.com/watch?v=WInKH0uv0K8.
9. Widad Nabi is a writer from northern Syria whose work was featured in the anthology of Mathias Bothor *et al.*, *Weg sein – hier sein: Texte aus Deutschland* [Being away: Being here: texts from Germany] (Zürich: Zürich Secession Verlag für Literatur, 2016).
10. 'Baynatna, The Arabic Library in Berlin', *Baynatna*, http://www.baynatna.de (accessed 11 April 2020).
11. Amro Ali lists many of these in 'On the Need to Shape the Arab Exile Body in Berlin': 'A number of institutions and initiatives have been central to

the German–Arab cultural exchange and collaboration. Among them: Free University, Humboldt University, Forum Transregionale Studien, the Goethe Institute (and its support of institutions such as the Arab Image Foundation); German Academic Exchange Service (DAAD) and its support of Arab artists and intellectuals (e.g., Akram Zaatari, whose films often show in the short competition of the Berlin Film Festival); Transmediale (which formerly ran the Arab Shorts Program); the Barenboim-Said Academy which is not only a site for Arab arts, intellectual exchanges, and conferences but, perhaps, the largest scholarship program for Arab musicians in the world. Overall, the spectrum is wide, from the various foundations of the political parties and the Foreign Office to the neighborhood dynamics in Neukölln along Sonnenallee street.'
12. See, for example, Mohamed Abou Laban, Ziad Adwan and Mario Münster (eds), *A Syrious Look: Syrians in Germany, a Magazine about Culture in Exile*, 2016.
13. The term 'post-migrant' is not meant to imply that migration has ended, but rather that migration shapes all social structures after the fact of migration. The term emerged from the theatre world but has also entered political discourse. In Germany, the term 'post-migrant' is often used to designate sociopolitical processes that follow migration (not that migration has ended) as well as the art of second- and third-generation migrants. The German Federal Agency for Civic Education (Bundeszentrale für politische Bildung), a German government agency tasked with promoting civic education, defines the term post-migration as the social processes that take place after migration. They argue that the term (1) entails a recognition that social structures have been transformed by migration, (2) immigration and emigration are widely recognized as impactful social phenomena whose impact cannot be reversed, and (3) political structures and institutions have adapted to a post-migration reality (from https://www.bpb.de/gesellschaft/migration/kurzdossiers/205295/post-migrant-society). Theatre director Shermin Langhoff is often credited with founding post-migrant theatre through her work as founder of Ballhaus Nynaunstrasse theatre in Kreuzberg, Berlin.
14. 'Shermin Langhoff', *Gorki*, https://gorki.de/en/company/shermin-langhoff (accessed 11 April 2020).
15. As of autumn 2019, a total of seven artists have formed part of the ensemble, participated in Gorki productions, and developed the group's own projects and performances. Many of the productions feature bilingual titles and

billing. Among the five plays created and produced by the exile ensemble are *Winterreise* رحلة الشتاء (The Winter Trip) (performed in January 2017, written and produced by Yael Ronan), a play about a two-week winter bus trip where newcomers travel through Switzerland and Germany and interact with each other, the bus driver, and 'the experts who try to explain Germany'. the debut Berlin production of established Syrian playwright and director Ayham Majid Agha *Skelett eines Elefanten in der Wüste* هيكل عظمي لفيل في الصحراء (An Elephant Skeleton in the Desert; performed in 2017–19) features an exploration of fragility and emotion during war.

16. Ali, 'On the Need'.
17. Ali, 'On the Need'.
18. Ali, 'On the Need'.
19. 'Co-Culture: the Hub of Cultural Growth', *Co-Culture*, https://coculture.de/index.html (accessed 12 April 2020).
20. 'Syrian Biennale: Roots En Route', *Co-Culture*, https://coculture.de/syrian-biennale.html (accessed 12 April 2020).
21. Rasha Abbas, *Adam Yakrah al-Talifiziyun* (Damascus: Al-Amana al-'Amma li-Ihtifaliyat Dimashq 'Asimat al-thaqafa, 2008).
22. Alexa Firat, 'Cultural Battles on the Literary Field: From the Syrian Writers' Collective to the Last Days of Socialist Realism in Syria', *Middle Eastern Literatures* 18, no. 2 (2015): 158.
23. Firat, 'Cultural Battles', 158.
24. Mohja Kahf, 'The Silences of Contemporary Syrian Literature', *World Literature Today* 75, no. 2 (Spring 2001): 230.
25. Kahf, 'The Silences', 228.
26. Hanna Minah, *Al-Rabi'wa-l-Kharif* (Beirut: Dar al-Adab, 1984).
27. Kahf, 'The Silences', 235.
28. Rasha Abbas, 'How Political Can We Get While Writing', *Schloss Post*, 20 October 2016, https://schloss-post.com/political-get-writing/.
29. Abbas, 'How Political'.
30. Rasha Abbas 'We Can't Compete in Writing', *Schloss Post*, https://schloss-post.com/we-cant-compete-in-writing/.
31. A slightly elevated and formal formulation in Arabic of how an action was undertaken or completed.
32. Abbas, *Kayfa Tamma*, 14.
33. Abbas, *Kayfa Tamma*, 17.
34. Abbas, *Kayfa Tamma*, 63.

35. Abbas, *Kayfa Tamma*, 63.
36. Abbas, *Kayfa Tamma*, 64.
37. Alice Guthrie, 'The Gist of It: Short Stories by Rasha Abbas: Reader's Report by Alice Guthrie', *English Pen*, https://www.englishpen.org/wp-content/uploads/2012/04/The-Gist-of-It-Short-Stories-by-Rasha-Abbas-Readers-Report-by-Alice-Guthrie.pdf (accessed 12 April 2020).
38. Hassan Blasim, 'Hassan Blasim', interview by Margaret Litvin and Johanna Sellman, *Tank Magazine* 8, no. 9 (2016): 239.
39. Haytham Bahoora, 'Writing the Dismembered Nation: The Aesthetics of Horror in Iraqi Narratives of War', *Arab Studies Journal* 23, no. 1 (2015).
40. Abbas, *Mulakhkhas*, 85.
41. Abbas, *Mulakhkhas*, 89.
42. Abbas, *Mulakhkhas*, 93.
43. Abbas, *Mulakhkhas*, 69.
44. Abbas, *Mulakhkhas*, 71.
45. Michal Raizen, email conversation with Johanna Sellman, 14 November 2019.
46. 'Please, Repeat after Me', *English Theatre Berlin*, https://www.etberlin.de/production/please-repeat-after-me/ (accessed 29 December 2019).
47. For one, the play's script notes the inspiration of Austrian playwright Peter Handke's 1966 *Publikumsbeschimpfung* (*Offending the Audience*), an experimental play that eschews plot and consistent characters in order to create a Brechtian alienation effect on the audience.
48. The professional actors [Selin Kavak (Hala), Gizem Akman (Reem), Enad Marouf (Sabah), Atilla Akinci, Hussein Shatheli, Ziad Adwan (Ziad)] are not playing themselves, although the initial introduction might lead the audience to assume this is the case.
49. Muhammad Dibo, 'Ziad Adwan: No Deeper Shock than that of Syrians', *Syria Untold*, 7 August 2018, https://syriauntold.com/2018/08/07/ziad-adwan-no-deeper-shock-than-that-of-syrians/.
50. Adwan, *Please, Repeat*, 13.
51. Litvin and Sellman, 'An Icy Heaven', 46.
52. Margaret Litvin, 'Syrian Theatre in Berlin', *Theatre Journal* 70, no.4 (January 2018): 447–8.
53. Adwan, *Please, Repeat*, 5.
54. Adwan, *Please, Repeat*, 7.
55. Adwan, *Please, Repeat*, 9–10.

56. Adwan, *Please, Repeat*, 12.
57. Adwan, *Please, Repeat*, 13–14.
58. Adwan, *Please, Repeat*, 20–1.
59. Adwan, *Please, Repeat*, 21.
60. Adwan, *Please, Repeat*, 33.
61. Ziad Adwan, interview with Johanna Sellman, Berlin, Germany, 19 June 2019.
62. Ibid.
63. Saadallah Wannous, 'On World Theater Day, the 1996 Message from Saadallah Wannous', *Arab Lit Quarterly*, 23 March 2013, https://arablit.org/2013/03/27/on-world-theater-day-the-1996-message-from-saadallah-wannous/.

6

Decentring the Metropole: Forced Migration Literature in London and Paris

While *Arabic Exile Literature in Europe* has for the most part foregrounded literary texts from more recent Arab diasporas, this final chapter highlights forced migration literature in the historical centres of Arabic literature in Europe, namely Paris and London, and their attendant national spaces. Although as a whole, the literary geography of Arabic forced migration literature decentres these metropoles, they continue to be home to important publishing houses, institutions, established Arab diasporas born of colonial histories, and prominent writers, all of which are contributing to the shifts in the politics and aesthetics of Arabic migration literature discussed in this book. This chapter revisits the questions raised in Chapter 1, which argued that the most urgent antihegemonic critiques in contemporary migration literature pertain to borders, citizenship and belonging, and shows how traditional literary centres in Europe participate in such an inquiry without necessarily being at the forefront of the aesthetic and political shifts that we see in contemporary Arabic literature of forced and precarious migration. There are similar trends in terms of the presence of speculative and defamiliarising modes of writing explored in the book, though they partake in a broad, highly connected, and varied Arabic-European literary space.

In the section on Paris, I briefly discuss representation of clandestine space in the 2006 novel *La géographie du danger* (The Geography of Danger) by Algerian writer Hamed Skif. Here, I put Skif's writing and critical reception in dialogue with *harraga* literature as well as French *beur*[1] writing and *banlieue* fiction, literature of urban peripheries. In contrast to these literary genres and spaces, many international writers in Paris are positioned as world writers contributing to their national literatures as well as a world literary heritage. Querying these distinctions of genre and literary consecration and their significance for contemporary Arabic exile literature, I turn to the prominent Paris-based authors Samar Yazbek and Hoda Barakat and their most recent novels, which both stage mobility and forced migration. The central character of Yazbek's 2017 novel, *Al-Masha'a (Planet of Clay)*,[2] is a potent metaphor for the constraints and forced mobility created by the war in Syria. Although the adolescent narrator of *Al-Masha'a* never leaves her city, her telling of the war offers an incisive exploration of mobility, constraint and forced displacement. She is afflicted with a mysterious condition that causes her to walk ceaselessly unless fettered. As war erupts around her, creating new borders and forced movement, she narrates her story in a way that defamiliarises movement, agency and violence. Hoda Barakat's novel *Barid al-Layl*[3] (*Voices of the Lost*), which won the 2019 International Prize for Arabic Fiction (IPAF), is an epistolary novel written from the perspective of travellers, undocumented migrants and immigrants. Through a chain of letters in which each character confesses secrets, pain and longings, and which are then intercepted by an anonymous other, a sense of a collective is forged from shared loneliness, vulnerability and the intimacy of intercepting confessions and life stories. The effect is far from the kinds of tropes and narratives that are often conjured in news media and elsewhere to render mass migration.

The chapter then turns to recent literary narratives of migration in London and in England more broadly. While there are numerous well-known Arabic diasporic novels based in London (examples from the early 2000s include Hanan al-Shaykh's *Innaha London ya Azizi* (*Only in London*; 2000) and Haifa Zangana's *Nisa' 'ala Safar* (*Women on a Journey*; 2001)) in addition to a thriving scene of English-language British Arab literature, there is also a more recent thriving literature and theatre scene that is integrally connected to the themes of the book, from the staging of plays (such as the adaptation of Hassan Blasim's story 'The Nightmares of Carlos Fuentes' by Rashid Razaq) to the hosting of prominent film and literary festivals showcasing forced migration themes and the publishing of Arabic speculative fiction in translation (for example the future-writing collections published by Manchester-based Comma Press *Palestine + 100* and *Iraq + 100*). The novel *Silence is a Sense* (2021)[4] by Kuwaiti writer Layla AlAmmar delves deeply into the representation of forced migration. In this novel set in an unnamed English town and narrated by a young Syrian woman who, like the narrator of Yazbek's *al-Masha'a*, refuses to speak, the fantastic acts as a stand-in for the unspeakable and becomes part of the novel's exploration of the limits of language in representing trauma.

It is not my intention here to overstate the differences between the literary and cultural production of Arab diasporas in the literary and cultural centres of London and Paris and that taking place in newer diasporas in Europe. There is significant overlap in terms of networks, collaboration across borders, and patterns of migration. At the same time, there are important factors that shape the dynamic of the Arabic migration literature in Europe. This chapter teases out some of the distinctions of these cities and attendant national spaces while also calling attention to overlapping trends in writing Arabic literature of forced and precarious migration in these locations. It does so through both close readings of selected literary texts and broad assessments of the landscape and conditions of Arabic literature in these cities. As colonial and postcolonial metropoles and as homes to large and historically rooted Arab diasporas, these cities are important sites for Arabic literary production, each linked to a formidable corpus of Arabic literature written in Arabic and in French and English respectively. This chapter outlines some of the dynamics of Arabic and Arab immigration, diaspora and migration literature in London and Paris, and the UK and France more broadly. As literary and cultural centres they are important sites of production, publication, curation and translation of Arabic literature and Arab migration literature more specifically. When it comes to Arabic literature of forced and precarious migration, these literary centres play a less prominent role, save for the way they curate and legitimise literary trends from locations that far exceed the boundaries of the nation. That said, the literary narratives of forced and precarious migration written in and about these spaces defamiliarise forced and precarious migration through literary means in ways that are like those of more recent diasporas. This comparative discussion and the examples discussed in this chapter highlight the importance of viewing this literature as transnational.

Literary Centres

In her ground-breaking 1999 book, *The World Republic of Letters*,[5] Pascale Casanova maps out a world literary order based on competition for literary legitimacy, where the literary centres of London, New York and Paris in particular have the power to consecrate authors and legitimise aesthetic trends and literary forms. The system of prestige that she delineates is distinct yet deeply intertwined with global systems of economic and political dominance. Although this model does not fully elucidate systems of prestige and legitimacy in Arabic literature, especially literature that is not translated and does not pass through these centres, it does point to important dynamics that pertain to travel migration literature historically, where London and Paris figure prominently due to colonial histories. Although a full discussion of the place of world literary centres in Arabic literature is beyond the scope of this book, it is important to consider the place of London and Paris as world literary capitals in our discussion of Arabic migration literature being written within and about these spaces. As discussed in Chapter 1, the history of writing modern Arabic travel, immigration and migration literature is deeply intertwined with the modernising discourses of the *Nahda* as well as colonial and postcolonial relationships. The history of writing Europe in modern Arabic literature focuses on London and Paris especially. The significant production of French literature by writers of North African descent and anglophone Arab British literature further enriches these literary spheres and any discussion of Arabic migration literature within them.

London is home to many major houses that publish Arabic-language works and works in English. There are many more, of course, but in London these include Saqi books, Darf Publishers, Gilgamesh Publishing and Medina publishing. Actes Sud, with its Arles and Paris locations, has played an important role in publishing Arabic literature in French translation. Institutions such as Institut du monde arabe in Paris and the Arab British Centre in London regularly host events and exhibits curated by local and international Arab artists, writers, and others. Numerous film and literary festivals in each location add to a robust Arab and Arabic literary scene. As we will see in the following discussion, the conditions for writing, disseminating, translating and interpreting Arabic migration literature about and in these locations is shaped by questions of positionality. Who is positioned as a literary figure writing from a literary centre and who is positioned as an immigrant writer? Furthermore, the presence and absence of institutions focused on Arabic-language arts and literature (and their translation) can be interpreted as either facilitating the presence of Arabic literature and culture in a particular location or creating constraints. As the following two examples suggest, centres of literary prestige and diasporic culture can offer both important opportunities and limitations.

In an email conversation about the Arabic-speaking arts and theatre community in Berlin, director and playwright Ziad Adwan offered his perspective on the difference between arriving in a city like Berlin versus Paris or London. He suggested that the relative absence of older Syrian and Arab diasporas as well as cultural institutions meant that their access to opportunities was not guarded by gatekeepers of Arab culture and they were not forced to conform to established artists' visions or goals. He noted, 'When we arrived in Germany no older generation was there to guide the lines of the actions and projects that take place in Germany.'[6] This emphasis on the relatively open horizons of Berlin's arts culture in the past few years is in line with Amro Ali's description of Berlin as offering a unique space for building new understandings and practices of exile. Some writers and critics, however, take a different perspective on what the ideal way of promoting and curating the writing of new arrivals looks like.

For example, in a February 2020 panel entitled 'Arab Writers – Going Global: Hoda Barakat, Jokha alHarthi & Marilyn Booth'[7] that took place during the Emirates Airline Festival with host Bilal Orfali, Paris-based writer Hoda Barakat made a case for the establishment of an Arabic-language system of support like *Francophonie*, a formal organisation that promotes the French language, representing countries and areas where French is spoken or is an important official or minority language, only for Arabic. A unified and transnational system that supported Arabic-language writers beyond the limited (and highly uneven) kinds of support available for writers on the national level, she conjectured, could provide residencies as well as support for publishing and translation. This kind of financial support, she notes, could raise the profile of Arabic literature worldwide and counter negative stereotypes of the region. In making the case for a new kind of cultural politics, Barakat turned to established and emergent cultural centres. What if the UAE, which already funds many institutions and projects in the region, could back such a project? Referring to her fellow IPAF award-winning novelist, Omani writer Jokha alHarthi, she asked, 'why can't they find us a support system, for people like Jokha? No one knew about Jokha. Jokha was discovered in London.' She continued:

> Okay, what about Syrians? Who would support them? Syrians are now supported by Germany and Germany is not choosing what should be chosen from Syrian literature. There is chaos. There are no institutions that are effective and credible that can support writers. For example, if an institution like *Francophonie* existed, if those institutions existed, it would be possible for Marilyn [Booth] to suggest a translation and to suggest that they communicate and collaborate … as a big institution, with an important publishing house.

These two different perspectives – the perception that new diasporas offer writers and other cultural actors important spaces of freedom for creativity versus the prioritising of the kinds of brokering and curating that established cultural centres can offer – exist as an important polarity in Arabic migration literature. Of course, the situation on the ground does not conform precisely to this binary. Previous chapters of this book have shown that migration literature interacts with local and transnational cultural institutions and cultural brokers such as publishing houses, translators, critics, and audiences. For instance, *harraga* literature is distinctly multilingual and published on both the northern and southern shores of the Mediterranean. It shares the challenge of literary legitimacy with other migration literature, as it is often relegated to expectations of social commentary on migration 'crises', expectations that may raise interest in sales and translations but often detracts from a consideration of its literary and artistic qualities. Furthermore, relatively recent diasporas in northern Europe showcase a diversity of ways that Arabic migration literature is framed and discussed. From varying degrees of state support for publishing and translating to the transformation of national canons to include the work of writers with roots elsewhere, to the confrontation with nationalist and exclusionary conceptions of belonging as well as outdated mappings of Arabic literature in Europe that omit newer diasporic sites, contemporary Arabic migration literature is navigating a complex arena of constraints, possibilities and aspirations.

Paris is a global and postcolonial literary centre. Today, the city is home to numerous writers with roots in the Arabic-speaking region who write in Arabic or French, or both. There are prestige and circulation fault lines that demarcate who is positioned as an immigrant writer and who is positioned as an international writer residing in a global literary centre. Laura Reeck, who writes about Arabic and Arab literary narratives in France in *The Oxford Handbook of Arab Novelistic Traditions*, notes that many writers of Egyptian and Levantine origin residing in France are not typically categorised as immigrant writers. Furthermore, those who write in French are situated not as minoritised writers but rather as writers contributing to both national and world literatures through the universal qualities of (the French) language. Such prominent writers include Lebanese-born Amine Maalouf, who won the prestigious Prix Goncourt in 1993; Egyptian-born Albert Cossery, recipient of the Grand Prix de l'Académie française in 1990; and Andrée Chedid, an Egyptian-French writer with Lebanese roots whose oeuvre of poetry and novels made her a Grand Officer of the French Legion of Honour in 2009. Reeck writes,

> In contrast to the Maghribi Francophone writers, these writers in exile have not endured the same critical scrutiny for writing in French, and they are often claimed by both their native country and France, and also by the annals of world literature. Despite the fact that they write in a language other than Arabic, rarely is their loyalty to their native country questioned, as is obvious in the following statement on Cossery: 'How else could he express his loyalty to Egypt than by bringing to French the sounds of dialectical Arabic – a mixing that brings him close to the Lebanese Farjallah Haïk and the Moroccan Driss Chraïbi' (Combe 2001, 67). His 'accented' written French expressed a valued hybridity,

placing him alongside novelists known for their literary language set in vernacular. Interestingly, the linguistic invention of early second-generation Maghribi writers (i.e., Beur novelists) has not been seen in like terms, but rather as a contamination of the French language, a pulling away at the standard held by the Académie Française.[8]

Hoda Barakat and Samar Yazbek write in Arabic and are thus positioned slightly differently than Cossery and Maalouf. However, they share the status of being claimed by their countries of origin and a world literary sphere without the constraints imposed upon immigrant and migrant literatures. The following section discusses this dynamic within the context of novels that use innovative narrative strategies to explore migration, mobility and constraint.

Inhospitable Space in *Banlieue* and Migration Literature: Hamid Skif's *La géographie du danger*

This section discusses the representation of space in Hamid Skif's novel *La géographie du danger*[9] within the context of French *banlieue* fiction as well as *harraga* writing, and then turns to Samar Yazbek's novel *Al-Masha'a* and Hoda Barakat's *Barid al-Layl* (*Voices of the Lost*). Barakat, who has resided in Paris since the 1980s and whose previous, award-winning novels have been set during the Lebanese Civil War, has recently turned to writing about diaspora and displacement. Yazbek has primarily resided in Paris since the Syrian uprising. Her novel *Al-Masha'a* follows the publication of two non-fiction books on the Syrian war, a hiatus in Yazbek's writing of novels. Barakat and Yazbek's work are not typically positioned as migration literature, yet they explore contemporary mobility in incisive ways and in ways that resonate with the defamiliarising modes of writing explored in this book. Reading these works together reveals a shared sense of urgency in using the literary to defamiliarise the collectivising tropes and discourses on forced and precarious migration as well as the variegated positionalities that authors occupy and their wide-ranging approaches to writing migration in a global literary centre.

The large populations in France with North African roots[10] are an integral part of the country's cultural landscape. Paris, a colonial metropole, was long a hub for intellectuals, writers and political actors coming from France's colonies, protectorates and mandates in Africa, the Middle East and Asia. The group of francophone writers from the Maghreb known as 'generation 52' began writing nationalist and anticolonial novels in the years leading up to the Algerian war of independence. In the 1960s and 70s, a number of prominent North African authors living in Paris as students or exiles wrote novels in an experimental vein, many of them exploring alienation and the figure of the immigrant. Post-World War II labour migration from North Africa, which was promoted to offset worker shortages, meant the establishment of sizable communities. The children and grandchildren of these labour migrants were the first to articulate the experiences and identities of these communities in literature. The first generation of *beur* fiction tended to be semi-autobiographical. Novels such as *Le gone du Chaâba* (1986) (*Shanty-town Kid*) by Azouz Begag, *Le Thé au harem d'Archimède* (1983) (*Tea in the Harem*) by Mehdi Charef, and *Georgette* (1986) by Farida Belghoul depicted the lives of young immigrants living on the outskirts of France's cities and navigating their own path between the languages and cultures of their parents and their French environs. Alec Hargreaves has called attention to the contours of the genre of *beur* writing, observing that the novels published in the 1980s tended to be semi-autobiographical and use a colloquial tone that incorporates both Arabic and French youth slang. He notes that many of these early novels explored the double-edged role of education and literacy as passageways toward social mobility, on the one hand, and as forces that distanced the protagonists from their roots, on the other.[11]

In contrast to this early wave of *beur* literature, the literature of second- and third-generation North African immigrants in France includes a vast array of styles and genres. Writing that depicts the urban peripheries of France is now often referred to as *banlieue* fiction. As a literary genre it has explored new ways of imagining the urban peripheries that are economically and politically marginalised. Rebecca Blanchard has noted that a number of authors who previously published semi-autographical novels aligned with the genre of *beur* fiction later began to write 'polyphonic, multi-voice narratives that shift their focus from the self to the collective'.[12] In fact, there are interesting parallels between *banlieue* fiction and some of the speculative modes of writing in Arabic migration literature, with its transindividual qualities that both honour individual narratives and locate them in contexts of large-scale migration and ways of imagining the self in intersection with others. Blanchard points to the emergence of speculative and defamiliarising ways of writing in *banlieue* fiction, including science fiction, fantasy and the *roman policier*, that challenge discourses that reinforce dominant narratives about the urban periphery. She does, however, caution the reader against reading the genre only in relation to categories such as *beur*, migration, or the postcolonial. She writes,

> As the category of the 'banlieue novel' tends to be instrumentalized by the literary and editorial establishment, it is of ever-increasing importance not to view these novels in a reductive manner – neither as the natural progression of Beur or migrant fictions, nor as a mere subcategory of postcolonial or diasporic literature. Broader approaches and hermeneutical tools that privilege new ways of thinking about these narratives will allow banlieue fictions to be repositioned from the margins to the centre of contemporary French literature. Novels that draw upon multiple genres and a diverse literary heritage therefore become all the more important as they necessitate a reconsideration of the paradigm of the banlieue novel and the usefulness of such terminology in literary criticism. And so, the problematic, yet seemingly unavoidable term 'banlieue novel' remains a point of reference by which the transgression of this category can continue to be examined.[13]

This move to privilege literary genre and style serves to reconnect these narratives to broader literary trends within France and, more broadly, world literature. Genres of note include dystopian writing as well as *fiction d'anticipation*, fiction that situates contemporary questions and issues within alternate, imagined histories. For example, French rapper Disiz's 2012 novel *René* is set in 2025 in an imagined near future in which the far right has come to power, a referendum on re-establishing the death penalty is being held, and the urban peripheries are being patrolled by paramilitary groups. *Zone cinglée* (Crazy Zone) by Kautar Harchi is set in a dystopian version of the *banlieue* that embellishes on current social realities. In the novel, space is divided into different zones: the Mothers' southern zone; land belonging to 'La cause'; 'Antre', a space that represents hope; and Ville-Centre, a refuge for youth in the neighbourhood. In the novel, humans are given animal qualities. For instance, mothers are depicted as wolves and leeches. Blanchard notes the carceral geography of *Zone cinglée*: 'Ultimately, the world described resembles a "carceral network" because all levels of society have been infiltrated and penetrated in the novel.'[14] The protagonist's mother is confined in their apartment by the father. She loses touch with reality and becomes obsessed with cleanliness – the apartment becomes a kind of asylum.

The dystopian and speculative trends within *banlieue* fiction resonate with French and world literature more broadly, but also with trends in contemporary Arabic migration literature. The turn to speculative and dystopian fictions and other defamiliarising narrative strategies unsettle dominant narratives and representations of forced and precarious migration. The transfiguration of the mothers in *Zone cinglée* conjures the wolves that appear in Hassan Blasim's fiction, for example. The creation of imagined borders and geographies in *banlieue* fiction calls attention to the contingency of borders within urban settings in ways similar to migration literature's attempt to 'denaturalise' national borders. In some ways, Hamid Skif's *La géographie du danger* bridges the genres of *harraga* and *banlieue* fiction with its simultaneous and interconnected exploration of borders and hostile zones within both urban space and irregular migration.

Hamid Skif's 2006 novel *La géographie du danger* (The Geography of Danger) shares some elements of writing inhospitable, even dystopian, urban space with *Zone cinglée*. The novel reads as the diary of an unnamed irregular migrant hiding in a city where migrants are being hunted down by the authorities. Hidden away in a small maid's chamber in an unspecified European city, he recounts his past life in his country of birth, the dangerous passage through the Pyrenees Mountains to his current location and a period of working to survive before going into hiding. In the cramped space of the maid's chamber, rented by the geography student Michel Delbin, 'a sympathizer of lost causes',[15] he observes the outside world through a small window. With each chapter of the book, the round-ups and arrests of clandestine immigrants intensify. As the narrator waits for Michel to arrive with food and news, he invents fantasy worlds about his neighbours and individuals implicated in human trafficking, characters that inhabit his past and his present.

Hamid Skif (1951–2011) had a long career as a writer in Algeria before the 1990s' civil war. In a climate where intellectuals were increasingly becoming targets, Skif survived several assassination attempts before relocating to Hamburg in 1994 through the PEN International's 'Writers in Exile' programme and the 'Hamburg Foundation for 29'. Though Skif resided in Hamburg until his death in 2011, several references in the novel point to Paris as the setting. At the same time, the novel appears to be making a more general case about inhospitable space in European cities. In Skif's own description of the book he states:

> In this book I have attempted to take the consequences of fear and confinement to their limits by describing what would happen if the cities of the west were to become the scene of a gigantic hunt for human beings ... This is not a delusion, it is foreseeable reality.[16]

Here, Skif blurs the line between speculation and verisimilitude, at once exploring what *would* happen if cities of the West were to hunt migrants while stating that this is an emergent reality. The dystopian qualities of the novel are also located in this space of ambiguity and interplay between the narrator's fantasy and his environs.

The 'geography' of the novel is structured around the danger of public space, on the one hand, and the fear that permeates the narrator's inner world, on the other. Public space becomes a 'geography of danger' where heightened state and media rhetoric on security and threat fuels a massive roundup of clandestine migrants. In contrast, the narrator's small hideout, which functions as an extension of his psychic space, is rendered as a 'geography of fear'. In the novel, public space in the city, or the geography of danger, is figured as a forest-like hunting ground where clandestine migrants are legitimate targets. It is a space that pushes out, intent on expelling all outsiders. The narrator describes his own condition in the geography of fear as a kind of 'metamorphosis' into rodent and insect life. In contrast to the geography of danger, the geography of fear pushes the migrant *in*, that is, into the hidden crevices of the city.

Even in his confinement to the maid's chamber, the narrator is privy to the news and radio reports of the ongoing effort to capture and deport *sans papiers*. The city is in the process of pushing its undocumented inhabitants out, a process that appears as a joint effort between the media, the security apparatus and the populace. Reports on the efforts to round up and expel punctuate the narrative. With the escalating discourse of threat and appeals to the population for solidarity with the state's policing efforts, the narrator begins to imagine the outside world through military terms. In his observations of his neighbours, he periodically presumes their complicity in this collective effort. 'The little old woman has reappeared at her window. It appears that she is standing guard.'[17] Likewise, the old lady on the ground floor becomes a 'sentinel'[18] when she steps outside to walk her dog. The language of security translates into what appears as a military intervention.

The idea of letting oneself be rounded up, *se faire cueillir*, signals resignation rather than resistance. Indeed, the narrator holds no illusions that his own fate will be different:

> I am at the end of my rope. I needn't do more than stick my nose outside (this great snout with its proliferation of little black spots) to be gathered up. The evening news has transformed itself into a sordid hunting scene. They have stopped keeping track of how many have fallen into the trap. The convoys are bursting at the seams. The laws that prohibit raids before sunrise have been rendered void. They are cleaning the city with a pressure washer.[19] Soon, I will be part of one of those convoys.[20]

In the hidden crevices of the city, he identifies with those other unwanted creatures of the city that also specialise in the art of provisional survival, figuring himself as a cockroach or a rat.

In a 2008 article, Russell West-Pavlov likens the intertwining of fantasy and reality in *La géographie du danger* to what Gaston Bachelard calls '*à la fois une réalité du virtuel et une virtualité du réel*',[21] showing how 'collective fantasy can pose as reality, and on the other hand, collective desire can pose as reality'.[22] On both shores of the Mediterranean, he argues, dreams and fantasy are stand-ins for the realities of migration. In Europe, a collective panic over immigration as an imminent security threat fuels draconian measures against migrants. South of the Mediterranean, the collective fantasy of Europe as a paradise continues to lure new migrants even as it disguises the precariousness of clandestine migration. Collective fantasy is constitutive of that which is believed to be 'real', whether this means seeing migrants as a security threat or imagining a better life in Europe. West-Pavlov points to the work that literary narrative can do to weave fantasy and reality into more synthesised perspectives. Far from a geography of fear, 'the novels weave complex relationships between fantasy and the reality of stubborn but all too often disappointed dreams. They weave them back and forth just as they weave Africa and Europe back together.'[23]

If the novels discursively undermine the policed boundary between the two continents, in *La géographie* fantasy also plays a role in critically addressing the forces that perpetuate clandestine migration and its policing. Although collective fantasies of threat on one side of the Mediterranean and paradise on the other obscure the histories that link the two shores, and although the narrator constructs imaginary worlds as protective fictions based on longing, so does fantasy become an important means to grapple with the underlying causes of the narrator's predicament. Set apart from the rest of the novel by the use of italics, the narrator's notebooks contain a series of first-person accounts of characters implicated in human trafficking between North Africa and Europe. In his notebooks, he fictionalises the lives of 'Kamel la Braguette', a migrant who has resorted to prostitution to stay alive; the policeman who tortured him in his own country for founding a league of unemployed university graduates; and the trafficker who brought him to Europe. The act of narrating these lives represents recuperation of agency. For example, by introducing the torturer's section, he reflects: 'I am going to make him tell me about his life, just as he made me repeat mine with the aid of a baton.'[24] In his first-person account, he describes how he became a trafficker and how he conducted the investigation of the narrator and arrested him on the charge of suggesting that the money for creating jobs had been siphoned off by the 'barons'.[25] In another section of the notebook, he writes in the voice of a trafficker in Tangiers who reflects cynically on the profitable collaboration between the authorities and the traffickers.

On a generic level, *La géographie* both bridges the *harraga* literature of clandestine immigration to Europe and shares many of the themes of refuge and (in)hospitality with literature that renders the asylum process. Although a novel of clandestine migration, its focus on urban space in a European city sets it apart from most *harraga* novels, which tend to focus on the journeys of irregular migration.

Mobility and Constraint in *Al-Masha'a*

A vocal journalist, activist and participant in the 2011 Syrian uprising, Samar Yazbek was forced to flee Syria soon after the revolution began. Since 2012, the prominent author and journalist has primarily resided in Paris. Like Hoda Barakat and many international writers in the city, she is not typically positioned as an immigrant writer but rather as a writer contributing to both world literature and her own national literature. Yazbek tends to speak of herself as a temporary exile and activist for the Syrian cause. At the same time, her literary contributions are categorised within the universalising discourses of world and Arabic literature rather than as contributions by immigrant or migrant writers. Her novel *Al-Masha'a* (*Planet of Clay*), which was published in 2017, is Yazbek's first novel since the beginning of the Syrian revolution and war. Its publication marked Yazbek's return to writing novels after a period of publishing short stories and autobiographical eyewitness accounts of the war. Her acclaimed 2012 book, *Taqatu' Niran: min Yawmiyat al-Intifada al-Suriyya* (*A Woman in the Crossfire: Diaries of the Syrian Revolution*),[26] offers a personal account of the Syrian uprising[27] and her 2015 book, *The Crossing: My Journey to the Shattered Heart of Syria*,[28] is based on several undocumented trips into Syria where she interviewed fighters and others living in war zones. In *The Crossing* she makes a point to include the perspectives of women as much as possible. In an interview in 2016, she noted that as the revolution became radicalised with the spread of ISIS and other jihadist groups, women's roles were marginalised: 'Their role in the movement disappeared, which is why I wanted to focus on them.'[29] *Al-Masha'a* shares with these latter works the aim of rendering life in Syria during the uprising and war.

Although the adolescent girl who narrates *Al-Masha'a* never leaves her city, the novel offers an incisive exploration of mobility in a war that has created unprecedented levels of displacement. For as long as the young narrator of *Al-Masha'a* can remember, she has been afflicted with a mysterious condition that causes her to walk ceaselessly unless fettered. While her feet seek movement, her tongue refuses it: she does not speak other than reciting the Qur'an. Instead, she expresses herself through colourful drawings and by writing her life story for an unknown future reader (the novel itself). Even before the war, her walking is deemed dangerous and necessary to curtail. First, her mother uses a rope to tie her in place. After her mother's death at a military checkpoint, her brother, who is part of the opposition, moves her into a rebel-held area and takes over the responsibility of keeping her contained. After particularly intensive bombings and a chemical attack that kills many of those she lives with and causes others to flee the area, the girl finds herself confined, shackled and abandoned alone in a basement, where she writes her story. Her tenacious and seemingly innate desire for mobility thus coexists with various forms of shackling, on the one hand, and with a proliferation of roadblocks and boundaries erected as the city around her erupts into war, on the other.

Several critics have described the novel as a surrealistic account of the war. The novel calls attention to the nightmarish qualities of organised violence, such as that seen in the Iraqi war and migration literature discussed in Chapter 2. Indeed, the mysterious condition of the young narrator lends a surreal and enigmatic dimension to the story. However, the defamiliarising aspects of the narrative are more closely linked to the protagonist than the setting. In describing the horrors of war, she often foregrounds literature and aesthetics, for instance, by describing a chemical attack through the colours it produces in the sky, likening the dead to statues, or interpreting events through her favourite books. The effect is far from trivialising; rather, seeing the events of the novels through the girl's eyes invites a tender and fresh perspective. For her part, the young narrator addressing the reader insists early on, on a kind of realism that refutes the literary. She writes, 'Don't think that what you are reading right now is a novel. What I am writing is the truth, and I am doing it to try to understand what happened.'[30] Her insights stand in contrast to the judgments of others who see her as mentally ill or disabled. Hers is a perceptive, sensitive, and for the reader, defamiliarising way of seeing the world.

In a 2017 review of the book in *Qantara* titled 'Samar Yazbek Narrates the Syrian War with a Bound Tongue', Maya al-Hajj writes:

> Yazbek didn't stray from readers' expectations when she made the Syrian war the main theme of the novel. After all, the war is the shared root of all the articles and literary narratives that she has written since the revolution broke out. However, in *Al-Masha'a*, the war is not rendered through narrative that closely mirrors reality. Rather, the novel reshapes reality by narrating the story from the first-person perspective of a girl who is afflicted with the ailment of walking. She is as far as one can be from the devastating war that is governed by savage forces both from within the country and without.[31]

The novel is narrated directly in a conversational tone to the reader. The opening of the novel frames the story; the author is confined and alone in a shelter. Bombs are dropping from the sky, though we do not fully come to understand the framing or setting until the end of the novel. She writes for posterity, for a reader who may or may not find the large pile of papers she is leaving behind. To introduce herself is to introduce her enigmatic condition:

> Everything I'm writing to you could vanish, and it will be a strange fluke if you have a chance to read it, like the fluke that made me so different from other people.
>
> I was born, and I can't stop walking. I stand up and I set off and I keep walking and walking. I see the road, and it has no end. My feet take over and I walk – I just follow them. I don't understand why it happened, and I'm not expecting you to either. This enchantment of mine doesn't care what people might understand.[32]

The young narrator wonders whether this drive to walk is a spell or a curse, or perhaps even a mistake that God made while creating her, a mistake that nonetheless reveals some divine wisdom. At times, she imagines the merging of her intellect and her feet – a coming together of high and low, of body and mind. She longs to keep walking until she loses or transcends her individual consciousness or simply to find out where her feet will ultimately lead her. Her walking, which encompasses both a yearning for and imposed movement, offers an important commentary on mobility and even migration that is transindividual. In her, mobility coexists with multiple constraints, both individual and collective. Though it takes place within a single city, this dynamic connects it to literature of contemporary forced migration.

At the same time that the girl dreams of walking wherever her legs may take her, borders, military roadblocks and checkpoints begin proliferating as the fighting between Bashar al-Assad's Syrian Arab Army and the Syrian Free Army of the rebels creates shifting yet rigid demarcations of space. For example, in one critical turning point during the early phases of the war, the girl's mother is shot and killed at a military roadblock. As their bus comes to a standstill, the mother and daughter witness a brutal beating. After the girl accidentally becomes untied, her mother chases after her and is killed by soldiers. They were on their way to visit the school librarian Sitt Souad, who has decided to leave the country. Before her death, the mother had been working as a school janitor. Sitt Souad invited the girl to spend time in the school library instead of being tied next to her mother. There, she taught the girl how to read and introduced her to a world of literature and art that remains a vivid part of the girl's imagination. *The Little Prince* and *Alice in Wonderland* in particular became lenses through which she sees and interprets the world around her. After waking up injured in a military hospital following the shooting, the girl notes:

> You can imagine what happened to me! I had thought, when I fell asleep as the man carried me after my mother fell down and we crossed the checkpoint, that the sinking I had felt as I collapsed in the midday heat was me going into a forest that changed every now and then, like in *Alice in Wonderland*, and this room was the forest. This is what happened – the light suddenly came on! And instead of the white rabbit, there was a nurse in white clothes.[33]

In the person of the girl, this mobility with unknown endpoints is directly tied to freedom and unknown horizons, making her condition of movement (constraints notwithstanding) not only a potent metaphor for contemporary displacement and migration, but also for freedom. Maya al-Hajj remarks that 'perhaps *Al-Masha'a* by Samar Yazbek is an imagined paradigm of

Syrians' longing for liberation after decades of constricted life. Or rather, shackled life where the walls of prisons, streets, and houses were always listening.'[34]

The girl's desire for physical mobility coexists with a refusal to move her tongue. This decision to remain silent builds on and extends the strategic use of silence in Syrian literature that Mohja Kahf analysed in her 2001 article, 'The Silences of Contemporary Syrian Literature'. In it, she argues that strategic silences in the face of censorship and surveillance have constituted an important feature of modern Syrian literature from the late Ottoman period through the twentieth century. 'Manifold silence, evasion, indirect figurative speech, gaps and lacunae',[35] constitute creative responses to political oppression and surveillance, and have sometimes even been figured as a form of exile without physical displacement. The conditions of life in Syria have, of course, changed markedly since Kahf's intervention. Silence is also a barrier that protects the young girl and prevents others from seeing the rich inner worlds that she reveals to the reader. Furthermore, the narrator's silence must be interpreted in dialogue with the theme of barriers and mobility.

Her silence and the silent absences of those around her (she says people have 'disappeared' instead of saying that they died) are the crux of the narrator's desolate state when the novel ends. After a massive attack on the rebel-held neighbourhood, her brother is killed along with countless others. Hassan, her brother's friend, carries the girl to safety after a chemical attack. He leaves her in a basement and promises to return yet he, like the others, 'disappears'. In the last section of the book, we return to the narrative present of the novel with the girl, abandoned and starving, writing the end of her story for a future reader.

As her body starves and weakens, she delves deeper into the fanciful worlds or 'planets' she has created in her life (there are four), her synesthetic understanding of colour and words, and the way she sees letters as pictograms. Through a small window, she peers out of the basement to catch glimpses of the rubble that used to be the neighbourhood. Once in a while, a stray dog appears, as do two brothers gathering grass and scrap metal in a wheelbarrow. One day, she decides to use her voice to get their attention. Her otherworldly scream attracts their attention. They are not able to see her and conclude, 'It's a monster!'³⁶ before walking away. Unable to free herself from the knot that Hassan tied around her wrist before leaving to take photographs documenting a bombing, she remains alone, writing her story through the expansive capacities of her imagination and observation. Like the narrator of *Season of Migration to the North* whose call for help at the end of the novel represents a grasping for agency amidst predetermined and binary narratives, the girl ends her narrative with the statement 'And I must scream.'³⁷ In the end, her voice begins to move as her vitality and mobility are being stilled.

Lonesome Communities in *Voices of the Lost*

When celebrated Lebanese author and journalist Hoda Barakat won the 2019 IPAF award for her first novel on migration in Europe, *Barid al-Layl* (*Voices of the Lost*), it was one accolade among many. Barakat had made the long list in 2013 with her fifth novel, *Malakut hathihi al-Ard* (The Kingdom of This Earth),³⁸ while her first novel, *Hajar al-Dahk* (*The Stone of Laughter*),³⁹ won the *al-Naqid* Prize and *Harith al-Miyah* (2000) (*The Tiller of Waters*),⁴⁰ the Naguib Mahfouz Prize. Barakat, whose literary oeuvre is known for its exploration of marginalised identities within the context of the Lebanese Civil War (1975–90), has resided in Paris since 1989 and continues to write literature in Arabic, though as a journalist, she writes in both Arabic and French. She grew up in Lebanon, graduated with a degree in Arabic literature from the Lebanese University in 1975, and began pursuing her PhD in Paris in 1975 before returning to Beirut the following year to work as a journalist, teacher and translator.

As an author, Barakat is positioned very differently than many writers of North African origin in France. Rather than being perceived as an immigrant writer, she is celebrated as a writer contributing to Arabic and world literature. In France, she received the 'Chevalier de l'Ordre des Arts et des Lettres' title in 2002 and was designated 'Chevalier de l'Ordre du Mérite National' in 2008, awards bestowed by the French Ministry of Culture to recognise significant contributions to the arts.

In a review of *Barid al-Layl* titled 'The Mail of the Species: A Novel by Hoda Barakat', American author Rumaan Alam notes the novel's focus on the 'psychic ramifications' of each characters' mobility. In the epistolary novel, each character writers a letter containing confessions, longings, and explorations of alienation and loneliness, letters that are intercepted by strangers (but fellow readers of Arabic) in unnamed locations in Europe. Each letter inspires the next, creating a chain of letters that do not reach their intended destination yet set the narrative in motion. Each character has their own experience and story of displacement or being out-of-place. Several are undocumented migrants – one is travelling to seek out a lost lover, another escaping a family – but now long to return home. Alam writes, 'This isn't heavy-handed, and it's not even altogether political; Barakat isn't writing about "the immigrant". She's writing about the human.'[41] Alam's review renders explicit the often unspoken and implied hierarchy between immigrant literature and literature, between the category of the immigrant and that of the human. Writing about 'The Mail of the Species', the title of his review also hearkens to the universalism implied in the category of the human.

Barakat herself is a staunch defender of the universal qualities of literature; the particularities of setting and characters represent portals into universal questions and experiences. Speaking about *Barid al-Layl*, Barakat, whose previous fiction has primarily been set during the Lebanese Civil War, notes a desire to write about recent large-scale migration: 'I chose the novel's final form when scenes of migrants fleeing their countries had penetrated my imagination. Those people who have lost their homes and are scattered all over the earth.' She continues,

> At this time, we are seeing a regression in the humanitarian dimension of those civilisations, as countries protect themselves by closing their doors. I hope that this novel, somehow or other, will have given voice to brittle lives, which are judged by others without understanding them or investigating what brought them to their current state.[42]

Barakat makes a case for literature's capacity to shift perceptions of migrants away from discourses that render them as an undifferentiated mass toward a recognition of the complexity of individual yet intertwined lives. 'Even when we see them as innocents and victims, we don't see them in the ways we normally see each other.' She continues, 'We see them as a very low group of people ... like sheep, numbers of sheep ... as masses of human beings.'[43]

Voices of the Lost is not the first novel that Barakat has written on migration and diaspora. Her 2004 epistolary memoir, *Rasa'il al-Ghariba* (The Stranger's Letters),[44] however, explores the meaning of diaspora through a series of personal vignetters or letters reflecting on the Lebanese diaspora in France. The book was serialised in *al-Hayat* newspaper before being published in book form. Here too, form reflects meaning. The disjointed narrative structure as well as the narrative *I* stage resistance to articulating a shared or continuous narrative of displacement and diaspora. For example, in the first vignette, 'The return of the non-prodigal children', Barakat establishes a tension between the first-person plural narration of the Lebanese diaspora in France and the repeated insistence that there is no 'we' or community to speak of. The phrase 'we do not form a community' (*lasna nushakkil jama'a* or *lasna jama'a*) is continually repeated in this first vignette, as Barakat narrates fleeting encounters between members of the Lebanese diaspora in France that are quickly abandoned, even avoided. The text thus evokes a sense of shared experience even as it evades it.

In *Rasa'il al-Ghariba* it is often the experiences and effects of the mundane that give rise to poetic reflections on what it means to be a stranger and a part of a community of strangers. *Khajal*, the spontaneous sense of being exposed, embarrassed, shy, or ashamed takes centre stage as a way of theorising ties to others. In *Rasa'il al-Ghariba*, Barakat is exploring the affective dynamics of diaspora rather than forced or precarious migration, yet her simultaneous affirmation and negation of a *we*, a community, is similar to the transindividual qualities of migration literature explored in this book. The transindividual, as described by Etienne Balibar, is found in border spaces where individual and communal relationships to the world are negotiated. The simultaneous attention to individual narrative and the way it is constituted by collective dynamics of mass migration, I have argued, gives rise to a transindividual awareness that challenges the binaries and hierarchies used to analyse and categorise exile and migration literature. Though Barakat's work is not typically categorised as migration literature, it participates in this broader project of exploring how both individual and collective categories are irreducible to the other. In *Voices of the Lost*, she brings this lens to an exploration of contemporary migration and displacement.

The main body of *Voices of the Lost*, 'Those Who Are Lost', consists of five letters composed by five different characters, each a migrant or traveller and each from an unnamed Arab country (the letters suggest Lebanon, Iraq and Egypt) and currently residing or passing through an unnamed European city. The next two sections, 'Those Who Are Searching' and 'Those Who Are Left Behind', contain the short narratives of those to whom the letters were addressed (but never received) and the narrative of a postman in a war-torn country who, instead of delivering letters, now archives them. Although each letter is addressed to an intimate other, they are intercepted by chance by another character who can read the Arabic and become inspired to write their own letter. The chain continues, creating a sort of story-within-a-story or story-invites-a-story and connecting characters who will never meet or reciprocally communicate. To invoke the title of Barakat's previous work, they are truly the letters of strangers even as the characters experience intimacy by virtue of reading these others' secrets and confessions. It is not similar life stories or experiences as migrants that unite them, but rather a shared sense of loneliness and alienation. The paradox of community builds on a shared sense of isolation at the heart of the book and works to unsettle narratives of mass migration.

The narrative begins with the letter of a young man who is residing without papers in the unnamed country. In his letter, addressed to an unnamed lover, he begins by recounting his mother's abandonment and his time spent writing articles and translating for an exiled political leader. It is clear in his letter that he was physically and emotionally abusing the lover he is addressing. He is both consumed and repelled by his desire for her. Later, a woman in a hotel room finds his letter tucked into a directory. She has just arrived in the country to reunite with a lover from decades past. Her reading of this letter inspires her to write to the man she is expecting, a man she knew in her youth and who has now promised to fly in from Canada to reunite with her. In writing, she recalls their youthful trysts when he was travelling as a tourist in her country and contemplates the aging body. Another man, observing her in the Arrivals hall at the airport, sees her tear the letter apart and toss it in a trash can before leaving the airport alone. He fishes out the letter, reads it, and writes his own letter of confession addressed to his mother. His letter reveals a longing for the mother even as he reproaches her for not protecting him from his father's beatings when he was a child. He relates how his torture in prison as an adolescent paved the way for him to become a feared torturer himself. When the dictator in his country fell, he joined those who were fleeing the country but retracted his asylum claim when others in the camp recognised him from the prisons of their home country. Living undocumented in an unnamed European city, he committed a major crime and is now fleeing from the police. His letter is found by a woman who is on the plane with him when he is arrested. She writes to her brother with her own confessions. She is hoping for reconciliation with him after years of sex work and domestic labour in Europe, work that allowed her to fulfil their mother's demands that she send money. Her letter is found by a young man who begins to pen a letter to his father. He recounts his lover's death by AIDS and his subsequent homelessness and odd work, seeking redemption and return to his family.

The chain of letters forges a collective out of a shared loneliness and the intimacy of intercepting confessions and life stories. Far from the kinds of collective tropes and narratives that are often conjured in media and elsewhere to render mass migration, the sense of a shared lot that generates communal affect in the novel is built not on shared identity or similar life stories but rather on shared loneliness and affective identification with the vulnerability of the other. The structure of the novel, with each writer initiating a chain of confessional narratives among people who will remain strangers to one another, creates a butterfly effect and a sense of shared experience that both forges and defies community. In her letter to her former lover, the second letter writer asks:

> Why am I telling you all this? To entertain myself a little while I am waiting, and also because the loneliness of that man, the letter writer, sounds a lot like my loneliness. Even if his story doesn't resemble my life in any way. But I sensed, felt, his cry of pain as though I were an old friend, or as though I myself was the woman to whom he was

complaining. Maybe I felt that way because after reading his letter, there were things I thought about telling him, things I wished I could say to him, and because I wanted to wrap my arms around him.[45]

Her warmth toward the first writer is not based on similar experiences of migration or in intimate relationships. Though they share 'a language foreign to this country' she struggles to read his handwriting, his 'letters curling into themselves like dead insects'.[46] Instead, she identifies with his pain and loneliness, that is, the effect that lies beneath the details of his life story. 'It was as if, as soon as my fingers even touched the written page, I sensed that the man who had left it here was someone familiar, a person I already knew.'[47]

This connection through *waḥsha* (loneliness and longing) becomes the basis of the sense of togetherness that inspires each writer. The last of the letter writers, a young man addressing his father, notes, 'What gave me courage to write, finally, was a letter written by a woman who was all on her own, lonely and deserted just like me. It's a letter I stumbled across a long time ago in my little storage locker in the bar I worked in.'[48] He senses that their fates are intertwined and in this case that their life stories are similar – he, a young gay man who finds himself homeless after his lover dies, and she, a mother who allows both her abusive mother and boss to die rather than offer assistance in their final moments. It takes him two years to put pen to paper, but when he does, it is also a shared sense of loneliness and vulnerability that forges a shared experience rather than the details of their life stories or experiences of migration.

The question of similarity and difference is at the heart of the way each writer imagines and experiences intimacy and something shared, even in the absence of mutual communication. Abandonment and betrayal at the hands of family members is a source of deep pain for many of the writers even as it fuels a longing for reconnection and redemption. The last writer delves deeply into the pain, unfulfilled longings, and betrayals that can be part of family bonds, so often imagined as a space of unconditional belonging. Despite the material conditions of his life in the new country (undocumented, periodically homeless), he has come to feel at home in his body and sexuality, a belonging that does not depend on his father's approval or on citizenship. He recounts seeing photos from his childhood where he appears to be an extension of his father's body and recalls his adolescence, when his father's disapproval severed him from paternal care and protection. In a dream he sees his father diminished, on a sickbed or deathbed, while his own body has grown larger. As his father takes on the shape of a foetus, the roles are reversed. The exiled son wraps himself around the foetus-father to protect him. Protection and violence intermingle. The father's protection was premised on his capacity for violence, his feared role in an army or maybe a militia.

> No one can put himself in another's place. What I mean is, in another person's exact place. And in my case there is a crucial detail, which is that my body – which has made me who I am, in my deepest self – is not your body. My body, which you see as a betrayal.[49]

In the letters, these polarised binaries, repulsion and love, reversed roles and irreversible roles, coexist in internal contradiction, just like the community built on each writer's isolation and loneliness.

The epistolary form also conjures an important tension. The epistolary form is often used to create a sense of realism and lend the documents that form the narrative an air of authenticity. Each letter writer seeks to confess important truths about their own life, actions and emotions. In contrast, the places of origin as well as the places of residence remain obscured, as do the characters themselves. The first letter writer's sentences often trail off, leaving out information. We cannot know for sure how to understand the geography of the characters' lives, at least with any specificity. The factual form and details of each character's confessions contrast with the vague, almost allegorical layer of the narrative. The testimonial qualities of the novel are thus distinct from the testimonial forms associated with migration, such as the asylum interview or the humanitarian account of suffering. In many of the letters, the binary of victim and perpetrator comes undone as we meet an abusive boyfriend who has also been mistreated, a murderer who was abused as a child and became a torturer after being tortured in prison. This defamiliarising of testimony and the confessional serves to create a nuanced reflection on the ties that bind us to one another. And in an age of mass migration, the narrative creates a different sense of belonging, one that arises from the shared experience of loneliness and alienation. Such a narrative offers a poignant counterpoint to prevalent media images of migrants as an undifferentiated mass.

London

London, like Paris, is both a historic and contemporary centre of Arab culture in Europe. The long historic Arabic literary presence in the city and the place of London in Arabic literary narratives that explore *Nahda* modernising ideologies, anti-colonial discourses and postcolonial realities make for multi-layered significations of the city. These material and discursive histories also shape the presence and circulation of contemporary Arabic literature of forced and precarious migration. While London and the attendant national space of the UK remains a centre for Arabic literature, theatre and culture in Europe, its centrality to Arabic literature of forced or precarious migration seems to reside mostly in the realms of the circulation and translation of forced migration by virtue of the hegemony of the English language and the publishing houses, theatres and festivals where Arabic literature, theatre and culture in Europe is curated and showcased.

In comparison to the literary landscape in France, especially in *beur* and *banlieue* fiction, there is less of an emphasis on and anxiety about transforming the English language in Arab British writing. Furthermore, the global hegemony of English means that translations, publications and performances in the English language can potentially reach a wider audience, even without an equivalent to *la Francophonie*, a fact that amplifies the role of London and UK-based institutions and events. As a literary centre London, and the UK more broadly, is a crossroads and a space that, in Pascale Casanova's terms, bestows legitimacy on authors and literary styles and creates the possibility for broader circulation and audience.

The hegemony of English and the centrality of London and the UK to world literature means that publishers and translations shape what genres, aesthetics and writers that, in Casanova's terms, find literary acclaim and legitimacy. One example to mention, since it is close to the speculative and defamiliarising approaches of many narratives discussed in this book, is the role Comma Press in Manchester has played in soliciting and publishing future writing by Arab authors. In the 2016 collection *Iraq+100*,[50] which was edited by Finland-based Iraqi writer Hassan Blasim,[51] ten Iraqi writers imagine the country 100 years from the 2003 invasion, each setting their story in a different city. The writers draw on science fiction and magical realism in their rendering of the future. Some stories imagine the future shaped by continuous occupation whereas others write futures liberated of forceful foreign interference and war. In *Palestine+100*,[52] published in 2019 (also by Comma Press) and edited by Basma Ghalayini, ten Palestinian writers imagine Palestine 100 years from the 1948 Nakba. With approaches like science fiction and dystopian writing, many of the stories query future uses of technology to further displace and overpower Palestinian lives or create partial and ineffective solutions to the occupation. As speculative endeavours that seek to reimagine the impasses of the present through literary means, the approaches seen in these collections align with many of the literary narratives of migration explored in this book. Furthermore, the fact that these collections were published in English while the Arabic originals remain unpublished (though some authors contributed original stories in English) is also testament to the place of English as a predominant world literary language.

Although the history of Arabic and Arab literature in the UK is rich and varied and beyond the scope of this chapter, a brief delving into some of the dynamics of Arabic literature set in London and the UK and into what Edward Said called 'The Anglo-Arab Encounter'[53] will help situate some of the more recent trends of publishing and performing migration and theatre in London and the UK in a broader context.

In the classic postcolonial text *Mawsim al-Hijra ila al-Shamal* (*Season of Migration to the North*) (1966) by Tayeb Salih, the character Mustafa Said's journey and stay in London was represented as a venture into a 'heart of darkness'. London was a site of violence and the novel confronted the modernising, romanticising and cultural encounter tropes that have been prevalent in Arabic migration literature and its representation of colonial metropoles. The text's critical intertextual engagement with Shakespeare's *Othello* and Conrad's *Heart of Darkness* rendered it both an indictment of Orientalism and the racialised violence of colonialism as well as the *Nahda* discourses that sought to build a future based on 'western' technology and 'eastern' culture. As Rasheed El-Enany argues in *Arab Representations of the Occident*, *Season of Migration to the North* represents a turning point in Arabic literary representations of Europe with many post-1967 literary narratives critiquing the intellectual and political underpinnings of the early postcolonial Arab states.

More recent Arabic literary renderings of London have emphasised the complexities of diaspora and have continued to reimagine the cultural encounter model of writing travel and migration. The 2001 novel *Nisa' 'ala Safar* (*Women on a Journey between Baghdad and London*) by Iraqi writer Haifa Zangana, for instance, explores the Iraqi diaspora in London in the 1990s through a polyvocal narrative of five women of different ethnic, class and political backgrounds who regularly meet at a café. The group encompasses a widow of a Baath official, a Kurdish mother and asylum seeker, an anti-regime activist and translator, a wife of a former and now disillusioned member of the Iraqi Communist Party, and a young divorced mother remaking a life in London. Each woman's journey is significantly different from the others' and, as Ruth Abou Rached has pointed out, the linguistic register of each woman echoes their different ethnic, social and political belongings.[54] Yet the interweaving of their stories and voices calls attention to how each suffered under the Iraqi regime and under the 1990s sanctions and to the shared challenges that the women face in their London-based lives.

Other Arabic-language writers based in London have re-written the cultural encounter framework within more recent diasporas. Hanan al-Shaykh's *Innaha London ya Azizi* (*Only in London*) offers another view on Arab diasporas in London, with a tone and scope quite distinct from Zangana's. Her novel follows a group of strangers who meet on a flight between Dubai and London. Lamees, an Iraqi divorcée, begins a romantic relationship with Nicholas, a British antique dealer. Ameera, a sex worker working in upscale hotels shares her flat with Samir, a gay man from Beirut, who has left his wife and children to find relationships in London. The novel explores how these characters make lives and selves that reflect hybridity and personal choice.

When discussing Arabic literature in the UK, it makes sense to also look to its anglophone counterpart, since a significant share of immigration and migration narratives are written in English, often by authors who are bilingual. In an overview of the anglophone Arab writing in Britain, Geoffrey P. Nash locates 'anti-colonialism, Orientalism, and hybridization as the main elements of Anglophone Arab writing up to the close of the twentieth century'.[55] Edward Said wrote on this topic too. In a review of Egyptian writer Ahdaf Soueif's English-language novel *In the Eye of the Sun* (1992) titled 'The Anglo-Arab Encounter', Edward Said celebrated Soueif's epic debut novel while pondering the dearth of English literature written in the Arabic-speaking region and its diasporas compared to French. Given the colonial relationship between Great Britain and Egypt and other Arab nations and the many English-language schools and universities, Said asks, 'Why did the Franco-Arab cultural encounter give rise to a more developed literary result?'[56] He notes that unlike many earlier Egyptian literary renderings of Europe, the main character Aya, an upper-class Egyptian woman pursuing a PhD in northern England, is not an allegory of the Arab woman but is resolutely individualised and living a life shaped by hybridity. The novel refuses the East–West, Arab–European binaries that Orientalist and *Nahda* discourses often took for granted.

Waïl Hassan discusses this new generation of writing in English by Arab authors residing in the UK in his 2011 book *Immigrant Narratives: Orientalism and Cultural Translation in Arab American and Arab British Literature*. Hassan argues that both Arab American and the smaller corpus of Arab British literature (written in English) is mediated by Orientalism, with English-language writers often positioned as cultural translators who navigate the binaries that are part and parcel of Orientalist conceptions of cultural difference as well an integral element of their host societies' conception of Arab immigrants. Neither Orientalism nor authors' efforts to meditate on it, however, are static. Geoffrey Nash points out that that each generation will experience hybridity differently in ways that are equally contingent on history.[57] As cultural stereotypes and material realities shift, so do authors' responses to them. As an example, the growth of Arab diasporas in the UK during the latter half of the twentieth century shifted Arab British literature from one of travel to one of immigration and hybridity. Furthermore, as Hassan discusses in *Immigrant Narratives*, a distinctive Muslim immigrant fiction has appeared in the post-1970s period following the collapse of the Arab secular nationalist project with the growing role of religion in public life in the Arab region and its diasporas. Leila Aboulela, a Sudanese writer residing in Scotland has made significant contributions to this genre with novels like *The Translator* (1999)[58] and *Minaret* (2005).[59] Other writers have arrived in London because of its role as a centre for media institutions and diplomacy. The 2002 English-language novel *The Last Migration* (2002) by London-based Lebanese *al-Hayat* journalist Jad al-Hage imagines the loves and losses of a Lebanese journalist based in London in the 1990s. British-Libyan author Hisham Matar's formidable oeuvre provides a different perspective. Matar, who was born in New York, grew up in London and Tripoli and was the son of a Libyan diplomat and dissident to the Gaddafi regime. His father was disappeared in Cairo in 1990. Matar's work as a memoirist, author and essayist explores and reimagines different dimensions of these geographies and histories and has won him numerous awards and accolades.[60]

The Return of Danton: Staging the Syrian Revolution via France, Germany and London

A world capital of theatre, London stages showcase the work of well-known international and local Arab artists. International collaborations, such as an ongoing project at the Royal Court Theatre, to bring in plays by Lebanese and Syrian playwrights[61] and high-profile festivals such as the biennial Shubbak festival play a role in making the work of Arab theatre makers visible in the city. This is also the case for theatre of forced and precarious migration in Europe. For instance, playwright and journalist Rashid Razaq expanded and adapted Finland-based Hassan Blasim's short story *The Nightmares of Carlos Fuentes* for the stage. The dark story of an Iraqi migrant who renames himself Carlos Fuentes in a futile effort to leave his past behind, it was performed at the Arcola Theatre in London in 2014.

The Return of Danton,[62] an Arabic-language play performed by Mülheim-based Collective Ma'louba ('an intercultural theatre lab' led by Syrian theatre makers in Germany) was written by Syrian playwright Mudar al-Haggi, the artistic director of the collective, and directed by London-based Omar Elerian, who is of Palestinian and Italian descent.

Premiering in summer 2021, *The Return of Danton* was staged by the Shubbak festival with the support of several theatres based in London and Germany. Due to COVID-19, it was performed online. The play is about a group of Syrian actors in Germany preparing to perform the classic 1835 play *Danton's Death* by the German writer Georg Büchne. *Danton's Death*, a play about the life and death of the French revolutionary leader Georges Danton during the period between the second and third terrors, seems to offer interesting fodder for comparing the French and Syrian revolutions. It also highlights the politics of securing funding for the arts in Germany. The director, dramaturg and actors in *The Return of Danton* disagree on casting choices, how the troupe should make decisions, and the appropriate balance between artistic integrity and the expectations of a German funding agency. And, they wonder, is there actually a relationship between the French and the Syrian revolutions? While the troupe does not end up answering this last question to their own satisfaction, their interpersonal and professional struggles while rehearsing the play create significant parallels between *Danton's Death* and their own hopes for and disappointments in the Syrian revolution. The play also includes commentary on German and European expectations on Syrian theatre makers in contemporary Europe.

Mudar al-Haggi has previously explored similar themes in a play written for al-Masrah al-Arabi fi Stockholm, the Arabic Theatre in Stockholm, namely the 2018 *Shafaq Qutbi/Norrsken* (Northern Lights), the first of two plays based on in-depth interviews with Arabic-speaking asylum seekers and refugees in Sweden. *Shafaq Qutbi* is composed of a series of sketches framed by the story of a group of Arab actors (who play the various characters in the sketches) working under a director (represented as a disembodied voice) who is well-established in the country, often reminding the troupe that he controls their career destinies. The sketches or vignettes that the play presents centre on themes of illusion, mental health and disappointment.

In *The Return of Danton*, as well, much of the drama lies in the question of staging and struggles between members of the troupe to have their voices heard. The director Eyas (played by Kinan Hmeidan) seeks to assert his vision over the dramaturg Rahaf (Amal Omran) and the actors Rida (Mohamed Alrashi) and Steve (Mohammad Dibo), who play Robespierre and Danton respectively. However, his quest for authority comes to naught when speaking to the German gatekeepers of culture. In an English-language phone conversation, we see him trying to explain his vision for *Danton's Death* to Karina, a German culture worker, but instead having to respond to questions like whether 'the refugees' will come to the play and about his journey to Germany. 'I came to Germany by plane ... no boat. Sorry, sorry ... no boat. Yes, Schengen visa.' His efforts to maintain control over the play also flounder when faced with his own troupe's attempts to subvert his authority by proposing alternate visions for the play. A couple of comical hash-induced dance scenes are particularly effective in angering Eyas, the director, but also in suggesting experimental interpretations of the German play. Alongside the troupe's efforts to evade the director's authority and the director's attempts to navigate the expectation that he will tell his personal story are three big questions: what would it mean for a revolution to succeed? What do previous political allegiances mean to those acclimating to a new country a decade after the revolution? To what extent should art be adapted to audience expectations and the whims of funding agencies?

This play about a play is also a play about theatre, especially Arabic and Arab migration theatre in contemporary Europe. The self-reflexive qualities of the play are reminiscent of some of the works that were discussed in the previous chapter on Arabic migration literature and theatre in Berlin, which scrutinised expectations about art and literature vis-à-vis those categorised as 'refugees'. Like so many others, the play's route to London was paved by transnational collaborations and networks in which London is an important node. In the following section, a novel on writing and representing forced migration, the 2021 English-language novel *Silence is a Sense* by Kuwaiti writer Layla AlAmmar, set in an unnamed English city, provides an equally self-reflexive commentary on the process of creating art with and against expectations of migration art in the wake of displacement and arrival.

Silence is a Sense

Written in English, the novel *Silence is a Sense* (2021) explores the questions of how to write forced and precarious migration, given the limitations of language to narrate trauma and with particular regard to the context of contemporary Syria. It is the second novel of Layla AlAmmar, a bilingual Kuwaiti novelist and academic pursuing a PhD in Arab women's writing and trauma theory in the UK. She earned an MA in creative writing from the University of Edinburgh and has published short stories in UK- and US-based literary journals and online sites and was a British Council International Writer in Residence at the Small Wonder Short Story Festival in 2018.

The narrator of *Silence* is a twenty-six-year-old Syrian writer from Aleppo residing in an unnamed town in England. We initially encounter her as a fastidious observer of life around her. From the window of her apartment, she witnesses and narrates the everyday lives of her neighbours residing in the apartment complex facing hers: 'No-Lights-Man', 'The Dad', 'The Old Couple', 'The Juicer', to name a few. Like the narrator of *La géographie du danger*, the young woman studiously observes the neighbours, ascribing stories and identities to each one. Her attentiveness to the details of their lives is incisive and insightful, yet as her monikers suggest, her observations are also a way to circumscribe complexity, much like the way she creates imagined borders in her town that demarcate where she allows herself to walk. The sense of borders demarcating permissible spaces creates a sense of safety. This effort to contain parallels her efforts to keep unspeakable trauma at bay. In fact, like the narrator of *al-Masha'a*, the narrator does not speak at all, causing many of her neighbours to assume that she is deaf and mute. From within her apartment, she pursues an online degree in Political Science and writes op-eds for a national paper under the pen name *the Voiceless*.

The novel contains a multitude of narrative forms, from the young woman's astute observations of her surroundings, her columns as *the Voiceless* and her email exchanges with her editor Josie to the emergence of traumatic memories that cannot be contained and thus intrude upon dreams, fantasy and waking life. Fragments of memory from her activism in the early Syrian revolution appear, along with memories of the extreme violence of war, encounters with sexual violence and death along the routes between Syria and the UK. Nightmares become interspersed in the narrative, both adding to her story and calling attention to the limits of language to describe trauma.

The young woman's pen name, *the Voiceless*, is both literal and paradoxical given that the narrator has not spoken since her arrival in the UK and, at the same time, has a large platform and readership in a column in a national paper. However, even here, the question of *how* her voice can be heard and perceived takes centre stage. Her editor Josie solicits personal accounts of the war in Syria and her experience as an irregular migrant and asylum seeker and gently admonishes her when she writes on topics such as politics, citizenship and Islamophobia. Yet, when *the Voiceless* does write about her journey, she is told that the story will not be credible to the newspapers' readership and that she needs to make it more palatable for her audience. As an unnamed refugee in the UK, she is expected to narrate a collective yet personal experience, similar to the director Eyas in *The Return of Danton*. Her expertise in political science and her creativity as a writer are seen as departures from the kinds of stories she should be telling.

Central to the way that the narrator navigates these expectations is the question of the human. Who counts as human and who counts as a statistic? Whose death is named and mourned and whose death is one number among many? Yet, *the Voiceless* does address these questions directly in her column. In one, she writes:

> They – and by 'they', I mean my editor and the people at the magazine you're currently reading and some of you who have left comments in the empty spaces below – want me to reveal myself as some microcosm of refugee society. They want to see, in me, all the hopes and ills and frustrations and struggles and singular stories of some five million plus people. They want me to speak for the chaos of the world, to weave the abstracts of cultural convulsions and scapegoats and simple apathy into my story, so that by seeing 'me', by knowing 'me', you might know them all, and I suppose – by extension – might feel some degree of empathy for them all. Humanize. That's what they say, when they're fawning over certain books and documentaries and films. A word uttered easily and without too much thought. A well-intentioned word that nevertheless concedes the argument that some people are not people and so require some art form to render them human.[63]

The next chapter contains an email response from the editor where she suggests that *the Voiceless* be careful about making sweeping statements such as the idea asylum seekers do not pose a danger to society. She cites a recent attack, the 2017 Westminster Bridge attack, saying that one of the assailants may have been an asylum seeker at one point and 'real people' died that day. The email, of course, raises the question of who is and is not a 'real' person.

> I find it ironic that this incident is what breaks [the editor] Josie. Seven or eight dead. In the war at home, some five hundred thousand have died. But I suppose there is a critical threshold after which numbers cease to have any meaning and people stop being 'real'.[64]

The narrator reflects on how to represent large-scale migration in a way that does not resort to statistics and a homogenisation of experience, on the one hand, while also acknowledging the dynamics of mass migration and the shared and overlapping stories of those who have been forced to flee war zones and take to irregular routes, on the other. This makes her a keen observer of the transindividual and of how meaning is contingent on how we narrate. She writes, 'People aren't interested in the truth so much as the narrative.'[65]

The many different narrative forms incorporated into the novel create a kind of spaciousness where different narrative forms can be tried out and commented on, often revealing the limitations of each form. The novel's attention to trauma and narration is also an attention to the limits of language. The most prevalent forms of defamiliarisation in the novel have to do with the return of the narrator's traumatic memories of the war and journey of irregular migration from Syria. Here, surreal images and events abound. As memories return in nightmares and waking consciousness, they arrive in fragments and often through elements of fantasy or the surreal. The description of the revolt in Syria and the ensuing war appears as brief episodes and in nightmares. Her tight-knit group of friends, including her romantic interest, make posters that they surreptitiously drop over buildings. In some memories, the letters slide right off the posters revealing a blank canvas. In others, the group reveals their posters to an imagined theatre of onlookers who turn violent. One member of the group has been hanged and dangles in a corner. Jinn abound in these memories and, with these spirits, the angel of death (*malak al-mawt*) is ever-present, gathering human lives. There is an all-seeing eye, a representation of pervasive state surveillance made literal. In the present, hallucinations appear in her everyday waking life in the UK. In one instance she sees a mirage of her lover merged with that of Edgar Allen Poe. The surreal elements of the novel are less about speculative narrative forms and more about attempts to capture the nightmares and fragmentation of narrative caused by trauma.

As the novel progresses, the attention of the narrator shifts from the intensive focus on her immediate surroundings toward a synthesis of the past and present, the internal and external. She writes about Islamophobia in her column and becomes an up-close witness to several violent incidents in her neighbourhood. An evolving friendship with an activist in one of the buildings moves from a reluctance to participate in anything resembling a protest to joining him despite reservations about the efficacy of their actions and memories of loved ones who were killed for similar acts in Syria. The recuperation of memory goes hand in hand with the recuperation of voice and finally the utterance of her name, both in her intimate relationships, and as a writer. If language begins as an impossibility, it becomes a major conduit for moving toward healing and speaking on her own terms.

The novel reflects more on the capacity of language and narrative in general than questions of English and Arabic literature in London's literary spaces discussed above. However, its concerns (such as Islamophobia and Orientalist representations of immigrants and migrants) link it both to Anglophone Arab-British literature and Arabic literature of forced and precarious migration.

Conclusion

Compared to Berlin, London and Paris offer different visions for what it means to be a capital of Arab culture in Europe. As global literary centres, the cities play an important role in shaping literary trends and legitimising authors, genres and aesthetic approaches. If we add to this their role as colonial and postcolonial metropoles and as homes to large and historically rooted Arab diasporas, it will come as no surprise that there is a formidable corpus of Arabic literature written in those metropoles in Arabic, as well as in French and English. It is this history and the way it shapes the present that makes their cultural and literary scenes distinct from a city like Berlin, where Arab diasporas are relatively new and where cultural and literary production is being promoted and shaped by different dynamics and gatekeepers. The recent flourishing of Arabic literature, arts and theatre in Berlin and Germany discussed in Chapter 5 offers an interesting and important counterpoint to London and Paris.

Yet, an important distinction between London and Paris and newer diasporas is that its literature of forced migration is co-present with significant immigrant literatures written in Arabic, French and English. In both London and Paris there are Arab diasporas with roots that date back to the mid-twentieth century and they each have their own established literatures. Furthermore, there are many prominent Arab writers who reside in Paris and London. Their work is often celebrated as belonging to world literature or national canons rather than as immigrant or migration literature, even when it explores these topics. As shown in this chapter, these writings contribute to an emergent genre of forced and precarious migration even when they are not classified as such. Like the work discussed in previous chapters, they use literary means to defamiliarise borders, citizenship and belonging as well as dominant fear-based and humanitarian discourses on contemporary migration, approaches that are distinct from immigration literatures' focus on hybridity and minoritised identities, even as there are important overlaps.

When it comes to Arabic literature of forced and precarious migration, the literary centres of London and Paris seem to play a less prominent role compared to what they do in other arenas of Arabic literature and culture in Europe. That said, their publishers and cultural and educational institutions play an important role in curating and legitimising literary trends from locations that far exceed the boundaries of the nation. Furthermore, the dominance of both French and English (and especially English) in the world means that works translated into and published in these spaces can reach wider audiences. However, as a whole, it is important to read this work comparatively and across borders since it is truly part of a broad, highly connected and varied Arabic-European literary space.

The many examples of migration literature and theatre in this chapter point to a shifting geography of Arabic migration literature in Europe; the traditional literary centres remain central but the literary geography of Arabic forced migration literature in Europe is coming as much from newer diasporas as the older literary centres. The literature itself is, of course, highly transnational given its subject matter. However, it is also transnational in the sense that taken-for-granted categories of belonging are defamiliarised, evoking questions that remain relevant as they cross borders.

Notes

1. The term *beur* refers to descendants of North African immigrants to France and comes from the creative re-mixing of *arabe*.
2. Samar Yazbek, *Al-Masha'a* (Beirut: Dar al-Adab, 2017); Samar Yazbek, *Planet of Clay*, trans. Leri Price (London: World Editions, 2021).
3. Hoda Barakat, *Barid al-Layl* (Beirut: Dar al-Adab, 2017).
4. Layla AlAmmar, *Silence is a Sense* (Chapel Hill: Algonquin Books, 2021).
5. Pascale Casanova, *The World Republic of Letters*, trans. Malcolm Debevoise (Cambridge, MA: Harvard University Press, 2007).
6. Email conversation in April 2021.
7. 'Arab Writers – Going Global: Hoda Barakat, Jokha alHarthi & Marilyn Booth', *YouTube*, https://www.youtube.com/watch?v=4rDudm1usE4 (accessed 29 November 2020).
8. Laura Reeck, 'France', in Waïl Hassan (ed.), *The Oxford Handbook of Arab Novelistic Traditions* (Oxford: Oxford University Press, 2017).
9. Hamed Skif, *La géographie du danger* (Paris: Editions Naïve, 2006).
10. The French government does not keep official statistics on race, ethnicity, religion, or national origins of its populations. It is estimated that about 7–9 per cent of the population is Muslim, and that the majority of this population has roots in North Africa. See 'France: North Africans', *Minority Rights*, https://minorityrights.org/minorities/north-africans/ (accessed 29 November 2020).
11. Alec Hargraves, 'Beur Fiction: Voices from the Immigrant Community in France', *The French Review* 62, no. 4 (1989): 661–8.
12. Rebecca Blanchard, 'Carceral States in Kaoutar Harchi's *Zone Cinglée*', *Romance Studies* 36, no. 1–2 (2018): 63.

13. Blanchard, 'Carceral States', 74.
14. Blanchard, 'Carceral States', 68.
15. Skif, *La géographie*, 17.
16. Naima El Moussaoui, 'The Refrain of a Shadowy Existence', *Qantara. de*, 21 September 2007, http://en.qantara.de/The-Refrain-of-a-Shadowy-Existence/8893c8969i1p507/.
17. Skif, *La géographie*, 49.
18. Skif, *La géographie*, 61.
19. This idea references Nicolas Sarkozy's statement during the June 2009 riots in suburban Paris: '*On va nettoyer au Karcher la cité*' ('We will clean up the projects with a pressure washer').
20. Skif, *La géographie*, 123.
21. Quoted from Russell West-Pavlov, 'The Fictions of Clandestinity: Dream and Reality in Ben Jelloun and Skif', *Australian Journal of French Studies* 45, no. 2 (2008): 170.
22. West-Pavlov, 'The Fictions of Clandestinity', 170.
23. West-Pavlov, 'The Fictions of Clandestinity', 177–8.
24. Skif, *La géographie*, 65.
25. Skif, *La géographie*, 72.
26. Samar Yazbek, *Taqaṭu' Niran: min Yawmiyat al-Intifaḍa al-Suriyya* (Beirut: Dar al-Adab, 2012); Samar Yazbek, *A Woman in the Crossfire: Diaries of the Syrian Revolution*, trans. Max Weiss (London: Haus Publishing, 2012).
27. She won the PEN/Pinter Prize 'International Writer of Courage' for the book. In 2012 she also won the Tucholsky Prize and the Dutch Oxfam Pen Prize.
28. Samar Yazbek, *The Crossing: My Journey to the Shattered Heart of Syria*, trans. Nashwa Gowanlock and Ruth Ahmedzai Kemp (London: Rider Books, 2015).
29. Stephanie Papa, '"The Most Important Way to Love and Peace Is Justice": A Conversation with Samar Yazbek', trans. Emma Suleiman, *World Literature Today* 90, no. 6 (November/December 2016): 16–20.
30. Yazbek, *Planet of Clay*, 19.
31. Maya al-Hajj, 'Samar Yazbek Tarwi al-Harb al-Suriyya bi-Lisan Marbut', *Qantara.de*, https://ar.qantara.de/node/26828 (accessed 29 November 2020).
32. Yazbek, *Planet of Clay*, 13–14.
33. Yazbek, *Planet of Clay*, 65–6.
34. Al-Hajj, 'Samar Yazbek Tarwi'.

35. Mohja Kahf, 'The Silences of Contemporary Syrian Literature', *World Literature Today* 75, no. 2 (Spring 2001): 235.
36. Yazbek, *Planet of Clay*, 297.
37. Yazbek, *Planet of Clay*, 314.
38. Huda Barakat, *Malakut hathihi al-Ard* (Beirut: Dar al-Adab, 2012).
39. Huda Barakat, *Hajar al-Dahk* (London: Riad al-Rayyes, 1990); Huda Barakat, *The Stone of Laughter*, trans. Sophie Bennett (Northampton: Interlink Books, 1998).
40. Huda Barakat, *Harith al-Miyah* (Beirut: Dar al-Nahar, 1998); Huda Barakat, *The Tiller of Waters*, trans. Marilyn Booth (Cairo: American University in Cairo Press, 2004).
41. Rumaan Alam, 'Voices of the Lost', *4Columns*, https://4columns.org/alam-rumaan/voices-of-the-lost (accessed 29 November 2020).
42. Sanjana Varghese, 'Lebanese author Hoda Barakat wins International prize for Arabic fiction', *The Guardian*, 24 April 2019, https://www.theguardian.com/books/2019/apr/24/lebanese-author-hoda-barakat-wins-international-prize-for-arabic-fiction#:~:text=Lebanese%20author%20Hoda%20Barakat%20has,translate%20the%20book%20into%20English.
43. Hoda Barakat in Interview: Comments on Displacement from Hoda Barakat, 2019 Arabic Fiction Winner', *Publishing Perspectives*, https://publishingperspectives.com/2019/05/interview-comments-on-displacement-and-migration-from-hoda-barakat-2019-arabic-fiction-winner/ (accessed 29 November 2020).
44. Hoda Barakat, *Rasa'il al-Ghariba* (Beirut: Dar al-Nahar lil-Nashar, 2004).
45. Barakat, *Voices*, 48.
46. Barakat, *Voices*, 54.
47. Barakat, *Voices*, 54.
48. Barakat, *Voices*, 141.
49. Barakat, *Voices*, 144.
50. The collection was published with support of the British Institute for the Study of Iraq.
51. Hassan Blasim (ed.), *Iraq+100* (Manchester: Comma Press, 2016).
52. Basma Ghalayini (ed.), *Palestine+100* (Manchester: Comma Press, 2019).
53. Edward Said, 'The Anglo-Arab Encounter', *Reflections on Exile and Other Essays* (London: Granta, 2001), 405–10.
54. Ruth Abou Rached, 'Feminist Paratranslation as Literary Activism: Iraqi Writer-Activist Haifa Zangana in the Post-2003 US', in Olga Castro and

Emek Ergun (eds), *Feminist Translation Studies: Local and Transnational Perspectives* (London: Routledge, 2019).
55. Geoffrey P. Nash, 'Britain', in Waïl Hassan (ed.), *The Oxford Handbook of Arab Novelistic Traditions* (Oxford: Oxford University Press, 2017).
56. Said, 'The Anglo-Arab Encounter', 406.
57. Nash, 'Britain'.
58. Leila Aboulela, *The Translator* (New York: Grove Press, 1999).
59. Leila Aboulela, *Minaret* (London: Bloomsbury, 2005).
60. His 2006 debut novel, *In the Country of Men* (New York: Viking Press, 2006), was longlisted for the 2007 Man Booker Prize and won a host of awards, including the 2006 Arab American Book award. Written from a child's perspective it stages familial drama and life under the Gaddafi regime. His 2016 memoir *The Return: Fathers, Sons, and the Land in Between* (Toronto: Knopf Canada, 2016) about his search for his disappeared father won a Pulitzer Prize and a Pen America award in 2017, and his 2011 novel *Anatomy of a Disappearance* (New York: Viking Press, 2011) is a fictional account of the disappearance of a dissident father.
61. 'Syria', *Royal Court Theatre*, https://royalcourttheatre.com/whats-on/syria/ (accessed 29 November 2020).
62. I saw this play in an online streaming format offered through the Shubbak festival due to 2021 COVID-restrictions.
63. AlAmmar, *Silence*, 141.
64. AlAmmar, *Silence*, 147.
65. AlAmmar, *Silence*, 181.

Conclusion
Imagining Mobility

أثينة – يونان Athens – Greece

    The truck exited the parking lot of the Central Bank and started driving through the noisy streets of the city. We didn't know where we were or where it was taking us.

    We were stacked on top of one another in paper tubes that were piled up inside wooden boxes. When our paper wrapping was removed, we flowed like rushing water into one of several small bank drawers, where our journey ended. In the process, I collided head on with an old Euro coin and together, we created a ringing sound that transported me back to a recent memory: the moment in the coin factory when I entered life and uttered my first ringing sound, like the cry of a baby at the moment of birth.[1]

This is how Nadhir Zuʻbi's 2016 fantasy novel *Yuru* (Euro) begins, a novel that contains two consecutive narratives that take place in the same speculative world. The first narrative is written from the perspective of a Greek Euro coin named Euro and the second from the perspective of a young man who begins to consume metal, gradually turns into steel, and abandons his human relations to join the parallel society that Euro inhabits. In this first section of the novel, Euro (who is gendered male) recounts his earliest memories and awakening to awareness. Here, as elsewhere in the novel, the process of expanding his self-awareness unfolds in relation to the category of the human. In the section above, Euro likens the moment when he produces his first ringing sound to the sound of a new-born baby's cry. Similarities between the coins and humans abound; for instance, the capacity of voicing emotion and communicating histories, stories and ideas is as central to the lives of coins as it is to the humans around them. Indeed, storytelling is what the coins of the novel do as they gather in constantly changing group formations: in pockets, wallets, banks and vending machines. But Euro and his shifting coin communities also marvel at what sets humans apart from them. In this first chapter Euro recalls: 'I remember when I saw a human being run for the first time. I laughed really hard because I didn't understand what he was doing. However, with time, I learned that this was the way that humans roll.'[2] Euro returns to this question of human mobility with some frequency, often expressing envy that they seem to have more agency and choice over their movement and travel.

Yuru can be read as an extended experiment in defamiliarising human mobility, even an inventive approach to considering questions of forced migration. For instance, the first section quoted at the beginning of this conclusion bears a resemblance to narratives about human trafficking such as Hassan Blasim's short story 'Shahinat Berlin' ('The Truck to Berlin') discussed in Chapter 3. The coins crammed together in the truck share a condition of (im)mobility and disorientation within the secured money transport. The novel is haunted by references to contemporary forced migration at other junctures as well. For example, when Euro leaves Greece for the first time, travelling with a Bulgarian couple who had been vacationing in the coastal town Thessaloniki, he reflects on his time spent in the house of a fisherman living on the Aegean coast.

> How I longed for him to take me with him on one of his fishing trips so that I could see how fish are caught. But he never did … and maybe this was for the best. I had seen coins drown right in front of me after falling off the tourist boats that travel between the islands. When coins drown, it means that they will spend the rest of eternity scattered across the loneliness (*waḥsha*) of the ancient ocean floor, enveloped in salty water and complete darkness as rust and algae grow on their faces and edges. Have you ever seen just how terrifying this kind of drowning is?[3]

Is it possible to read this description of drowning in the Aegean and not think of the border crossings and many lives lost on these routes in recent years? The invocation of *waḥsha*, indicating both wilderness and loneliness – the longing that comes from separation from community – also links the novel *Yuru* to the literary explorations of wilderness in the migration literature explored in this book. The idea of coins drowning is of course a defamiliarising take on unfolding tragedies, but Euro the coin addresses the reader directly, asking them to consider how terrifying this kind of loss is, one that has direct parallels in our own world. Indeed, Euro frequently inserts such direct questions into his narrative, asking the reader to consider the world from his vantage point, often in reference to either terrifying or strange experiences. (In Bucharest, Romania: 'Have you ever tried being a tool in the hands of a magician?'[4] In Lyon, France: 'Have you ever imagined yourself dangling on a washing line on colourful plastic clothespins?'[5]) If Euro is constantly understanding his own existence through the category of the human, these recurring questions ask readers to put themselves in his position, or rather, to consider how the experiences we consider human are shaped by other categories, capacities and larger histories.

Yuru probes the relationship between border crossings, value and the boundaries of the human. On the one hand, the coins are forcibly displaced over and over again; they are swept up in the vicissitudes of commerce, chance, and the choices and mistakes that humans make. Their communities are forcefully dissolved each time they are spent, gifted or traded. Theirs is a kind of forced migration at the hands of humans, commerce and economies. Furthermore, as the novel explores the mutual interdependence of human and coin lives and affect, it simultaneously calls attention to key differences in mobility, raising the question of who can cross borders, how, and at what consequence. While Euro longs for choice and agency over his travels, it is also apparent that he enjoys a kind of mobility not available to many humans; Euro does not face border controls and retains relevance and value as he moves across borders (though at one point, he fears becoming irrelevant due to the Greek fiscal crisis that threatened the country's standing in the EU). The structure of the narrative attests to this preoccupation as each chapter is titled according to the location Euro finds himself in. The travel narrative of a coin, *Yuru* takes estrangement far along the spectrum of speculative worlds.

Should we consider *Yuru* part of the genre of literature of forced migration discussed in this book? To do so would be to define the parameters of the genre not in relation to the settings or perspectives of refugees and asylum seekers, or the normative bounds of citizenship (as I have suggested in this book) but rather around an extended narrative exploration and questioning of contemporary borders, displacement and mobility. Though this book has focused on literary narratives and plays that reimagine contemporary migration contexts that are well known, there is a case to be made for expanding the genre and our attention to the preoccupations and questions underlying conventional understandings and representations of forced and precarious migration.

In this book, I have identified defamiliarisation as a widely variable but shared tool of resistance to the violence of both the material and discursive realities of forced migration. The repurposing of common tropes, the use of speculative modes of writing, and the insistence on the artistic integrity of literature that explores precarious and forced migration all support a project of destabilising common language and discourses on borders and migration and point to the necessity of imagining mobility in novel ways.

On one level, defamiliarisation is a useful way to think about what literature and art do in general. But more than that, it is a tool whose discursive impact shifts when used within specific concepts and realities. In this book, I have drawn attention to a variety of defamiliarising modes in literature and hold that these techniques – though drawn from different genres – are an invitation to reimagine categories of borders and citizenship that underpin forced, precarious and irregular migration and that are often taken for granted or reified as inevitable aspects of global relationality. To see these categories from a distance or from a novel vantage point is also to find space for reflection and, perhaps, movement.

The previous chapters have considered multiple types of defamiliarisation. For one, there is the project of unsettling the tropes and language that are staples of media representations of forced migration and which often render the migrant as a victim, statistic, or even an invader or threat. This kind of flattening in media representations of migration (somewhat paradoxically) renders migrants simultaneously hypervisible and invisible, both as threats and as voiceless victims. Through such means, literary narratives resist the idea that art about migration should provide direct testimony and explain the causes and effects of migration that neatly complement discourses that are already circulating. Instead, these narratives ask us to consider how art can disrupt and reimagine the very categories on which such discourses are built. Some literary renderings and performances avoid representation of precarious migratory routes altogether. Instead, they invite readers and audiences to delve deeply into the subjectivity of their characters and themselves (as readers/audience members) and to consider their own desires and choices in fashioning new, perhaps yet unformulated, responses and imaginings of mobility, ones that do not rely on binaries that assume clear demarcations between Europe and the Middle East, audience/reader and refugee. By doing so, they invite diverse audiences to grapple with their own preconceived notions of what they expect from a performance or literary narrative and, in dialogue with these art forms, perhaps create shifts in perception.

Defamiliarising modes of writing and the speculative worlds in some literary narratives of forced migration create space for perceiving categories of mobility and migration differently. For example, many of the texts discussed in the book defamiliarise the category of citizenship and collapse the boundary between exile literature and refugee literature. The literature's insistence on individual stories within an evocation of the larger contexts that regulate belonging (by producing citizenship as well as precarity and illegality) are part of an effort to write the transindividual and also to collapse the boundaries between exile literature and refugee literature in a literature of forced and precarious migration. The defamiliarising modes in the Arabic migration literature discussed here are participating in a broader call for taking nonrealist perspectives seriously, one that goes beyond the realm of Arabic literature and Arabic literary studies per se. For instance, Judith Butler's recent reflection on nonviolence (*The Force of Nonviolence*) asserts the need for a counter-realism in this moment:

> In response to the objection that a position in favour of nonviolence is simply unrealistic, this argument maintains that nonviolence requires a critique of what counts as reality, and it affirms the power and necessity

of counter-realism in times like these. Perhaps nonviolence requires a certain leave-taking from reality as it is currently constituted, laying open the possibilities that belong to a newer political imaginary.[6]

The departures from realism in the literature of migration discussed in this book cannot be boiled down to a counter-realism that opens up visions for more just worlds (however important it is as a resource for political imagining). The speculative worlds in Arabic literature of forced and precarious migration are frequently infused with violence and anxiety, exploring liminal spaces and the violence that those living in borderlands or spaces outside of citizenship are more exposed to. However, as argued in the book, defamiliarising modes of writing can destabilise some of the highly contingent 'truths' that dominant understandings of citizenship, mobility and borders are constructed through (the defence of which are often anchored in politics that claim realism). The turn to the speculative in this moment, even its more dystopian strains, is one way to both create and invite more expansive imaginings of mobility and a sense of how our current understandings of it are highly contingent and subject to change.

Furthermore, the question about what constitutes nonrealism has much to do with perspective. While the idea of a cognisant and verbal coin in *Yuru*, for example, is a departure from what is real or plausible, it calls attention to the very present way that human mobility and migration are conceived against and in relation to capital and information. Literary realism is, historically and in the present, linked to how the nation is imagined and narrated. Alexandra Chreiteh has argued that magical realism in Arabic literature has created space for minoritised languages and belongings against the dominance of literary realism within twentieth-century nation-based political and literary discourses. Similarly, speculative and defamiliarising modes of writing in migration literature have created imaginative possibilities within the very spaces outside of citizenship that are so often *not* imagined in political and social discourse.

Though it is nothing new, our sense of both individually and collectively inhabiting vulnerable and porous bodies has been heightened in the past year and a half of living in a global pandemic, creating shifts in perspectives. Our being what Rosi Braidotti calls 'posthuman subjects of knowledge', 'embedded, embodied and yet flowing in a web of relations with human and non-human others'[7] has been particularly palpable and apparent during this time. In addition to the ways that our collective being is predicated on the porousness and interconnectedness of our bodies, we have been called to see ourselves from the perspective of a virus. From this perspective, we are less sovereign subjects than we are hosts that move, carry, transmit and experience infection. However, even as a sense (and reality) of a shared vulnerability is heightened, vulnerability is unequally distributed along familiar lines. Globally, unequal public health and capacities of medical systems create increased risk for some. Incarcerated individuals have been subject to increased exposure to infection and death. Border detention camps in Greece and on the US-Mexico border as well as refugee camps are particularly vulnerable because of the restricted mobility and close living quarters within them. What could calls to stay 'home' mean to the many who are displaced or confined in migrant camps? The pandemic and its responses have heightened both existing precarity of those living in borderlands and the contingency of borders and their meanings. In the context of a pandemic, our experience of choice and narratives of self have been refigured not in terms of individual impact but within a macro-logic of local and global spread and curves. This kind of transindividual perception is distinct from the Arabic literary explorations of migration and borderlands explored in this book yet there is a shared concern about opening the borders of the sovereign self and nation and instead an openness to how the individual and collective intersect, each irreducible to the other.

In the migration literature explored in this book, the way that vulnerability and the transindividual are expressed is also linked to literary genre. The form of the novel, and emergence of 'world literature', is, as Joseph Slaughter has argued, closely linked to the development of the human rights discourses in the twentieth century.[8] The narrative arc of individual becoming most strongly associated with the *Bildungsroman*, Slaughter argues, performed the cultural work of naturalising human rights, particularly the premises of individual human rights tied to citizenship emphasised in the United Nations Declaration of Human Rights. In a similar way, the tension between exile and refugee literature discussed in this book parallels the tension between international migration law, where proving individual persecution is the key to making effective asylum cases, and the parallel knowledge that migration and displacement affect many at once and are caused by forces that far exceed the individual. As argued throughout this book, contemporary Arabic literature of forced migration collapses some of the binaries that pit the singular and artistic qualities of exile literature against the testimonial expectation and 'mass politics'[9] attendant on refugee writing. Instead of upholding this binary, the transindividual perspectives emphasised in the book reimagine the individual within the flow of mass politics and migration and write the borderland spaces of forced and precarious migration. But like the *Bildungsroman*'s plot of becoming a rights-endowed citizen, focus on the transindividual zooms out to the mobile individual and collective and the way that the construction of borders and citizenship comes to define both. The speculative and imaginative qualities of the modes of writing explored in the book intensify our perception of the way that these categories are constructed, and how they could be otherwise. Fiction, here, creates new narratives, and ways of thinking, about borders and citizenship.

As a final note, a few years ago, a blog on teaching literature caught my eye and its implications have remained with me. Matthew Salesses writes,

> We don't want to simply be. We don't want to let ourselves be overtaken by cultural production, be defined by other people's stories. We want to tell stories because we want to become. To accept the status quo, to read or tell a story uncritically, is a kind of death.[10]

Indeed, the stakes of creating different systems of mobility in this moment are no less than life and death. But the potential to make mobility safer and more equitable is also anchored in the imaginative capacity to create other narratives, other ways of becoming. While the migration literature discussed here is by no means prescriptive, it calls attention to the borders that make and unmake belongings, defamiliarises them, and invites a curiosity to see the familiar anew.

Notes

1. Nadhir Zuʻbi, *Yuru* (Beirut: Al-Dar al-ʻArabiyya lil-ʻUlum Nashirun, 2016), 11.
2. Zuʻbi, *Yuru*, 12.
3. Zuʻbi, *Yuru*, 19–20.
4. Zuʻbi, *Yuru*, 53.
5. Zuʻbi, *Yuru*, 81.
6. Judith Butler, 'Judith Butler on the Case for Nonviolence', *Literary Hub*, 18 February 2020, https://lithub.com/judith-butler-on-the-case-for-nonviolence/.
7. Rosi Braidotti, 'A Theoretical Framework for the Critical Posthumanities', *Theory, Culture and Society* 36, no. 6 (2019): 34.
8. Joseph Slaughter, *Human Rights Inc.: The World Novel, Narrative Form, and International Law* (New York: Fordham University Press, 2007).
9. Edward Said, *Reflections on Exile and Other Essays* (London: Granta, 2001): 176.
10. Matthew Salesses, 'CW Workshop and Trump: 7 Things I Teach (Salesses)', *Pleiades Literature in Context*, http://www.pleiadesmag.com/cw-workshop-trump-7-things-i-teach-salesses/ (accessed 14 April 2020).

References

Abbas, Rasha, *Adam Yakrah al-Talifiziyun* (Damascus: Al-Amana al-ʿAmma li-Ihtifaliyat Dimashq ʿAsimat al-thaqafa, 2008).

——, *Die Erfindung der deutschen Grammatik: Geschichten*, trans. Sandra Hetzl (Berlin: Mikrotext, 2016).

——, 'How Political Can We Get While Writing?', *Schloss Post*, 20 October 2016, https://schloss-post.com/political-get-writing/.

——, Interview (unpublished) with Johanna Sellman, Berlin, Germany, 13 August 2018.

——, *Kayfa Tamma Ikhtiraʿ al-Lugha al-Almaniyya* (Beirut: Heinrich Boll Stiftung, 2016).

——, *Mulakhkhas Ma Jara* (Milan: Manshurat al-Mutawassit, 2018).

ʿAbd alʿAl, ʿAli, *Aqmar ʿIraqiyya Sawdaʾ fi al-Suwayd* (Damascus: Dar al-Mada, 2004).

Abderrezak, Hakim, *Ex-Centric Migrations: Europe and the Maghreb in Mediterranean Cinema, Literature, and Music* (Bloomington: Indiana University Press, 2016).

——, 'The Refugee Crisis and the Mediterranean "Seamentary"', Lecture at the Ohio State University, Columbus, OH, 2 November 2018.

Abou Laban, Mohammad, Ziad Adwan and Mario Münster (eds), *A Syrious Look: Syrians in Germany, a Magazine about Culture in Exile* (2016).

Aboulela, Leila, *Minaret* (London: Bloomsbury, 2005).

——, *The Translator* (New York: Grove Press, 1999).

Abou Rached, Ruth, 'Feminist Paratranslation as Literary Activism: Iraqi Writer-Activist Haifa Zangana in the Post-2003 US', in Olga Castro and Emek Ergun (eds), *Feminist Translation Studies: Local and Transnational Perspectives* (London: Routledge, 2019).

Adwan, Ziad, *Please, Repeat After Me*, unpublished play script.
Agamben, Giorgio, *Homo Sacer: Sovereign Power and Bare Life*, trans. Daniel Heller-Roazen (Stanford: Stanford University Press, 1998).
Agier, Michel, *Borderlands*, trans. David Fernbach (Cambridge: Polity Press, 2016).
Ahmad, Ibrahim, 'Lajiʾ ʿind al-Iskimu', *Baʿd Majiʿ al-Tayr: Qisas min al-Manfa* (Budapest: Saḥārī, 1994).
——, 'The Arctic Refugee', in Shakir Mustafa (ed. and trans.), *Contemporary Iraqi Fiction: An Anthology* (Syracuse: Syracuse University Press, 2008).
Alam, Rumaan, 'Voices of the Lost', *4Columns*, https://4columns.org/alam-rumaan/voices-of-the-lost.
AlAmmar, Layla, *Silence is a Sense* (Chapel Hill: Algonquin Books, 2021).
Ali, Amro, 'On the Need to Shape the Arab Exile Body in Berlin', *Alsharq Blog* (now *dis:orient*), 25 January 2019, https://www.disorient.de/blog/need-shape-arab-exile-body-berlin.
Andalzúa, Gloria, *Borderlands/La Frontera: The New Mestiza* (San Francisco: Aunt Lute Books, 1987).
Apter, Emily, *The Translation Zone: A New Comparative Literature* (Princeton: Princeton University Press, 2006).
'Arab Writers – Going Global: Hoda Barakat, Jokha alHarthi & Marilyn Booth', *YouTube*, https://www.youtube.com/watch?v=4rDudm1usE4.
Arendt, Hannah, *The Origins of Totalitarianism* (New York: Harcourt, Brace and Co., 1951).
——, 'We Refugees', in Marc Robinson (ed.), *Altogether Elsewhere: Writers on Exile* (Winchester: Faber and Faber, 1994).
El-Ariss, Tarek, 'Hacking the Modern: Arabic Writing in the Virtual Age', *Comparative Literature Studies* 47, no. 4 (2010): 533–48.
——, 'Return of the Beast: From Pre-Islamic Ode to Contemporary Novel', *Journal of Arabic Literature* 47, no. 1–2 (2016): 90.
——, *Trials of Arab Modernity: Literary Affects and the New Political* (New York: Fordham University Press, 2013).
Bahoora, Haytham, 'Writing the Dismembered Nation: The Aesthetics of Horror in Iraqi Narratives of War', *Arab Studies Journal* 23, no. 1 (2015).
Balibar, Etienne, 'At the Borders of Citizenship: A Democracy in Translation?', *European Journal of Social Theory* 13, no. 3 (2010): 315–22.

Barakat, Hoda, *Barid al-Layl* (Beirut: Dar al-Adab, 2017).

——, *Malakut hathihi al-Ard* (Beirut: Dar al-Adab, 2012).

——, *Rasa'il al-Ghariba* (Beirut: Dar al-Nahar lil-Nashar, 2004).

——, *Voices of the Lost*, trans. Marilyn Booth (New Haven: Yale University Press, 2021).

Barakeh, Khaled, 'The Role of Cultural Organizations', talk at the *'Beyond Trauma' Conference*, Berlin, Germany, 13 June 2019.

Barghouthi, Hussein, *Al-Daw al-Azraq* (Jerusalem: Bayt al-Maqdis li-l-Nashr wa- l-al-Tawzi', 2001).

——, *Al-Difa al-Thalitha li-Nahr al-Urdun: Riwaya* (Jersulalem: Dar al-Katib, 1984).

'Baynatna, The Arabic Library in Berlin', *Baynatna*, http://www.baynatna.de (accessed 11 April 2020).

Bell, Anna, and Karim Mattar, *The Edinburgh Companion to the Postcolonial Middle East* (Edinburgh: Edinburgh University Press, 2018).

Bhungalia, Lisa, 'Elastic Sovereignty: A Global Geography of US Terrorism Law', Yi-Fu Tuan Lecture Series Talk, Department of Geography, University of Wisconsin-Madison, WI, February 2018.

Binebine, Mahi, *Cannibales* (Paris: Fayard, 1999).

——, *Welcome to Paradise*, trans. Lulu Norman (London: Granta Books, 2003).

Blanchard, Rebecca, 'Carceral States in Kaoutar Harchi's *Zone Cinglée*', *Romance Studies* 36, no. 1–2 (2018): 63–75.

Blasim, Hassan, 'In Conversation with Hassan Blasim', *Finnish Institute*, http://www.finnish-institute.org.uk/en/articles/1511-in-conversation-with-hassan-blasim.

——, 'Hassan Blasim', interview by Margaret Litvin and Johanna Sellman, *Tank Magazine* 8, no. 9 (2016), 238.

—— (ed.), *Iraq+100* (Manchester: Comma Press, 2016).

——, *The Iraqi Christ*, trans. Jonathan Wright (Manchester: Comma Press, 2009).

——, *Lu'bat al-Qubba'at al-Raqamiyya* (trans. Jonathan Wright as *The Digital Hats Game*) (unpublished script).

——, *The Madman of Freedom Square*, trans. Jonathan Wright (Manchester: Comma Press, 2009).

——, *Majnun Sahat al-Huriyya* (Beirut: al-Mu'assasa al-'Arabiyya lil-Dirasat wa-l-Nashr, 2012).

Bothor, Mathias, *et al.*, *Weg sein – hier sein: Texte aus Deutschland* [Being away: Being here: texts from Germany] (Zürich: Zürich Secession Verlag für Literatur, 2016).

Braidotti, Rosi, *The Posthuman* (Malden: Polity Press, 2013).

——, 'A Theoretical Framework for the Critical Posthumanities', *Theory, Culture & Society* 36, no. 6 (2019): 31–61.

——, *Transpositions: On Nomadic Ethics* (Cambridge: Polity Press, 2006).

Brandzel, Amy L., *Against Citizenship: The Violence of the Normative* (Champaign: University of Illinois Press, 2016).

Brecht, Berthold, 'On Chinese Acting', trans. Eric Bentley, *The Tulane Drama Review* 6, no. 1 (September 1961): 130–6.

Bunz, Mercedes, Birgit Mara Kaiser and Kathrin Thiele (eds), *Symptoms of the Planetary Condition: A Critical Vocabulary* (Lüneburg: Meson Press, 2017).

Butler, Judith, *Frames of War: When is Life Grievable* (New York: Verso Books, 2010).

——, 'Judith Butler on the Case for Nonviolence', *Literary Hub*, 18 February 2020, https://lithub.com/judith-butler-on-the-case-for-nonviolence/.

——, *Notes toward a Performative Theory of Assembly* (Cambridge, MA: Harvard University Press, 2015).

'Capital of Culture', *BBC News Arabic*, Berlin, *YouTube* video, 52:25, 21 May 2018, https://www.youtube.com/watch?v=WInKH0uv0K8.

Casanova, Pascale, *The World Republic of Letters*, trans. Malcolm Debevoise (Cambridge, MA: Harvard University Press, 2007).

Castells, Manuel, *Networks of Outrage and Hope: Social Movements in the Internet Age* (Cambridge: Polity Press, 2012).

Castles, Stephen, and Mark J. Miller, *The Age of Migration*, 4th edn (New York: Palgrave Macmillan, 2009).

Chamberlain, Lori, 'Gender and the Metaphorics of Translation', *Signs* 13, no. 3 (1988): 454–72.

Chreiteh, Alexandra, 'Fantastic Cohabitations: Magical Realism in Arabic and Hebrew and the Politics of Aesthetics', PhD dissertation, Yale University, 2016.

'Co-Culture: the Hub of Cultural Growth', *Co-Culture*, https://coculture.de/index.html (accessed 12 April 2020).

Deckard, Sharae, *Paradise Discourse, Imperialism, and Globalization* (New York: Routledge, 2010).

Dibo, Muhammad, 'Ziad Adwan: No Deeper Shock than that of Syrians', *Syria Untold*, 7 August 2018, https://syriauntold.com/2018/08/07/ziad-adwan-no-deeper-shock-than-that-of-syrians/.

El-Enany, Rasheed, *Arab Representations of the Occident: East–West Encounters in Arabic Fiction* (London: Routledge, 2006).

Fadel, Youssef, *Hashish* (Casablanca: Dar al-Fanak, 2000).

Faist, Thomas, 'Diaspora and Transnationalism: What Kind of Dance Partners', in Rainer Baubröck and Thomas Faist (eds), *Diaspora and Transnationalism: Concepts, Theories and Methods* (Amsterdam: Amsterdam University Press, 2010).

Fayyad, Sulayman, *Voices*, trans. Hosam Abou-Ela (New York: Marion Boyars, 1993).

Fiddian-Qasmiyeh, Elena, 'Disrupting Humanitarian Narratives: Reflections from the Refugee Hosts Project', paper presented at *Refugee Hosts International Conference: Without Execution – the Politics and Poetics of Local Responses to Displacement*, University College London, 24–25 October 2019, https://www.youtube.com/watch?v=XflyWu7kVqs&feature=emb_logo.

Fiore, Teresa, 'From Crisis to Creative Critique: The Early Twenty-First Century Mediterranean Crossing on Stage and Screen in Works by Teatro delle Albe and Andrea Segre', *Journal of Modern Italian Studies* 23, no. 4 (2018): 522–42.

Firat, Alexa, 'Cultural Battles on the Literary Field: From the Syrian Writers' Collective to the Last Days of Socialist Realism in Syria', *Middle Eastern Literatures* 18, no. 2 (2015): 153–76.

'France: North Africans', *Minority Rights*, https://minorityrights.org/minorities/north-africans/.

'The Future Now: 10 African Artists to Watch', *ARTnews*, http://www.artnews.com/2018/07/18/future-now-10-african-artists-watch/ (accessed 29 November 2020).

Ghalayini, Basma (ed.), *Palestine+100* (Manchester: Comma Press, 2019).

Ghanim, Fathi, *Al-Sakhin wa-l-Barid* (Cairo: Dar al-Jumhuriyya li-l-Sihafa, 1960).

Greenslade, R, *Seeking Scapegoats: The Coverage of Asylum in the UK Press* (London: Institute for Public Policy Research, 2005).

Guthrie, Alice, 'The Gist of It: Short Stories by Rasha Abbas: Reader's Report by Alice Guthrie', *English Pen*, https://www.englishpen.org/wp-content/uploads/2012/04/The-Gist-of-It-Short-Stories-by-Rasha-Abbas-Readers-Report-by-Alice-Guthrie.pdf (accessed 12 April 2020).

Al-Hajj, Maya, 'Samar Yazbek Tarwi al-Harb al-Suriyya bi-Lisan Marbut', *Qantara.de*, https://ar.qantara.de/node/26828.

Al-Hakim, Tawfiq, *'Usfur Min al-Sharq* (Cairo: Dar al-Sharq, 1938).

Halabi, Zeina, *The Unmaking of the Arab Intellectual: Prophecy Exile and the Nation* (Edinburgh: Edinburgh University Press, 2017).

Handke, Peter, *Publikumsbeschimpfung und andere Sprechstücke* (Frankfurt am Main: Suhrkamp, 1966).

Hanoosh, Yasmine, 'Beyond the Trauma of War: Iraqi Literature Today', *Words Without Borders*, https://www.wordswithoutborders.org/article/beyond-the-trauma-of-war-iraqi-literature-today.

——, 'Unnatural Narratives and Transgressing the Normative Discourses of Iraqi History: Translating Murtada Gzar's Al-Sayyid Asghar Akbar', *Journal of Arabic Literature* 44 (January 2013): 145–80.

Haqqi, Yahya, *The Lamp of Umm Hashim and Other Stories*, trans. Denys Johnson-Davies (Cairo: American University of Cairo Press, 2004).

——, *Qandil Umm Hashim* (Cairo: Dar al-Ma'arif, 1944).

Harchi, Kaoutar, *Zone cinglée* (Paris: Editions Sarbacane, 2009).

Hargraves, Alec, 'Beur Fiction: Voices from the Immigrant Community in France', *The French Review* 62, no. 4 (1989): 661–8.

Harlow, Barbara, in Ferial Jabouri Ghazoul and Barbara Harlow (eds), *The View from Within: Writers and Critics on Contemporary Arabic Literature* (Cairo: AUC Press, 1994).

Hassan, Waïl S., *Immigrant Narratives: Orientalism and Cultural Translation in Arab American and Arab British Literature* (Oxford: Oxford University Press, 2011).

——, 'Postcolonial Theory and Modern Arabic Literature: Horizons of Application', *Journal of Arabic Literature* 33, no. 1 (2002): 45–64.

——, 'Postcolonialism and Modern Arabic Literature: Twenty-First Century Horizons', *Interventions: The International Journal of Postcolonial Studies* 20, no. 2 (2018): 157–73.

——, *Tayeb Salih: Ideology and the Craft of Fiction* (Syracuse: Syracuse University Press, 2003).

Hedetoft, Ulf, *The Global Turn: National Encounters with the World* (Aarhus: Aalborg University Press, 2003), 146.

Idriss, Yusuf, 'Al-Sayyida Fiyinna', in *Al-'Askari al-Aswad wa Qisas Ukhra* (Cairo: Dar al-M'arifa, 1962).

Inghilleri, Moira, *Translation and Migration* (New York: Routledge, 2017).

Iraq Body Count, https://www.iraqbodycount.org/.

Kahf, Mohja, 'The Silences of Contemporary Syrian Literature', *World Literature Today* 75, no. 2 (Spring 2001).

Kanafani, Ghassan, *Men in the Sun and Other Palestinian Stories*, trans. Hillary Kirpatrick (Boulder: Lynne Rienner Publishers, 1999).

Kareem, Mona, 'To Translate Octavia Butler: Race, History, and Sci-Fi', Online Lecture, Princeton Institute for International and Regional Studies, 7 December 2020.

'Key Migration Terms', *International Organization for Migration (IOM)*, https://www.iom.int/key-migration-terms (accessed 21 October 2018).

Khaal, Abu Bakr, *African Titanics*, trans. Charis Bredin (London: Darf Publishers, 2014).

——, *Taytanikat Ifriqiyya: Riwaya* (Beirut: Dar al-Saqi, 2008).

Khemiri, Jonas Hassen, *Ett öga rött* (Stockholm: Norstedts, 2003).

——, *Invasion!*, trans. Rachel Wilson Broyles (New York: Samuel French, 2013).

Khider, Abbas, *Deutsch für alle: Das endgültige Lehrbuch* (Munich: Carl Hanser Verlag, 2019).

——, *The Village Indian*, trans. Donal McLaughlin (New York: Seagull Books, 2013).

Litvin, Margaret, 'Syrian Theatre in Berlin', *Theatre Journal* 70, no. 4 (January 2018): 447–8.

Litvin, Margaret, and Johanna Sellman, 'An Icy Heaven: Arab Migration on Nordic Stages', *Theatre Research International* 34, no. 1 (2018): 45–62.

Löytti, Olli, 'Follow the Translations! The Translational Circulation of Hassan Blasim's Short Stories', in Heidi Grönstrand, Markus Huss and Ralf Kauranen (eds), *The Aesthetics and Politics of Linguistic Borders: Multilingualism in Northern European Literature* (New York: Routledge, 2019): 27–47.

Malkki, L. H., 'Refugees and Exile: From "Refugee Studies" to the National Order of Things', *Annual Review of Anthropology* 24 (1995): 495–523.

Malm, Sara, 'Arabic Overtakes Finnish to Become the Second Most Common Language in Sweden after Migrant Influx', *Daily Mail*, 7 April 2016, http://www.dailymail.co.uk/news/article-3528381/Arabic-overtakes-Finnish-second-common-language-Sweden-migrant-influx.html (accessed 25 April 2018).

Masmoudi, Ikram, *War and Occupation in Iraqi Fiction* (Edinburgh: Edinburgh University Press, 2015).

Matar, Hisham, *Anatomy of a Disappearance* (New York: Viking Press, 2011).

——, *In the Country of Men* (New York: Viking Press, 2006).

——, *The Return: Fathers, Sons, and the Land in Between* (Toronto: Knopf Canada, 2016).

Mignolo, Walter D., and Madina V. Tlostanova, 'Theorizing from the Borders: Shifting to Geo- and Body-Politics of Knowledge', *European Journal of Social Theory* 9, no. 2 (2006): 205–21.

Minah, Hanna, *Al-Rabiʿ wa-l-Kharif*, 2nd edn (Beirut: Dar al-Adab, 1986).

Miyoshi, Masao, 'Turn to the Planet: Literature, Diversity, and Totality', *Comparative Literature* 53, no. 4 (2001): 283–97.

Moraru, Christian, '"World", "Globe", "Planet": Comparative Literature, Planetary Studies, and Cultural Debt after the "Global Turn"', *ACLA State of the Discipline Report*, 2015, https://stateofthediscipline.acla.org/entry/%E2%80%9Cworld%E2%80%9D-%E2%80%9Cglobe%E2%80%9D-%E2%80%9Cplanet%E2%80%9D-comparative-literature-planetary-studies-and-cultural-debt-after (accessed 25 June 2018).

Morén, Jonathan, 'Inverting the Stranger: Salīm Barakāt in the Land of the Living Dead', in *Arabic Literature in a Posthuman World: Proceedings of the 12th Conference of the European Association for Modern Arabic Literature (EURAMAL), May 2016, Oslo* (Wiesbaden: Harrassowitz, 2019), 119–27.

Al-Mousawi, Nahrain, *The Two-Edged Sea: Heterotopias of Contemporary Mediterranean Migrant Literature* (Piscataway: Gorgias Press, 2021).

El Moussaoui, Naima, 'The Refrain of a Shadowy Existence', *Qantara.de*, 21 September 2007, http://en.qantara.de/The-Refrain-of-a-Shadowy-Existence/8893c8969i1p507/.

Al-Nadawi, Hawra, 'Interview with Hawra al-Nadawi, the only woman on the IPAF longlist', *The Tanjara*, 26 November 2011, http://thetanjara.blogspot.co.uk/2011/11/interview-with-hawra-al-nadawi-only.html.

——, *Tahta Samaʾ Kubinhaghin* (Beirut: Dar al-Saqi, 2016).

Nash, Geoffrey P., 'Britain', in Waïl Hassan (ed.), *The Oxford Handbook of Arab Novelistic Traditions* (Oxford: Oxford University Press, 2017).

Nutall, Sarah, *Entanglement: Literary and Cultural Reflections on Post-Apartheid* (Johannesburg: Wits University Press, 2009).

Nyers, Peter, *Rethinking Refugees: Beyond States of Emergency* (New York: Routledge, 2006).

Papa, Stephanie, '"The Most Important Way to Love and Peace is Justice": A Conversation with Samar Yazbek', trans. Emma Suleiman, *World Literature Today* 90, no. 6 (November/December 2016): 16–20.

Paynter, Eleanor, 'Autobiographical Docudrama as Testimony: Jonas Carpignano's *Mediterranea*', *Auto/Biography Studies* 32, no. 3 (2017): 659–66.

——, 'The Liminal Lives of Europe's Transit Migrants', *Contexts* 17, no. 2 (2018): 40–5.

Pireddu, Nicoletta, 'A Moroccan Tale of Outlandish Europe: Ben Jelloun's Departures for a Double Exile', *Research in African Literatures* 40, no. 3 (2009): 29.

'Please, Repeat after Me', *English Theatre Berlin*, https://www.etberlin.de/production/please-repeat-after-me/ (accessed 29 December 2019).

Pratt, Mary Louise, 'Harm's Way: Language and the Contemporary Arts of War', *PMLA: Publications of the Modern Language Association of America* 124, no. 5 (2009): 1515–31.

Raizen, Michal, 'Hebrew-Arabic Translational Communities and the Recuperation of Arab-Jewish Literary Memory', *Dibur* 8 (Spring 2020): 29–42.

Ramsey-Kurz, Helga, and Geetha Ganapathy-Doré, 'Introduction: Some Uses of Paradise', in Helga Ramsey-Kurz and Geetha Ganapathy-Doré (eds), *Projections of Paradise: Ideal Elsewheres in Postcolonial Migrant Literature* (Amsterdam: Rodopi, 2011).

Reeck, Laura, 'France', in Waïl Hassan (ed.), *The Oxford Handbook of Arab Novelistic Traditions* (Oxford, Oxford University Press, 2017).

Roseneil, Sasha, *Beyond Citizenship?: Feminism and the Transformation of Belonging* (London: Palgrave Macmillan, 2003).

Said, Edward, 'The Anglo-Arab Encounter', in Edward Said, *Reflections on Exile and Other Essays* (London: Granta, 2001): 405–10.

——, *Orientalism* (New York: Pantheon, 1978).

——, *Reflections on Exile and Other Essays* (Cambridge, MA: Harvard University Press, 2002).

Sakr, Rita, 'The More-than-human Refugee Journey: Hassan Blasim's Short Stories', *Journal of Postcolonial Writing* 54, no. 6 (2018): 766–80.

Salesses, Matthew, 'CW Workshop and Trump: 7 Things I Teach (Salesses)', *Pleiades Literature in Context*, http://www.pleiadesmag.com/cw-workshop-trump-7-things-i-teach-salesses/ (accessed 14 April 2020).

Salih, Tayeb, *Season of Migration to the North*, trans. Denys Johnson-Davies (New York: New York Review Books Classics, 2009).

Al-Samman, Hanadi, *Anxiety of Erasure: Trauma, Authorship, and the Diaspora in Arab Women's Writing* (Syracuse: Syracuse University Press, 2015).

Sellman, Johanna, 'The Ghosts of Exilic Belongings: Maḥmūd al-Bayyātī's *Raqs ʿalā Al-Māʾ: Aḥlām Waʿrah* and Post-Soviet Themes in Arabic Exile Literature', *Journal of Arabic Literature* 47, no. 1–2 (2016): 111–37.

Al-Shaykh, Hanan, *Only in London*, trans. Catherine Cobham (New York: Anchor Books, 2002).

'Shermin Langhoff', *Gorki*, https://gorki.de/en/company/shermin-langhoff (accessed 11 April 2020).

Shklovsky, Viktor, 'Art as Device', trans. Benjamin Sher, in Viktor Shklovsky, *The Theory of Prose* (Bloomington: Dalkey Archive Press, 1991).

Siebers, Tobin, *Disability Theory* (Ann Arbor: University of Michigan Press, 2008).

Skif, Hamed, *La géographie du danger* (Paris: Editions Naïve, 2006).

Slade, Christina, *Watching Arabic Television in Europe: From Diaspora to Hybrid Citizens* (Basingstoke: Palgrave Macmillan, 2014).

Slaughter, Joseph, *Human Rights Inc.: The World Novel, Narrative Form, and International Law* (New York: Fordham University Press, 2007).

Squire, Vicki, 'Researching Precarious Migrations: Qualitative Strategies Towards a Positive Transformation of the Politics of Migration', *The British Journal of Politics and International Relations* 20, no. 2 (2018): 441–58.

Stan, Corina, 'Novels in the Translation Zone: Abbas Khider, *Weltliteratur*, and the Ethics of the Passerby', *Comparative Literature Studies* 55, no. 2 (2018): 292.

Statistics Finland, https://www.stat.fi/til/muutl/2018/muutl_2018_2019-06-17_tie_001_en.html (accessed 4 February 2020).

Suvin, Darko, *Metamorphoses of Science Fiction: On the Poetics and History of a Literary Genre* (New Haven: Yale University Press, 1978).

'Syria', *Royal Court Theatre*, https://royalcourttheatre.com/whats-on/syria/.

'Syrian Biennale: Roots En Route', *Co-Culture*, https://coculture.de/syrian-biennale.html (accessed 12 April 2020).

Tahir, Bahaʾ, *Al-Ḥubb fī al-manfa* (Cairo: Dar al-Hilal, 1995).

Thiele, Kathrin, 'Entanglement', in Mercedes Bunz, Birgit Mara Kaiser and Kathrin Thiele (eds), *Symptoms of the Planetary Condition: A Critical Vocabulary* (Lüneburg: Meson Press, 2017).

Tuan, Yi-Fu, *Place and Place, the Perspective of Experience* (Minneapolis: University of Minnesota Press, 2011).

Turner, Victor, *From Ritual to Theatre: The Human Seriousness of Play* (New York: PAJ Publications, 1982).

Varghese, Sanjana, 'Lebanese Author Hoda Barakat Wins International Prize for Arabic Fiction', *The Guardian*, 24 April 2019, https://www.theguardian.com/books/2019/apr/24/lebanese-author-hoda-barakat-wins-international-prize-for-arabic-fiction#:~:text=Lebanese%20author%20Hoda%20Barakat%20has,translate%20the%20book%20into%20English.

Wanner, Adrian, 'Moving Beyond the Russian-American Ghetto: The Fiction of Keith Gessen and Michael Idov', *Russian Review* 73, no. 2 (April 2014): 281–96.

Wannous, Saadallah, 'On World Theater Day, the 1996 Message from Saadallah Wannous', *ArabLit Quarterly*, 23 March 2013, https://arablit.org/2013/03/27/on-world-theater-day-the-1996-message-from-saadallah-wannous/.

West-Pavlov, Russell, 'The Fictions of Clandestinity: Dream and Reality in Ben Jelloun and Skif', *Australian Journal of French Studies* 45, no. 2 (2008): 164–78.

Wilson, Janet, 'Novels of Flight and Arrival: Abu Bakr Khaal, *African Titanics* (2014 [2008]) and Sunjeev Sahota, *The Year of the Runaways* (2015)', *Postcolonial Text* 12, no. 3/4 (2017): 13.

Wright, Terrence, 'The Media and Representations of Refugees and Other Forced Migrants', in Elena Fiddian-Qasmiyeh, Gil Loescher, Katy Long and Nando Sigona (eds), *The Oxford Handbook of Refugee and Forced Migration Studies* (Oxford: Oxford University Press, 2016): 463.

Yazbek, Samar, *Al-Masha'a* (Beirut: Dar al-Adab, 2017).

——, *The Crossing: My Journey to the Shattered Heart of Syria*, trans. Nashwa Gowanlock and Ruth Ahmedzai Kemp (London: Rider Books, 2015).

——, *Planet of Clay*, trans. Leri Price (London: World Editions, 2021).

——, *Taqaṭuʿ Niran: min Yawmiyat al-Intifāḍa al-Suriyya* (Beirut: Dar al-Adab, 2012).

——, *A Woman in the Crossfire: Diaries of the Syrian Revolution*, trans. Max Weiss (London: Haus Publishing, 2012).

Young, Robert, 'Postcolonial Remains', *New Literary History* 43, no. 1 (2012): 20–1.

Yousef, Farouq, *Fakiha Samita* (Beirut: Jadawil li-l-nashr wa-l-tawziʿ, 2011).

——, *La Shay la Ahad:* yawmiyat *fi-l-shamal al-urubi* (Beirut: Al-Mu'assassa al- 'arabiyya li-l-dirasa wa-l-nashr, 2007).

Zafzaf, Mohamed, *Al-Mar'a wa-l-Warda* (Beirut: Manshurat Galeri Wahid, 1972).

Zu'bi, Nadhir, *Yuru* (Beirut: al-Dar al-'Arabiya li-l-'Ulum Nashirun, 2016).

Index

abandonment, 69, 213, 215
Abbas, Rasha, 16, 17, 24, 148, 149, 159, 160
   short stories of, 157–65, 184–5
Abderezzak, Hakim, 14, 48
Aboulela, Leila, 29, 221
Académie française, 198
activism, 93–4
   hacker, 96
   open-borders, 97
Adam Yakrah al-Talifiziyun (Adam Hates Television) (Abbas), 157
''Adat al-Ta-'arri al-Sayyi'a' (The Bad Habit of Getting Naked) (Blasim), 101
Adwan, Mahmoud, 171
Adwan, Ziad, 16, 17, 148, 157, 170, 171, 172, 174, 175, 180, 181, 182, 183, 184, 195, 189n48
   theatre and, 185
aesthetics, 5, 12, 17, 50, 85, 206, 227
Agamben, Giorgio, 63, 93
'Age of Migration', 11
Agier, Michel, 27, 28, 36, 87, 102
Ahmed, Ibrahim, 1, 6, 19n1, 38
al-'Al, 'Ali 'Abd, 22
el-Ariss, Tarek, 14, 29–30, 94, 95
al-Assad, Bashar, 208
al-Bayati, Abd al-Wahhab, 33
al-Bayaty, Mahmoud, 24
al-Bustani, Butrus, 154
al-Haggi, Mudar, 221, 222
al-Hajj, Maya, 207, 208–9
al-Hakim, Tawfiq, 23, 31, 32
Al-Hubb fi al-Manfa (Love in Exile) (Tahir), 33

al-Ku'us al-Sab' (Seven of Cups) (Abbas), 158
Al-Mar'a wa-l-Warda (The Woman and the Flower) (Zafzaf), 32–3
Al-Masha'a (Planet of Clay) (Yazbek), 18, 192, 193, 198, 205–6, 207, 208–9, 224
Al-Masih al-'Iraqi (The Iraqi Christ) (Blasim), 84, 87, 91, 101
al-Masrah al-Arabi fi Stockholm (Arabic Theatre in Stockholm), 222
Al-Mousawi, Nahrain, 52
al-Nadawi, Hawra, 16, 24, 109, 112, 113, 144n5
al-Qazwini, Iqbal, 24
Al-Rabi' wa-l-Kharif (Spring and Autumn) (Mina), 33, 158
'Al-Sa'a al-Sabi'a fi Yawm Ams' ('Seven O'Clock Yesterday'), mobility in, 165–9
Al-Sakhin wa-l-Barid (The Hot and the Cold) (Ghanim), 31
al-Samman, Hanadi, 25, 128, 129
al-Sayyab, Badr Shakir, 33
al-Shaykh, Hanan, 18, 128, 192, 219
al-Sirr, Amir Taj, 29
Al-Siyyida Fiyina (Madam Vienna) (Idriss), 31
al-Takarli, Fu'ad, 92
Al-Tifl al-Shi'i al-Musum (The Shi'i's Poisoned Child) (Blasim), 91
Alaidy, Ahmed: on hacking, 94–5
Alam, Rumaan, 210–11
AlAmmar, Layla, 193, 224
Alemeddine, Youssef, 47
Algerian war of independence, 199, 202

Ali, Amro, 153, 183
   Berlin and, 155, 156, 195
   exile and, 155
   material conditions and, 154
   new Arab exile body and, 147–8
alienation, 33, 34, 118, 174, 183, 189n47, 199, 211, 213, 217
AlSharq blog, 153
'Anglo-Arab Encounter, The' (Said), 218, 220
anti-colonialism, 220
antifascism, 156
anti-imperialism, 158
Anxiety of Erasure: Trauma, Authorship, and the Diaspora in Women's Writing (al-Samman), 25, 128
Anzaldúa, Gloria, 87
Apter, Emily, 110
Aqmar 'Iraqiyya Sawda' fi al-Suwid (Black Iraqi Moons in Sweden (al-'Al), 22, 23
Arab, term, 5
Arab Representations of the Occident: East–West Encounters in Arabic Fiction (El-Enany), 30, 33
Arab Spring, 152, 155
Arab uprising, 49, 151, 153
Arabic language, 123, 127
Arabic literature, 11, 19, 25, 26, 30, 37, 114, 118, 129, 149, 191, 197, 205, 217, 227, 228, 237
   borderlands and, 112
   British, 192, 194
   European migrant literature and, 139
   exile and, 33
   history of, 218
   prestige/legitimacy of, 194
   profile for, 195–6
   reading, 36–40
   writing Europe in, 3, 4–5
Arabic migration literature, 101, 194, 197, 237
   aesthetics of, 19
   contemporary, 27–30, 41, 104, 201
   defamiliarisation in, 12
   exile of, 143
   geography of, 229
   politics of, 191
   writing in, 200
Arendt, Hannah, 10–11, 38
art, 35
   forced migration and, 185

migration, 223
   visible, 184
Aswat (Voices) (Fayyad), 32
asylum, 1, 2, 158, 201, 214, 240
asylum interviews, 163, 164, 175, 216
asylum seekers, 13, 22, 23, 25, 36, 47–8, 50, 86, 225, 226, 236
   perspectives of, 4, 24
authenticity, 122, 139, 143, 173, 180, 181
   cultural, 172
   discourses of, 16, 110
   disrupting, 174–9

Bachelard, Gaston, 203
B'ad Maji' al-Tayr: Qisas min al-Manfa (After the Bird's Arrival: Stories from Exile) (Ahmed), 1
Baghdad, 83, 86, 130
   as 'city of peace', 131
Bahoora, Haytham, 92, 164
Balibar, Etienne, 14, 37
Ballhaus Nynaunstrasse theatre, 152, 153, 187n13
banlieue fiction, 191, 217
   harraga literature and, 201
   inhospitable space in, 198–205
Barakat, Hoda, 18, 192, 195, 196, 198, 205, 210, 211, 212, 213
Barakat, Salim, 85
Barakeh, Khaled, 149, 156
Barghouthi, Hussein, 33
Barid al-Layl (Voices of the Lost) (Barakat), 18, 192, 198
   lonesome communities in, 210–11
Baynatna (Between us), 151–2
Begag, Azouz, 199
Being Abbas al Abd (Alaidy), 94–5
Belghoul, Farida, 199
belonging, 14, 40, 41, 114, 191
   alternate/multiple, 36
   citizenship and, 53
   defamiliarising, 228
   illegality and, 53
   legal/social, 37, 219
   modes of, 2, 7
   political, 219
   precarity and, 53
Ben Jelloun, Tahar, 14, 23, 47
Berlin, 99, 130, 148, 182
   Arab culture and, 149–57, 183–4, 195, 227

Berlin (*cont.*)
  Arabic literary/theatre/arts scene in, 16, 147–8, 150, 173–4, 228
  as 'city outside', 185
  grittiness of, 154
  immigration to, 154–5
  rendering of, 155, 160
Berlin Conference (1885–6), 156
Berlin Film Festival, 152, 187n11
beur fiction, 191, 198, 199, 200, 217
Bildungsroman, 239, 240
binaries, 110, 112, 129, 142, 185, 240
  oppositional, 128
  polarised, 216
  us–them, 139, 180–1
Binebine, Mahi, 14, 38, 46–7, 48, 55
biopolitics, 38, 41, 60–1, 88, 89
Blanchard, Rebecca, 199, 200, 201
Blasim, Hassan, 15, 18, 23, 38, 92, 97, 104, 192, 218, 221, 234
  borderlands/networks in, 86–91
  migration and, 79, 85, 87
  nightmare realism of, 91, 164
  short stories of, 39–40, 83, 88–9
  writing of, 84, 89, 90–1, 93, 95, 96, 98, 101, 105
border crossings, 39, 84, 97, 235
border studies, 4, 10, 15, 40
borderlands, 27, 79, 86–91, 94, 129, 132, 139, 238, 239
  liminal spaces of, 36, 78
  literary, 105
  rethinking, 14, 112
  violence in, 13
Borderlands: Towards an Anthropology of the Cosmopolitan Condition (Agier), 27, 36, 87
borders, 3, 7, 13, 14, 30, 39, 49, 52, 105, 191, 192, 208
  breaking down, 61, 85
  building, 12, 19, 26, 27, 37, 40, 41, 87, 101, 121, 240
  citizenship and, 4, 6, 53
  contingency of, 158, 239
  defamiliarising, 8, 228
  denaturalising, 201
  displacement and, 152
  function of, 98
  hacking, 93–101
  identities and, 8
  liminal spaces of, 36
  linguistic, 16
  opening of, 85, 103
  paradoxes of, 37
  policing, 9
  proliferation of, 206
  rethinking, 14
  transformation of, 37
  transgression of, 84
  wilderness and, 102
Braidotti, Rosi, 38, 40, 88, 94, 143, 239
Brandzel, Amy L., 36
Brecht, Berthold, 3
bureaucracy, 34, 160, 164
Butler, Judith, 26, 237–8

Cannibales (Welcome to Paradise) (Binebine), 14, 38, 48, 49
cannibalism, 2, 49, 61–8
  endemic, 67
  metaphor of, 62
  trope of, 66
Casanova, Pascale, 194, 217
Castells, Manuel, 90
censorship, 159, 209
  hacking and, 95
Chamberlain, Lori, 122
Charef, Mehdi, 199
Chedid, Andrée, 197
Chraibi, Driss, 197
Chreiteh, Alexandra, 5, 238
citizen
  nation and, 38, 40
  national, 38
  normative, 123
  transnational, 141
citizens-in-exile, 155
citizenship, 14, 22, 30, 36, 37, 41, 79, 105, 114, 134, 141, 143, 191, 216, 225, 236, 237, 238
  belonging and, 53
  biopolitical construction of, 61
  borders and, 4, 6, 53
  conceptions of, 88, 113
  construction of, 240
  defamiliarising, 228
  defining, 120, 121, 141
  documents, 47
  flexible, 128
  full, 38, 88
  human rights and, 239–40
  in-between, 78
  interconnections beyond, 23
  legal regime of, 61

migration and, 3, 7, 13, 24
national, 2, 38
nature of, 11
normative, 24, 112–13
Orientalism and, 34
protections of, 49
rights and, 62
space and, 7
spaces outside, 6, 12, 56, 88
understandings of, 12–13, 19, 238
civil conflict, 87, 92, 93
civilisation, 72, 141
   East–West notions of, 34
   humanitarian dimension of, 211
   wilderness and, 100
CoCulture, 156
collaboration, 150, 152, 193, 221, 223
   German-Arab, 187n11
Collective Ma'louba, 221
colonialism, 28, 49, 70, 71, 155, 218
   articulation of, 31
   European, 61
Comma Press, 18, 193, 217, 218
community, 39, 97, 214
   exile in, 118–22
   forced migration and, 114
   Iraqi Danish, 113, 115
   lonesome, 210–21
   loss of, 34
   Muslim, 114
   political, 2, 141
   self-aware, 153
consciousness, 91, 102, 105, 226
   altered states of, 17, 148, 164, 166, 169, 184
   individual, 207
   class, 158
constraint, mobility and, 205–10
Copenhagen, 114, 115, 119, 121, 123, 124, 131
   landscapes of, 128
Cossery, Albert, 197, 198
creativity, 36, 123, 134, 196
critical thought, 13, 28, 36, 53
Crossing, The (Yazbek), 205
cultural production, 28, 35, 95, 193
cultural studies, 11, 35
culture, 32, 35, 121, 153, 179, 228
   Arab, 150, 151, 155, 157, 184, 195, 227
   Danish, 113
   eastern, 219

   emergent, 154
   exilic, 155
   food, 181
   German, 223
   hipster, 148, 160
   Syrian, 150, 171, 178, 181

Damascus, 157, 163, 171, 176
Danton's Death (Büchne), 222, 223
'Day I Returned to the Ruins, The' (Abbas), mobility in, 165–9
Deckard, Sharae, 64
defamiliarisation, 3, 6, 7, 8, 12, 13, 15, 16, 34, 40, 49, 79, 114, 148, 169, 170, 183, 184, 191, 206, 216, 226, 228, 234, 235, 240
   types of, 236–7
   vanishing original and, 128–34
dehumanisation, 67, 69
Denmark, 113, 116, 140
   citizenship in, 120
   stereotyped representation of, 117
Der falsche Inder (The Village Indian) (Khider), 16, 23, 112, 129, 130, 131, 143
   meanings on, 109–10
   stories in, 142
Derrida, Jacques: 'hostipitality' and, 150
destabilisation, 129, 176, 236, 238
Deutsch für alle: Das endgültige Lehrbuch (German for Everybody: The Ultimate Textbook) (Khider), 131, 161
'Dhi'b' (Wolf) (Blasim), 101
diasporas, 12, 17, 28, 91, 147, 150, 157, 196, 197, 220, 221
   affective dynamics of, 212
   Arab, 25, 86, 111, 117, 151, 154, 184, 191, 193, 195, 212, 219, 227, 228
   encounter with, 14
   narrative of, 115, 212
   post-migration, 112, 113, 114
Dibo, Mohammed, 222
Die Erfindung der deutschen Grammatik (The Invention of German Grammar) (Abbas), 24, 148, 160
discourses, 139, 158
   anti-colonial, 217
   dominant, 78–9
   exclusionary, 118
   exile, 22
   fear-based, 228

discourses (*cont.*)
  gendered, 123
  humanitarian, 228
  literary, 54
  media, 110
  migration, 138
  orientation and, 141
  political, 238
  public, 52
  social, 238
Disiz, 200
displacement, 33, 79, 86, 152, 154, 156, 159, 164, 179, 183, 184, 206, 208, 209, 211, 212, 223, 240
  diaspora and, 12, 198
  forced, 192
  mass, 34, 35, 38, 40, 88, 150
  migration and, 18, 26, 148, 149, 213
  mobility, 7, 9, 11, 13, 34, 41, 91
divination practices, 162, 165, 166, 167, 169
Dream Search Engine, 102
drones, hacking, 94, 96
dystopian writing, 5, 13, 15, 84, 85, 88, 200, 201, 218, 238

Elerian, Omar, 221
El-Enany, Rasheed, 30, 31, 33, 219
English Theatre, 170, 183
Eritrea, 68, 69, 72, 74, 75, 76
Eritrean Liberation Front, 49
estrangement, 3, 6, 7, 33, 35, 118, 235
ethos, 151
  avant-garde, 150
  collaborative, 185
  internationalising, 147
Ett öga rött (One Eye Red) (Khemiri), 134, 135
Euro, 39, 233, 234, 235
Europe: as cannibal, 61–8
  idealisation of, 32
  as paradise, 65
Exil Ensemble, 153
exile, 3, 13, 33, 34–5, 147, 149, 212
  abstracting/idealising, 35
  Arabic-language, 152
  as collective practice, 155
  in community, 118–22
  concept of, 34, 36
  dehistoricization of, 35
  disability and, 118
  migration and, 128

  modernist idea of, 36
  narratives of, 32, 115
  refugee and, 35
  socialism in, 158
  as terminal loss, 35
  understandings of, 28, 157
  writing, 47
exile literature, 12, 22, 157–65, 237, 240
  emergence of, 33
  forced migration and, 10
  meanings/forms of, 1
  understandings of, 34

Fadel, Youssef, 14, 23, 38, 48
fantasy, 5, 7, 40, 202
  collective, 203, 204
Farman, Gha'ib Tu'umah, 92
Fayyad, Sulayman, 32
fiction d'anticipation, 200
Fiddian-Qasmieh, Elana, 9–10
Finland, 87, 101, 102
  Arabic speakers in, 86
  migration policy of, 86
Fiore, Teresa, 51, 78
firdaws, 59, 60
First Gulf War, 91, 131
Force of Nonviolence, The (Butler), 237
forced migration, 3, 5, 6, 16, 47, 50, 86, 112, 113, 129, 141, 147, 154, 167, 184, 227, 228, 235, 238
  Arabic literature of, 22, 30, 37, 38, 40–1, 150, 193, 217
  art and, 185
  circulation/translation of, 217
  community and, 114
  contemporary, 208
  defamiliarisation of, 193
  exile literature and, 10
  geography of, 17
  literature of, 4, 12, 13, 25, 48, 54, 104–5, 191, 193, 229, 240
  'multiplying'/'unfolding' of self and, 143
  narratives of, 8, 237
  post-Arab Spring, 147
  reality of, 40
  representations of, 236–7
  rethinking, 157
  season of, 23
  term, 8–9
  themes, 192–3

vocabulary/contexts of, 185
writing, 223–4
Foucault, Michel, 177
frameworks, 7
 borders studies, 10
 citizenship, 6, 19
 conceptual, 185
 cultural encounter, 4, 28
 literary, 13
 political, 41
Francophonie, 195, 196, 217
French Ministry of Culture, 210
From Ritual to Theatre: The Human Seriousness of Play (Turner), 57

'Gardens of Babylon, The' (Blasim), 89–90
gender, 16, 122, 128, 161
'generation 52', 199
Geneva Refugee Convention, 1, 2
Gennep, Van, 57
Georgette (Belghoul), 199
Ghalayini, Basma, 218
Ghanim, Fathi, 31
ghurba, 33, 118, 119
Global North/Global South, 61, 67
globalisation, 11, 26, 39, 43n18, 89, 181
Gus, Agustin Nsanzinesa: poem by, 9
Guthrie, Alice, 17, 164

hacking, 95, 97
 censorship and, 95
 drone, 94, 96
Haddad, Dana, 151
Haddad, Joumana, 90
Haïk, Farjallah, 197
Hajar al-Dahk (The Stone of Laughter) (Barakat), 210
Halabi, Zeina, 35, 36
hallucinations, 166, 167, 169, 227
halqa, 54, 62
Hamburg Cell, The (Spielberg), 171
'Hamburg Foundation for 29', 202
Hanoosh, Yasmeen, 91–2
Haqqi, Yahya, 23, 31
Harchi, Kautar, 200
Hargreaves, Alec, 199
Harith al-Miyah (The Tiller of Waters) (Barakat), 210
harraga literature, 14, 23, 48, 49, 50, 52, 54, 61, 67, 68, 77, 78, 79, 81n30, 149, 191, 196, 205

banlieue fiction and, 201
 genres of, 201
 term, 47
Hashish (Fadel), 14, 15, 38, 48, 49, 56, 57, 59, 60, 61, 64, 65, 67
Hassan, 56, 209, 210
Hassan, Waïl, 28, 29, 32, 33–4, 220–1
Heart of Darkness (Conrad), 218
Higher Institute of Dramatic Arts, 171
history, 48, 52, 168, 218
 Arab intellectual, 184
 colonial, 17, 155, 191, 194
 communicating, 234
 imagined, 200
 intellectual, 129
 Syrian, 184
homelessness, 214, 215
Homo Sacer: Sovereign Power and Bare Life (Agamben), 93
Hope and Other Dangerous Pursuits (Lalami), 14, 81n30
human rights
 citizenship and, 239–40
 groups, 51
 naturalising, 239
humanitarianism, 34, 51, 216
Hussein, Saddam, 86, 91, 92, 124, 130, 132
hybridity, 29, 67, 118, 129, 141, 197, 219, 220, 228

identity, 58, 85, 112, 129, 142
 borders and, 8
 bounded, 143
 crisis, 66
 gender, 177
 hyphenated, 128
 Iraqi, 123
 migrant, 112
 minority, 92, 228
 multiplied, 142
 national, 8, 9
 Syrian, 156
Idriss, Yusuf, 31
ightirāb, 118
ikhitirāq al-nizām, 95
'*ilān kaynūnatī*, 124
imagination, limits of, 140, 240
Immigrant Narratives: Orientalism and Cultural Translation in Arab American and Arab British Literature (Hassan), 220
 Orientalism and, 33–4

immigrants, 155, 192, 198, 211, 228
  clandestine, 201
  friendships of, 121
  invasion of, 51
  Orientalist representations of, 227
immigration, 154–5, 187n13, 219–20
  Arab, 193
  panic of, 203–4
  security and, 203–4
In the Eye of the Sun (Soueif), 220
individual, 90, 134
  collective and, 239
Inghilleri, Moira, 111
Innaha London ya 'Azizi (Only in London) (al-Shaykh), 18, 128, 192, 219
  characters in, 129
interconnectivity, 15, 40, 43n18, 83, 84, 85, 89, 91, 105, 143, 239
International Organization for Migration (IOM), 25
Invasion! (Khemiri), 16, 50, 109, 110, 112, 134, 134–9, 143
  central questions of, 141
  identities and, 142
  mistranslation of, 139
Invisible Stories, 171
Iran–Iraq war, 91, 93
Iraq, 85, 86, 133, 159, 213
Iraq + 100 (Blasim), 18, 89–90, 193, 218
Iraqi Arabic, 120, 121, 122
Iraqi Communist Party, 219
Iraqi literature, 47, 91–3
Iraqi war, 15, 85, 164, 206
Islamophobia, 225, 227

jurthuma, 15, 49, 70

Kafka, Franz, 61
Kahf, Mohja, 158, 209
'Kalimat Mutaqat'ia' ('Crosswords') (Blasim), 83
Kanafani, Ghassan, 99
Kaplan, Caren, 30
Kayfa Tamma Ikhtira' al-Lugha al-Almaniyya (The Invention of the German Language) (Abbas), 17, 148, 157, 158, 160, 161
Khaal, Abu Bakr, 14, 23, 38, 48, 49, 68
Khemiri, Jonas Hassen, 16, 50, 51, 109–10, 129, 134, 135, 139
Khider, Abbas, 16, 109–10, 129, 130, 139, 161

Kurdi, Alan, 149
Kurds, 73, 86, 87, 131

La géographie du danger (The Geography of Danger) (Skif), 18, 191–2, 198–205, 224
'Laji' 'ind al-Iskimu' ('The Arctic Refugee') (Ahmed), 1, 3, 4, 38
Lalami, Laila, 14, 23, 47, 81n30
Langhoff, Shermin, 152, 153, 187n14
Last Migration, The (al-Hage), 221
Le gone du Chaâba (Shanty-town Kid) (Begag), 199
Le Pen, Jean-Marie, 48
Le thé du harem d'Archimède (Tea in the Harem) (Charef), 199
Lebanese Civil War, 154, 198, 210, 211
Les clandestins (The Clandestines) (Elalami), 14
liminal spaces, 14, 36, 55–9, 65, 66, 67, 79, 98
literary centres, 193, 194–8
literary studies, 5, 27, 28, 35
literary texts, 5–6, 7, 17, 19, 22, 25, 29, 34, 36, 41, 46, 47, 90, 95, 110, 139, 142, 152, 184, 191
Literature and Revolution (Trotsky), 159
Litvin, Margaret, 137, 173
London, 70, 115, 116, 148, 151, 182, 184, 191, 221, 222
  Arab culture in, 195, 217–20, 227
  Arabic literary/theatre/arts scene in, 194–5, 219, 228
  colonial history and, 194
  literary/cultural centres of, 193
  violence in, 218
London School of Economics, 70
loneliness, 101, 102, 103, 211, 213, 216, 234, 235
  shared, 104, 214, 215, 217
Löytti, Olli, 90
Lu'bat al-Qubba' at al-Raqamiyya (The Digital Hats Game) (Blasim), 15, 84, 93–101

Maalouf, Amine, 197, 198
Madinah: City of Stories from the Middle East (Haddad), 90
Maghreb, 23, 47, 68
  francophone writers from, 199
Majnun Sahat al-Huriyya (The Madman

INDEX | 261

of Freedom Square) (Blasim), 15, 38, 84, 87, 90, 94, 98
Malakut hathihi al-Ard (The Kingdom of This Earth) (Barakat), 210
Malkki, Liisa, 34
manfa, 33, 36, 118
marginalisation, 26, 111, 113
M'arid al-Juthath (The Corpse of Exhibition) (Blasim), 15, 91
Masmoudi, Ikram, 93
Matar, Hisham, 221
Maus, 162
Mawsim al-Hijra ila al-Shamal (Season of Migration to the North) (Salih), 15, 23, 31–2, 49, 70, 71, 210, 218, 219
  colonial/postcolonial elite and, 32
  final scene of, 66–7
Mediterranean crossing, 14, 23, 46, 47, 54, 72, 78
Mediterranean Sea, 46, 68, 76, 79, 203
Metamorphosis (Kafka), 61
metropoles, 70, 191, 193, 227
migrants, 22, 36, 59, 61, 71, 73, 129, 213
  archetypes of, 51
  connecting, 49
  economic, 50
  exposure/arrest of, 97
  hostility for, 10
  hypervisible/invisible, 236
  images of, 69, 217
  irregular, 225
  liminal state for, 57
  Orientalist representations of, 227
  policing and, 101
  progression of, 99
  rooted citizens and, 140–1
  rounding of, 203
  as security threat, 204
  vulnerability of, 26
  would-be, 48, 98
migration, 3, 4, 8, 12, 15, 19, 27, 41, 58, 77, 83, 111, 129, 148, 174, 183, 191, 198, 200, 216, 240
  Arabic, 196–7
  Arabic literature of, 11, 22, 25, 30–6
  border, 36–40, 84, 139
  capital/information and, 238
  citizenship and, 7, 13
  clandestine, 54, 58, 91, 204, 205
  conception of, 140
  contemporary, 36, 79, 104, 228, 236
  as crisis, 149, 184

defamiliarising, 16–17, 68, 157
ecosystem of, 173
evocation of, 69–70
exile and, 128
experience with, 87, 215
future and, 59
global context of, 28
history of, 48, 52
imagining, 49, 54, 56
irregular, 132–3, 205
labour, 22, 199
large-scale, 36, 41, 85, 200, 211, 226
mass, 24, 88, 213, 214, 216, 226
making sense of, 50
mass politics and, 240
meanings of, 122
movement of, 133
patterns, 27, 193
phenomenon of, 68–9
postcolonial, 47, 171
publishing/performing, 218
racialisation and, 139
repositioning and, 110
representations of, 71, 149, 236–7
space and, 26
spectral condition of, 78
technology of, 185
transindividual, 208
trends of, 51
war and, 159, 169
water and, 68
writing, 5, 8, 10–11, 12, 77, 86–91, 101
  see also forced migration
migration literature, 4, 13, 37, 87, 163, 184, 194, 206, 228, 238, 239
  Arabic, 5, 30, 193, 195, 196
  contemporary, 36, 191
  examples of, 229
  inhospitable space in, 198–205
  multilinguistic dimensions of, 5
  postcolonial and, 26
  space/migration and, 2
  transindividual qualities of, 212
migration studies, 13, 27
migration theatre, 149, 170, 172, 184, 229
  Arabic/Arab, 173–4, 223
  expectations of, 171
  power dynamics of, 173
Minah, Hanna, 33, 158
Minaret (Aboulela), 221
mistranslations, 109, 110, 111, 112, 134, 136–7, 137–8, 139, 140

mobility, 7, 11, 14, 17, 39, 41, 94, 147, 149, 165–9, 192, 198, 234, 237, 240
  barriers and, 209
  capital/information and, 238
  constraint and, 205–10
  contemporary, 27
  defamiliarising, 157
  displacement and, 9
  expectations for, 183
  history of, 48
  imagining, 236
  managing/restricting, 37
  psychic ramifications of, 211
  rights to, 89
  transindividual, 208
  transnational, 38
Modern Standard Arabic (MSA), 49
Morocco, 55, 73
  representation of, 59
movement, 52, 133
  cross-border, 26
  metaphors of, 166
Mulakhkhas Ma Jara (The Gist of It) (Abbas), 17, 24, 148, 157, 158, 164, 165
multilingualism, 129, 142, 143

Nahda, 48, 154, 218, 220
  discourses of, 194
  ideologies, 32
Napoleon, 31
narratives, 10, 28, 36, 41, 54, 78, 91, 121–2, 129, 133, 168, 210, 212
  Arabic literary, 11–12, 197, 217
  confessional, 214
  dominant, 5, 55
  exile, 32, 115
  fictional, 160
  fragmentation of, 227
  literary, 4, 8, 11, 12, 19, 22, 32, 40, 47, 50, 53, 83, 84, 93, 192, 193, 218, 219, 237
  migration, 7, 14, 22, 24, 30, 32, 39, 50, 52, 53, 54, 55, 85, 88, 93, 192, 218
  modernist, 169
  multi-voice, 199
  realist, 85
  structures, 49, 90
  travel, 32, 33
nation, citizen and, 38, 40
nationalism, 16, 143, 158
  antimigrant, 152
  economic, 27
  far-right, 154
  populist, 48
networks, 68, 86–91, 102, 193, 223
  carceral, 201
  digital, 90, 91
  information, 68
  migrant, 68
  social, 90
  support, 26
nightmares, 15, 85, 91, 93, 165, 224
'Nightmares of Carlos Fuentes, The' (Blasim), 221
'Nightmares of Carlos Fuentes, The' (Razak), 18, 192
Nutall, Sarah, 89
Nyers, Peter, 8

occupation, 85, 87, 91, 93, 218
  violence of, 92
Orientalism, 30, 31, 33–4, 54, 156, 173, 175, 218, 220
Orientalism (Said), 29
original, 128
  binaries of, 123
  translation and, 16, 109, 114
Origins of Totalitarianism (Arendt), 38
Othello (Shakespeare), 71, 218
Others, 7, 51, 103, 182, 239
Oxford Handbook of Arab Novelistic Traditions, The (Reeck), 197

Palestine + 100 (Ghalayini), 18, 193, 218
paradise, 65, 81n19
  aiming for, 59–61
  war and, 176
Paris, 115, 116, 148, 151, 184, 191, 198, 202
  Arab culture in, 195, 217, 227
  Arabic literary/theatre/arts scene in, 228
  colonial history and, 194
  international writers in, 192, 197
  literary/cultural centres of, 193
Partir (Leaving Tangiers) (Ben Jelloun), 14
performance, 36, 147, 174, 178, 179
  literary, 237
Pireddu, Nicoletta, 50
Please, Repeat After Me (Adwan), 16, 17, 148, 157, 170–4, 179, 185
politics, 4, 5, 12, 17, 28, 34, 110, 137, 158, 179–83, 191, 194, 223, 225, 238

conventional, 39
mass, 35, 240
migration, 53
'post-migrant' theatre (*postmigrantisches Theater*), 152, 174
post-traumatic stress, 85
postcolonial, 26, 27–30, 32, 71, 200
postcolonial studies, 28, 29, 35, 36
postnationalism, 38, 88, 143
Pratt, Mary Louise, 141, 142
precarious migration, 25, 26, 40, 46, 113, 227, 236, 238
    Arabic literature of, 30, 38, 193, 217
    defamiliarisation of, 193
    large-scale migration and, 41
    routes, 149
    understandings/representations of, 236
    writing, 223–4

Qaiconie, Mohannad, 151
Qandil Umm Hashim (The Lamp of Umm Hashim) (Haqqi), 23, 31, 32
Qur'an, 206

racism, 173
Raizen, Michal, 169
rape, 56, 67, 95, 177
Rasa'il al-Ghariba (The Stranger's Letters) (Barakat), 212
Razak, Rashid, 18, 192, 221
realism, 89, 206, 216
    literary, 19, 92, 238
    magical, 5, 218
    nightmare, 15, 85, 91, 93, 164
    social, 92
    Socialist, 158
'Reality and the Record, The' (Blasim), 90
Reeck, Laura, 197–8
refuge, taking, 167, 168, 169
refugee camps, 137, 163, 164, 239
Refugee Hosts: Local Community Experiences of Displacement from Syria: Views from Lebanon, Jordan and Turkey, 9–10
refugee literature, 12, 169, 185, 237, 240
    post-human, 149
    as social document, 132
refugee status, applying for, 162
refugees, 8, 13, 22, 23, 25, 36, 47, 50, 147, 149, 150, 155, 164, 170, 173, 178–9, 182, 223, 236, 237
    accounts of, 53

arrival of, 10
as definable category, 9
exile and, 35
hostility for, 10
Iraqi, 101
perspectives of, 3, 24
playing, 171, 175
term, 34
time, 168
as victims, 10
relationships, 39, 128, 142–3
    colonial/postcolonial, 4, 220
    intimate, 215
    parasitic, 15, 91
    translational, 125
René (Disiz), 200
Rethinking Refugees: Beyond States of Emergency (Nyers), 8
Return of Danton, The (al-Haggi), 221–3, 225
rights, 57, 105
    citizenship and, 62
Rijal fi al-Shams (Men in the Sun) (Kanafani), 99, 100
Roseneil, Sasha, 37
Rousseau, Jean-Jacques, 157
routes, 132, 149
    imagining, 184
    migratory, 61, 85, 93, 133, 237
    roots and, 128
Royal Academy of Dramatic Art, 171
'Ruh al-'Asr' (al-Bustani), 154

Said, Edward, 29, 218, 220
    exile and, 34–5
Sakr, Rita, 88–9
Salesses, Matthew, 240
Salih, Tayeb, 15, 23, 31–2, 49, 66–7, 70, 218
Scheherazade, quest of, 54
science fiction, 5, 6, 7, 40, 218
Second Gulf War, 131
security
    immigration and, 203–4
    language of, 203
    place and, 7
Sellman, Johanna, 137, 174
Shafaq Qutbi/Norrsken (Northern Lights) (al-Haggi), 222
'Shahinat Berlin' ('The Truck to Berlin') (Blasim), 38, 93–101, 234
Shklovsky, Viktor, 3

Shubbak festival, 222, 232n62
Silence is a Sense (AlAmmar), 193, 223–7
Skif, Hamid, 18, 47, 191–2, 198–205, 201
Slade, Christina, 141
Slaughter, Joseph, 239
social conditions, 90, 154, 173
social critique, 160, 164, 196
social spaces, 113, 141
social structures, 7, 13, 137
sorcery, 71
   storytelling and, 72–3
Soueif, Ahdaf, 220
sovereignty
   citizenship and, 3
   elastic, 96
   individual, 70, 90
   state, 26, 37, 41
space, 238
   citizenship and, 7
   diasporic, 110
   migration and, 26
   national, 217
   understanding of, 8
Stan, Corina, 133
stereotypes, 117, 138, 170, 173, 174, 182
   anti-black, 70
   countering, 196
   cultural, 220
   Orientalist, 70
storytelling, 23, 39, 49, 55–9, 62, 79, 133, 175, 234
   in *African Titanics*, 68–77
   functions of, 15
   individual/collective practices of, 54–5
   migration, 112
   modalities of, 47
   sorcery and, 72–3
   theme of, 68
   undocumented migration and, 71
   ways of, 134
Strait of Gibraltar, 55, 61, 64, 65
subjectivity, 11, 17, 37–8, 46, 50, 83, 111, 128, 149, 165, 185
   changing, 41
   global/mobile, 88
   migratory, 141
   open-ended, 104–5
   repositioning, 110, 122–5
   translation of, 122–5
Surat Āl-ʿImran (Family of Imran), 127
Suvin, Darko, 6, 7

Sweden, 1, 2, 4, 19n1, 85, 134, 222
   Arabic speakers in, 86
'Sweetness of Being a Refugee, The' (Gus), text of, 9
Syria, 86, 148, 158
   migration from, 226
'Syria Cultural Index', 156
Syrian actors/artists, 87, 147, 174, 222
Syrian Arab Army, 208
'Syrian Biennale: Roots En Route', 156
Syrian Free Army, 208
Syrian literature, 158, 159, 164, 209
Syrian refugees, 16, 17, 24, 149, 164, 175
   arrival of, 147, 186n1
   challenges for, 160
Syrian revolution, 164, 175, 177, 181, 205
   staging/via France/Germany/London, 221–3
Syrian war, 18, 85, 150, 157, 174, 198, 205
Syrians, 149, 155, 164, 180, 181, 182, 183
   arrival of, 163
   displacement of, 179
Syrious Look, A, 171

Tahir, Bahaʾ, 33
Tahta Samaʾ Kubinhaghin (Under the Copenhagen Sky) (al-Nadawi), 16, 24, 109, 111–12, 112–14, 123, 129, 130, 131, 139, 140, 143
Tanween Theatre and Dance Company, 171
Taqatuʿ Niran: min Yamiyat al-Intifada al-Suriyya (A Woman in the Crossfire: Diaries of the Syrian Revolution) (Yazbek), 205
Tayeb Salih: Ideology and the Craft of Fiction (Hassan), 32
Taytanikat Ifriqiyya (African Titanics) (Khaal), 14, 15, 23, 38, 48, 49, 53, 54, 79
   postcolonial and, 71
   storytelling/literary in, 68–77
theatre, 174, 182, 185
   post-migrant, 153
   professional, 172
   publishing/performing, 218
Thiele, Kathrin, 89
Third Gulf War, 131
Tolstoy, Alexey, 159
torture, 138, 177, 204, 214, 216
tourism, escapist, 167, 168

traffickers, 47, 56, 61, 62, 68, 83, 87, 98, 99, 202
  authorities and, 204
transformation, 14, 41, 55, 58, 60, 61, 66, 111, 112, 114, 127, 128, 197
  hopes for, 142
transindividual awareness, 37, 39, 54, 121, 212
transindividuals, 14, 37, 78, 121, 133, 200, 208, 239
translation, 122, 127, 128
  accurate, 138
  binaries of, 123
  failed, 109
  hierarchies/anxieties about, 123
  with missing originals, 109, 110, 111
  multilingualism and, 143
  original and, 16, 109, 110, 114
  paradigm of, 37
  project, 111–12, 135
  understandings of, 125
  violence and, 142
Translation and Migration (Inghilleri), 111
Translation Zone, The (Apter), 110
Translator, The (Aboulela), 221
translators, 16, 109, 111, 114, 122, 123, 125, 126, 138, 141–2, 196, 210, 219
  cultural, 220
  relying on, 112, 134
  role as, 124
transnationalism, 141, 155
Transpositions: On Nomadic Ethics (Braidotti), 38, 40
trauma, 25, 86, 91, 92, 164, 165, 167, 177, 193, 224, 226, 227
  individual/collective, 84, 85
travel, 4, 13, 48, 51, 70, 72, 87, 132, 137, 166, 167, 180, 183, 194, 219, 220, 234, 235
  Arabic literature of, 30, 36
  narratives of, 32, 33
Trotsky, Leon, 159
Tuan, Yi-Fu, 7–8
Turner, Victor, 57

undocumented migrants, 23, 47, 48, 50, 55, 192, 203, 211, 214
  perspectives of, 3
undocumented migration, 4, 15, 23, 67, 71, 79
  Arabic literature of, 50–5

  narratives of, 24, 52, 54
  stories of, 79
  storytelling and, 71
United Nations Declaration of Human Rights, 239–40
Unmaking of the Arab Intellectual: Prophecy, Exile, and the Nation (Halabi), 35
'Usfur min al-Sharq (Bird of the East) (al-Hakim), 23, 31, 32

Verfremdungseffekt, 3
violence, 67, 72, 83, 91, 92, 93, 137, 166, 216, 218, 227
  colonial, 32
  cycles of, 15
  misrepresentation and, 139
  organised, 206
  renderings of, 85
  translation and, 142
'Visa?', 162, 163
Voiceless, the (pen name), 224, 225, 226
vulnerability, 26, 62, 67, 72, 93, 94, 97, 128, 192, 214, 215, 239

waḥsha, 101, 102, 104, 215, 234, 235
Wannous, Saadallah, 185
war, 83
  contemporary, 104–5
  literature/aesthetics and, 206
  migration and, 159, 169
  paradise and, 176
  violence of, 92
War (Fadel), 48
War and Occupation in Iraqi Freedom (Masmoudi), 93
War on Terror, 93, 181–2
'We Can't Compete in Writing' (Abbas), 160
'We Refugees' (Arendt), 10–11
Welcome to Paradise (Binebine), 14–15, 55, 56, 57, 59–60, 61, 64, 67, 68
  cannibalism and, 65
  trafficking and, 62
West-Pavlov, Russell, 203, 204
White Clay (Blasim), 86
wilderness, 1, 54, 101, 104
  border and, 102
  civilisation and, 100
  explorations of, 235
  metaphors of, 6
  tropes of, 67

wildness, 67
    metaphors of, 61–2
Wilson, Janet, 53, 77
wolf, 101, 102
'Wolf, A' (Blasim), 101, 102, 104
World Republic of Letters, The (Casanova), 194
Wounded Camera (Osman), 86
Wright, Jonathan, 90, 91
writing, 147
    fictional, 169
    modes of, 19, 54, 237
    speculative, 19

Yazbek, Samar, 18, 192, 193, 198, 205, 207
Young, Robert, 28
Yousef, Farouq, 38
Yuru (Euro) (Zuʻbi), 6, 18, 19, 39, 233, 234, 238
    forced migration and, 236
    wilderness and, 235

Zafzaf, Mohamed, 32–3
Zangana, Haifa, 18, 24, 192, 219
Zone cinglée (Crazy Zone), (Harchi), 200, 201
Zuʻbi, Nadhir, 6, 18, 39, 233

EU representative:
Easy Access System Europe
Mustamäe tee 50, 10621 Tallinn, Estonia
Gpsr.requests@easproject.com